Insights into environmental education

Insights
into environmental
education

Edited by George C. Martin and Keith Wheeler

Oliver & Boyd

Oliver & Boyd
Croythorn House
23 Ravelston Terrace
Edinburgh EH4 3TJ
A Division of Longman Group Ltd

ISBN 0 05 002798 0 (*paperback*)
    0 05 002799 9 (*cased*)

Printed in Great Britain by
Willmer Brothers Limited, Birkenhead

Contents

Section 3

George C. Martin

The original idea for this book was suggested by George C. Martin who died during the final stages of the preparation of the manuscript. His death at the age of fifty-one is a sad loss to the environmental education movement. He campaigned tirelessly for the introduction of environmental curricula into schools and colleges. He was a co-founder of the Society for Environmental Education, and from its inception in 1968 he served as Secretary, and then latterly Chairman. He was a member of the Council for Environmental Education, the Council for Urban Study Centres and the Institute of Environmental Sciences. He was author of numerous articles on environmental education, and co-editor of *Handbook of Environmental Studies* (Blond Educational, 1972).

Preface

This book consists of contributions by exponents of environmental education teaching in Britain or abroad, and is intended to give the reader insights into aspects of environmental education which either have not been dealt with elsewhere, or which are here brought together for the first time. It is offered, therefore, as a contribution to the search for a new curriculum in which understanding of, and involvement in, the processes of creating and conserving the environment forms an important part.

Environmental education is an emergent concept in the early stages of its development for which there is no precedent in other areas of education. Much already has been thought and written about this approach to learning. But this book is not concerned with repeating what has been said elsewhere; nor is it concerned with describing the contribution of the traditional disciplines, such as geography or biology, to environmental objectives. These subjects have their own publications for airing their ideas. Instead, here are presented a number of case studies describing inter-disciplinary insights which are potential growing points for curriculum development. For the fact is, perhaps, that environmental education has evolved on the fringes of subjects, rather than on the frontiers of knowledge, by a pragmatic involvement in environmental problems and teaching strategies. In addition, the book includes reviews of the advances made towards devising environmental education curricula in other countries.

Each chapter is provided with references to further reading which, along with the bibliographies, are a selected resource guide to environmental education. Discussion questions are also given at the end of the book. Not everyone will agree with the views expressed by the contributors; nor is the book intended to be exhaustive in its scope. But if these chapters stimulate discussion among teachers and students which eventually results in the introduction of better defined environmental education objectives into our schools and colleges, then the book will have performed its intended task.

Keith Wheeler

Contributors

James L. Aldrich

Senior Associate at the Conservation Foundation (USA), he also serves as a member of the IUCN Commission on Education, is Vice-Chairman of the US National Committee for MAB and Trustee of Threshold.

Bernard Aylward

School adviser for design education for over twenty-five years in West Riding and Leicestershire, he is an Associate of the Society of Industrial Artists and Designers, and has served on a number of educational bodies such as the Consultative Committees of the Schools Council Project in Design and Crafts, of the Royal College of Art research, 'Design in General Education', and the General Council of the East Midlands Regional Examination Board. He is currently Chairman of the National Association for Design Education, and contributes articles to the *Times Educational Supplement* and journals such as *Studies in Design Education* and *Craft*. He is a contributor to the book, *Attitudes in Design Education*, and is editor of a teachers' handbook, *Design Education in Schools*.

Anne M. Blackburn

She is a co-ordinator of a secondary school curriculum development project at The Conservation Foundation (USA), and also serves as Adviser to the District Youth Board of the Northern Virginia Soil and Water Conservation District and as Chairman of the Fairfax County Environmental Education Committee.

Colin and Mog Ball

Both have taught extensively in England, Asia and Africa. From 1970 to 1972 Colin was Director of the Advisory Service of Community Service Volunteers, and latterly he was Head of Community Education at a Leicestershire Community College. They are co-authors of *Education for a Change*.

John Burton

Senior Lecturer in Environmental Studies at Crewe and Alsager College of Education, he has taught in various types of schools, and was School Adviser in County Antrim before taking up his present post. He is author of a series of textbooks on environmental studies.

Frank Chippendale

Formerly Head of School of Architecture, Leeds School of Art, and visiting lecturer at King Alfred's College of Education, he has received research awards from RIBA for an enquiry into architectural education, and from the Leverhulme Trust for an enquiry into visual education in the curriculum of Colleges of Education.

Malcolm Elliott

Awarded a Ph.D. (University of Wales) for his researches on the hormonal regulation of root growth in 1967, he then spent two years as a research fellow at Yale University and afterwards two years as Lecturer in Plant Physiology at the University of Leicester. Since 1971 he has been a member of staff at the School of Biology of City of Leicester Polytechnic where he is Principal Lecturer in Biology and Course Tutor for the B.Sc. Science and the environmental degree.

Ivor Goodson

At present Head of Faculty of Man in Time and Place, Stantonbury Campus School, Milton Keynes, he formerly taught at Countesthorpe College, Leicestershire. He is co-author of *A History of the Hosiery and Lace Industry* and has also published articles in several educational journals.

John Holliday

He worked in planning and landscape design with Durham and Kent County Councils before moving into education at the Birmingham College of Art in 1961. He is currently Head of Department of Urban and Regional Planning, Lanchester Polytechnic, Coventry, and is a past member of the Council and Education Committee of the Royal Town Planning Institute. His publications include *City Centre Development*, which he edited, and various articles and research reports.

Carol Johnson

General Secretary of the Council for Environmental Education, Secretary of IUCN Commission on Education and editor of *REED*.

Dr Tom Pritchard

He is Vice-Chairman, IUCN Commission on Education, Director (Wales) of the Nature Conservancy Council and has been engaged in many aspects of environmental conservation since he joined the Nature Conservancy in 1967. His interests in environmental education, and particularly the training of environmental scientists, have been expressed through his activities in IUCN, the Council of Europe and many parts of the world.

Dr Paul Rogers

Senior Lecturer at Huddersfield Polytechnic where he is mainly concerned with the development of interdisciplinary courses in human ecology, he is an executive member of the Commonwealth Human Ecology Council, and has edited two books on human ecology. His main research interests are in the political aspects of the use of resources in less developed countries.

Tom Shaw

Head of Humanities, Wreake Valley College, Leicestershire.

David L. Smith

Lecturer in Geography Education at the University of Sydney Teacher Development Programme, where he is also leader of a one-term Seminar on Environmental Education. He is co-author of *Decline of the Environment: a source book for environmental education*.

Michael Storm

Dean of Environmental Studies, Berkshire College, Reading. He is particularly interested in urban and regional planning and in development studies, and has worked in Cyprus, Jamaica, West Africa and the Pacific. A new main course, Regional Development Studies, which focuses upon regional and global disparities in levels of development, forms part of Berkshire College's B.Ed programme recently approved by CNAA. He is author of *Urban Growth in Britain*.

Colin Ward

He worked for many years in architecture before training as a teacher at Garnett College, London. Formerly lecturer in charge of Liberal Studies at Wandsworth Technical College and presently Education Officer of the Town & Country Planning Association and co-editor of the *Bulletin of Environmental Education,* he is the author of several secondary schoolbooks, co-author of *Streetwork* and editor of *Vandalism.*

Bryan Waites

He researched into the geography of monasticism at the Institute of Historical Research, London University and has taught in Uganda, Kenya and Australia. He is a Fellow of the Royal Historical Society, Royal Geographical Society and the Society of Nautical Research, and is author of *Moorland and Valeland Farming in North East Yorkshire* and the schoolbooks: *Geography of a New Europe* and *Future Environments in Britain: Water.* He is also co-author of *Leicestershire Landscapes, Patterns and Problems in World Agriculture, Leicester Town Trail* and co-editor of *Environmental Geography.* At present he is Principal Lecturer in Geography at the City of Leicester College of Education.

Keith Wheeler

Formerly Secretary, Surrey Fieldwork Society, and Chairman, Leicestershire Association for Local Geographical Studies, he is a Fellow of the Royal Geographical Society, a member of the Council for Urban Study Centres and a founding member of the Society for Environmental Education whose bulletin, *SEE,* he edited 1968–70. He is co-editor of *Geographical Fieldwork: a handbook for teachers, Leicestershire Landscapes* and *Environmental Geography.* He is editor of *Geography in the Field* and co-author of *Patterns and Problems in World Agriculture* and *Leicester Town Trail.* He is author of *Future Environments in Britain: the Future City* and of numerous articles dealing with educational or environmental matters. He has taught in West Africa and specialised in the education of the non-academic older pupil, and is presently Senior Lecturer in Geography at the City of Leicester College of Education. He is a contributor to the IGU Commission on the History of Geographical Thought, and a member of the UNESCO/UNEP Environmental Education Programme Working Party.

Section 1

Defining environmental education

There is an urgent need to find a solution to the problem of defining the objectives of environmental education if it is to be implemented at all levels of school and higher education. The two chapters in this section, therefore, examine the origins and development of environmental education, together with the difficulties involved in obtaining a concensus of opinion among educationists and environmentalists on what exactly constitutes the field of environmental education, and what its curriculum objectives in school and college should be.

1   The genesis of environmental education

Keith Wheeler

Man cannot be separated from his environment: not only the environment of the natural world, but also the environment of his cultural background. He is both a creature and a creator of the surroundings he inhabits. Consequently, the infinite complexity of this relationship means that any discussion concerning 'environmental matters' is further complicated by the need to assess the evidence of conflicting facts and philosophies. Such a state of affairs is made even more involved when the educational implications of the environment are considered, because education deals with an equally intricate field of human concern. The result is that the terms 'environment' and 'education' are difficult to define for there are almost as many opinions about their meaning as there are people to express themselves on these subjects! Similarly, the history of environmental education reflects the many attitudes towards both 'environment' and 'education' found in society, now and in the past. It is important, therefore, if one is to clarify one's understanding of the significance and purpose of environmental education, to know first something about its genesis – for as D. G. Watts commented, 'The main plank in the environmental platform is neither philosophical, or psychological, but historical.'[1] This chapter outlines the salient developments which have brought the term 'environmental education' into general use by educationists in this country.

The discovery of the environmental concept

The modern concept of environment originated in the nineteenth century when the Industrial Revolution caused an unprecedented alienation of Man from Nature and the disruption of civilization's formerly unified cultural milieu. In addition, Darwin's book, *The Origin of Species* (1859), demonstrated how all living things, human beings included, are the product of the environment working through the processes of Natural Selection. He thereby substituted

2

the mechanisms of evolution for the power of God as the shaping force in the destiny of living things, and drew attention to the intimate connection between the natural environment and life.

Many thinkers, reflecting on the significance of this new view of environment, felt isolated without a theistic interpretation for support. The romantics, such as Wordsworth, mourned the passing of the rustic scene while some educationists, following the example of Rousseau, advocated the importance of nature studies in a child's education. This was at a time when people were becoming engulfed in a spreading manufactured environment of iron, glass and brick, propelled by steam power and creating cities on a scale unknown before. Ironically, it was the innocent study of botany which provided Victorians with two more important environmental ideas: ecology and sociology. The pioneer sociologist, Frederick Le Play (1806–82)[2] considered botany 'was the most significant factor for understanding the nature of society'; and the term 'ecology' was invented by the philosopher-biologist Ernst Haeckel (1834–1919) in 1874.[3]

By the late nineteenth century most working people were living in circumstances hardly conducive to the growth of human dignity, and Britain became the first country in the world to experience an urban environmental problem of modern proportions. Meanwhile, the exuberant spirits of the young were clamped down in the learning routines of the Board Schools; or, if more wealthy, were moulded in the strait jacket of public school conventions. Eventually it became apparent that Victorian society, underneath its armour of confident authority, was suffering from a malaise – as much evident in its art and architecture as in the palid faces of the poor. The critical rumblings of thinkers like Ruskin, William Morris and Herbert Spencer had set off a new search for a human environment preferable to the horrors perpetrated by the Industrial Revolution.

Into this social climate, compounded of romanticism and realism, entered Patrick Geddes (1854–1933), a Scottish Professor of Botany and student of Le Play sociology. In his work and thought were focused the interlapping strands of nineteenth century environmental concern, but he brought to it his own inventive contribution which was to have a great influence on the future development of education. He was dissatisfied with school and university learning methods and appalled by the overpowering growth of what he called 'conurbations' spreading through Britain. The sum of these deficiencies, he believed, resulted in a tragic waste of human beings. Geddes therefore dedicated himself to the improvement of both environment and education, and to this purpose he opened in 1889 a unique educational establishment, The Outlook Tower, in the Royal Mile, Edinburgh.[4] This building still stands as a reminder of Geddes' great achievements. His view was unique and before his time in that he saw a close connection between the quality of education and the quality of environment. He argued that a child brought into contact with the profound realities of his environment would not only be more likely to learn better, but also develop a creative attitude towards his surroundings. In fact, all the elements of the best of present day enlightened teaching were germinal to his thinking. For example, he wanted schools to adopt a 'psychological timetable' based on the 'Three H's: Head, Heart and Hand', rather than the oppressive imposition of the Three R's.

Ultimately, Geddes believed, human life could only flourish if we came to terms with our cities and towns by making them both beautiful and functional places to live in. For him the environment resulted from an interaction between place, work and folk: a trinity from which he was able to derive a whole environmental philosophy practically expressed in the methods of civic and regional surveying he disseminated from the Outlook Tower. Undoubtedly Geddes was the founding father of environmental education. Unfortunately, however, his ideas of education as a vehicle of urban rejuvenation were misinterpreted after his death by members of the post-First World War Le Play Society which encouraged many teachers to indulge in rural surveys appealing to historical sentiment, but having little relevance to Geddes' intention of radically improving the environment. Thus his most important idea was watered down and made impotent as a means of bringing about environmental change.

The essence of the Le Play Society approach was set out by C. C. Fagg and G. E. Hutchings in their book, *An Introduction to Regional Surveying* (1930), which was the prototype of educational fieldwork and an influential contribution to the development of environmental studies in schools. Meanwhile educational theorists, such as Dewey, Adams and Adamson, had ensured that during the inter-war period teachers were converted to the idea that learning for young children at least took place through contact with the environment. This really meant the use of concrete situations rather than abstract and the fostering of observations through nature study. It is significant, however, that the book, *Actuality in the School* by C. J. Cons and C. Fletcher (1938) is considered another key work in the development of environmental studies. The significance lies in the fact that the book dealt with bringing people into the classroom so that children could learn about the lives of the postman, policeman and fireman. Here, then, was a contribution to social education complementing the more prevalent 'nature' element in environmental learning.

It was not until the 1960s that new styles of school architecture and classroom design allowed freer contact with the outside world, reflecting the requirements of child-centred interdisciplinary learning. In addition, the abolition of 11+ examinations in many areas gave schools a freer hand to teach in a way consistent with child development. The term 'environmental studies' had finally entered the vocabulary of the teaching profession mainly through the advocacy of the post-1945 Training Colleges for this sort of schoolwork as part of an overall progressive teaching strategy. But nobody at that time saw environmental studies as the potential progenitor of a 'subject' with even 'subversive' undertones. The commendable Training College lady lecturers in tweed skirts, with map and camera in hand, leading students on forays into the countryside would hardly have believed that they were pioneers of an idea that would shake up many entrenched positions in the teaching profession and join forces with radical elements seeking to improve the quality of environment through political action. If they had such qualms they could turn to such bodies as the Field Studies Council which did, and still does, enormously important but uncontroversial work in propagating fieldwork methods concerned mainly with field biology and physical geography. In this way environmental teachers may have developed a sharp eye for country, but they have until recently been remarkably blind to the problems of the urban and technological world in which the majority of their pupils live. So much so, that D. G. Watts could write in 1969, 'The naturalist element remains a mainspring of the environmental studies movement.'[5] Nevertheless, the late 1960s were fateful years for the evolution of environmental education ideas, and marked the watershed between the apolitical, naturalist practices of environmental studies and the committed activism of environmental education which, in fact, grew out of germinal ideas propounded by a mid-Victorian American.

Conservation and amenity

In 1864, George Perkin Marsh (1801–82), American diplomat and scholar, published his book, *Man and Nature: or Physical Geography as modified by Human Action,* which was the first detailed examination of Man's erosion of Nature.[6] Contrary to the general tenor of nineteenth-century optimism, and at a time when large parts of the world remained unexplored, Marsh documented the extent to which the earth's resources were being depleted, and forecast that such exploitation could not continue without inevitably exhausting the 'bounty of Nature'. Marsh's warning, largely unheeded in Europe, was taken notice of in the USA where vast areas of trees and prairie had been laid waste within a few years. Inspired by his book, great efforts were made to protect some of the threatened places. In 1872 Yellowstone was declared the world's first National Park; in the same year Arbor Day was inaugurated, and during that year, too, the word 'conservation' was first used in the modern sense of 'conserving scarce natural resources'. However, it was not until the 1908 Conference of Governors at the White House, convened by President Theodore Roosevelt, that conservation became a major theme in the policy-making of the United States which thereby became the first industrialized country in the world to take seriously the preservation of its natural environment. Also, another important outcome was the introduction of conservation studies in American schools.

In Britain, mounting concern about the environment was most vocally expressed by people wishing to preserve the amenities of the countryside against the encroaching fingers of urbanization. On the whole, it was a nostalgic aesthetic movement worried about the decline of farming and with a patronizing attitude to the dying rustic ways of life. Naturalists, middleclass countrymen, leftwing rustic philosophers joined forces to create the Council for the Preservation of Rural England in 1926 as a co-ordinating body which 'put the accent strongly on country as against town, and on preservation as against management'.[7] Nevertheless, despite this selective approach it was the first pressure group to call for 'vigorous political and educative activity on a national scale' to protect the countryside. The approach of the amenity movement before the Second World War was summed up in books like *Britain and the Beast.*[8] Characteristically, of course, by Britain we meant the countryside, and the Beast was the urban intruder. C. E. M. Joad, a contributor, opined, 'What this education should be it is confessedly not easy to say. Certain steps are, however, obvious. Lessons in country lore should be given at every school and country manners taught as carefully as social.' However, whatever fears the supporters of the CPRE might have had concerning the fate of the countryside, they were reassured by the belief that Britain's population was declining. Little did they foresee the rapid rise in the birthrate that followed the last war, or the problems of affluence that accompany it.

Post-war environmental awareness

The war years provided an important period of incubation during which many plans for improving the environment were proposed. An enthusiasm for socialism gripped the nation, and an important impetus to this political idealism was the desire to improve the lot of the ordinary person by removing slums, building New Towns and by injecting new life into the decaying industrial regions of the north. These high hopes for post-war reconstruction reached practical expression in the Town and Country Planning Act of 1947, and from that time onwards planning became as much a political activity as an administrative one. The control wielded by planners over the environment caused controversy at both local and national level – arguments that were to increase in frequency and vehemence as planning legislation increased in a land which, by the 1961 Census, had become the most densely populated in the world. What to do about improving the quality of the urban-industrial environment had become as important a consideration as that of the countryside. Meanwhile, 'amenity' gave way to 'conservation of nature' as the prime concern to the ruralists. The Nature Conservancy, instituted in 1949, soon recommended to government the need for an educational policy to protect the countryside. The Conservation Corps, formed in the late fifties, 'opened countless eyes to constructive opportunities and values of nature.' In 1958, the Council of Nature was formed to popularize the problems of wildlife, particularly through such demonstrations as National Nature Week. Unceasingly, too, the mass media fired the public interest in nature conservation through photographic and broadcast accounts.

Nevertheless, despite the work of numerous official and voluntary organizations, it became apparent as a result of the 1963 *Observer* Wild Life Exhibition, that there was a lack of national leadership in initiating official policy towards countryside conservation. This weakness was noted by the Duke of Edinburgh who initiated a study conference entitled *The Countryside in 1970* from which it was hoped would come the machinery for removing the conflicting factions in the conservation movement, and give it a common purpose for the future. The first study conference, held in 1963, brought together representatives from over ninety national organizations. Numerous consultations, policy decisions and surveys followed – the development of nature trails being one, and the impetus given to saving the threatened coastline, another. Importantly, too, a decision was made to call a conference on education at the University of Keele in March 1965. It was here that the term 'environmental education' was heard for the first time in Britain, and where it was agreed that environmental education 'should become an essential part of the education of *all* citizens, not only because of the importance of their understanding something of their environment but because of its immense educational potential in assisting the emergence of a scientifically literate nation'.[9]

How to implement environmental education was another matter. The probable vehicle for this, it was thought, might be biology teaching. But to have reached the 1960s, as Max Nicholson acidly commented, 'with a type of biological education officially stigmatized as perhaps more than useless is an indication that it would be difficult to overstate the scale of default of British educationists.'[10] Of course, since then the Nuffield Biology Project and other schemes have done much towards putting right this bad state of affairs; but the same accusation could have been levelled also at much of geography and history, and not least, at the environmental study courses in Training Colleges. Indeed, the importance of the Keele Conference is that it recognized the essential breadth of environmental education and drew attention to the danger of solely equating environmental education with biology teaching, of neglecting human needs in favour of other living things, of concentrating on the academic ten per cent of the population and of failing to involve the teaching profession as a whole. Nevertheless, the conference saw environmental education as, essentially, conservation or applied ecology. The result was that in March 1968 the Council for Environmental Education was established as a co-ordinating body with Mr (now Sir) Jack Longland as its Chairman. Since then, too, it has given much valuable assistance to teachers through the resource lists and newsletters it has published.[11]

By a historic coincidence, another conference was convened in the same year by Messrs George Martin and G. Barnes at the City of Leicester College of Education with the purpose of bringing together teachers interested in developing environmental studies in school and college. Undoubtedly, there was a need for such a conference, but there is little evidence to suggest that the conveners had in mind more than a discussion of curriculum innovations allowing for pupil-centred, inter-disciplinary learning in the locality of the school. Few who attended dangled the spectre of the 'environmental crisis' before the eyes of the conference members – most had come looking backwards to the ideas of Rousseau rather than forward to the environmental problems confronting the world around them. When the guest speaker referred to environmental studies as 'the most revolutionary form of educational study within living memory',[12] the accent of interest was on method rather than content. This is made clear by Ian F. Rolls' comment on the meeting: 'It has been said that environmental studies is more a way of learning than a subject. It makes sense alongside the traditional disciplines, and as a part of the general education of students whose futures lie more with the teaching of children than with the teaching of a subject.'[13] In the event, the conference recommended the formation of a Society for Environmental Education, thereby allowing the various factions within the emergent Society to work together towards teaching for the betterment of the environment as they could not all agree to teach using the methods of 'environmental studies'. Significantly, Rolls does not mention the adoption of the term 'environmental education' at the conference, yet by March 1969 George Martin, the first Chairman of the Society for Environmental Education (SEE) and its major inspiration, perceptively commented 'It is the value of the contribution to our culture which environmental studies can make, using the environment for education and education for the environment, which must be judged.'[14] From then onwards the search for the identity of environmental studies has also involved defining its doppelganger, environmental education; and to that purpose SEE has devoted many of its valuable conferences and discussion papers.

This continuing problem of identifying the exact nature of environmental education and its relationship to environmental studies on the one hand, and academic disciplines on the other, is one important reason for today's inadequate inclusion of environmental education objectives in school and higher education curricula. In 1970, Report No. 9 of the Council for Environmental Education diagnosed the problem of defining environmental education thus: '. . . it is clear that different people mean different things by it, and also that some who use it are not really certain what they mean. Some of the confusion arises from the tendency for adherents of various disciplines to appropriate the word "environmental" to their own subject, whether this be ecology, geography, history, archaeology, architecture, planning, sociology or rural studies. In particular, some think almost exclusively in terms of the so-called "natural" environments, others of urban or at any rate "man-made" environments. Again, some stress the educational value of using man's biological and physical environment as a basis for studies at first-hand, viewing this environment as a *medium for education*; while others are more concerned with the need to promote a sense of personal responsibility for the state of the environment, which is thus seen as a *goal of education,* since man's health and happiness – and ultimately even his survival – depends on the way he manages it. Confusion also arises from the variable use of the term "environmental studies", sometimes as a synonym for environmental education, sometimes to describe a method of study within particular disciplines, and sometimes . . . as the name of a new and developing subject in its own right.'

In retrospect, however, 1968 can be regarded as the year when the somewhat ill-defined, but potent concept of environmental education made its first real impact on the thinking of teachers. In 1970, the Schools' Council set up Project Environment to explore the relevance of rural studies to environmental education, and by that year the number of environmental studies courses in Colleges of Education were almost double those in 1968; and in 1970, too, the National Rural Studies Association (later to be renamed the National Association for Environmental Education), with a strong country-based tradition going back to the early 1900s, supported the efforts of the Hertfordshire County Council to devise an 'A' level syllabus in environmental studies. The 1971 report of the conference called to formulate the syllabus is a fascinating record of environmental educationists creating out of the entanglement of conflicting opinions an examinable course in environmental studies.[15] At first the proposal was received with little encouragement from the Schools Council, but happily 1975 will see the first candidates taking the examination.

Meanwhile, interdisciplinary degrees studying environmental problems had been introduced into the universities and the expanding polytechnics,[16] mainly as 'environmental science'. Indeed, the creators of the Hertfordshire 'A' level environmental studies syllabus attempted to reconcile 'environmental science' with its emphasis on natural sciences, particularly ecology, with environmental studies having a greater emphasis on socio-economic content, although the

political implications of environmental education were only sketch-
ily touched upon. Exponents of environmental science have continued to make important contributions to school and higher education curricula through such agencies as the Centre for Science
Education, the Association for Science Education[17] and the more
recently formed Institute of Environmental Sciences.[18]

The sum result was that by 1971, following the added impetus
given by European Conservation Year, the environmental education
movement gathered even greater momentum. Although the
development of syllabuses for CSE, 'O' and 'A' levels was under-
way, nevertheless attempts, often ill-defined, to make environmental
studies a 'subject' suitable for non-academic children were being
made to a disturbing extent while the 'bright' pupils were encouraged to concentrate on their academic disciplines having little
or no environmental education content. Geography, traditionally
the main contender to be the subject in schools that taught most
about 'the environment', was now beginning to discard its interest in
the man-land relationship and adopt instead the techniques of
'spatial analysis'. As teachers swung over to teaching environmental
studies so geographers originated more of the techniques for teaching about the human environment, such as games and simulations,

Table 1

DEPARTMENTS INVOLVED IN ENVIRONMENTAL EDUCATION

	%
Geography	73
Biology	59
Science	42
General Studies	37
History	33
Religious Knowledge	23
Humanities	21
Environmental Studies/Science	20
Economics	11
Rural Studies/Science	7
Social Studies/Science	5
Other departments	16
No departments	8
No reply	8

Source: *National Survey into Environmental Education*, The Conservation Society, 1974

perception studies and issue-based enquiries. Yet the so-called 'new
geography', developed in the universities, has introduced into
schoolwork mind-bending exercises in statistics largely irrelevant to
the urgent problems confronting the environment we live in. Just as
the subject was, and is, undergoing traumatic change to a more
theory-based study so the loyalty of teachers has been torn between

11

allegiance to the abstractions of the new geography and conversion to the ideals and objectives of environmental education. Nevertheless, teachers trained in geography make up the greatest number supporting the environmental education movement as can be seen from Table 1.

Another powerful factor in the development of environmental education has been the growing interest in outdoor education ranging from mountaineering to camping, canoeing to orienteering, and many other activities.[19] Increasingly, therefore, the promoters of these expeditions, whether schools or organizations like the Youth Hostels Association, see their work as part of environmental education. In addition, many Educational Authorities have set up Outdoor Study Centres; and fieldwork excursions of all kinds (particularly now that fieldwork questions enter examinations) have increased considerably the number of study parties using the outdoors as a 'laboratory'. The result is that many of the popular areas are overused, for example the Lake District. The risks to students' lives in mountainous areas and the disruption fieldwork activities may cause to the environment, such as the removal of rare specimens, has today led to efforts by the Geographical Association and the Council for Environmental Education to control fieldwork activities by arguing for the introduction of a fieldwork qualification which teachers should have before leading students on this special kind of educational enterprise.

The environmental revolution

The growth of the environmental education movement after 1968 can only be understood in the light of what Max Nicholson has called the 'Environmental Revolution'.[20] By this he means a new and creative concern for lives and landscapes, about which Nicholson observed 'It has been said that the one thing in the world which is invincible is an idea whose time has come. Such an idea, in these days, is the care of man's environment, or in a word, conservation.' Many calamities, like the wreck of the Torrey Canyon spilling its oil along the south coast, have occurred to underline dramatically the urgency of his point. Why, then, did not environmental issues enter public awareness until the late 1960s despite the fact that as early as 1962 Rachel Carson published her disturbing book, *Silent Spring*? Other American writers had written copiously on the perils of destroying the world's soil ever since the disaster of the American Dustbowl; and in Britain, even before the war, Sir George Stapledon had pleaded for the adoption of human ecology as a means of preserving the earth's fertility.[21] Perhaps, like all revolutions, the environmental one began only after numerous uncontrollable pressures for change had built up to the point where they could be held back no longer. Ecologists and conservationists, while forming the most dramatic pressure groups were joined by economists like J. K. Galbraith who had acidly wondered in his book, *The Affluent Society*, why rich societies enjoyed so much private wealth in such dreadful public squalor of the communal environment. However, whatever the exact causes, in Britain the 'revolution' was finally triggered off by the 1969 BBC Reith Lectures, *Wilderness and Plenty*, given by the ecologist Sir Frank Fraser Darling, and almost overnight the environment became a topic debated on chat shows, pronounced upon by pop stars and even inspired the TV drama series, *Doomwatch*.

Already in the United States Professors Paul Ehrlich and Barry Commoner were popularizing ecology as the key word in the environmental debate.[22] In Britain their books were being eagerly discussed, and in 1970 the magazine *Ecologist* was launched as a powerful contribution to the ferment of environmental ideas – achieving its greatest coup, perhaps, with the publication in Spring 1971 of *Blueprint for Survival*,[23] describing a scheme (supported by many influential scientists and politicians) to get Britain into an ecologically healthy condition by taking some fairly strong social measures, such as the dispersion and decentralization of cities. A new prefix, 'eco-', was introduced into the English language so that people now talk about eco-farming, eco-houses, eco-mystics and many other variations. The prefix can be used either as a term of abuse or approval according to the extent one considers the eco-propagandists right in their prophesies of environmental doom. Another consequence of the 'revolution' is the discussion concerning man's need for a new morality towards nature proselytized by eco-evangelistic movements such as Friends of the Earth, and argued for by churchmen like the Bishop of Kingston. By 1972 a group of industrialists, calling themselves the Club of Rome, joined in the debate by publishing a calm scientific appraisal of the ecological future of the world in the book *Limits to Growth*.[24] They applied the methods of general systems analysis to arrive at their conclusions. It is interesting to note that the principles of systems analysis have not been used so far by advocates of environmental studies as a unifying philosophy for environmental education. Perhaps that has to come.

However, the 'Environmental Revolution' took a new direction, not entirely foreseen by the earlier environmentalists and resulting from the growing impact on people's lives of the decisions made by planners in their efforts to control the development of the built environment. In 1964 Colin Buchanan's masterly report, *Traffic in Towns,* caused wide public debate by arguing that it was a question of choice between whether we wanted a good environment for men to live in or for cars to move in. This was the first public issue to popularize the idea of 'environmental quality' in urban areas. During the late sixties, too, bitter controversy arose from the alleged need to build a third London Airport somewhere in southern England. This problem was examined by the Roskill Commission, and the conflicts of opinion it generated and the kind of evidence it uncovered resembled on a grand scale the many irksome conflicts over local planning issues occurring in many places of lesser national importance. Increasingly, too, the opinion grew that planning was not operating in accord with democratic procedures, and decisions were being taken over the heads of ordinary people without giving them a chance to influence the plans affecting their lives. In 1969, therefore, but without attracting anything like the same publicity as the dramatic gestures of the ecologists, the Government published the Skeffington Report *People and Planning* which recommended the setting up of machinery for the public to participate in planning and the teaching of planning in schools.[25] In 1970 the Department of Environment was created. So it came about that the word 'environment' was given official blessing, and came to include not only the natural but also the built environment which the ordinary person could, in principle at least, take part in planning. In fact, environmental action groups of various kinds sprang up to do just that. Until then Nicholson's 'Environmental Revolution' was the revolt of the *élite* and well-informed middle classes; but from the date of the publication of the Skeffington Report the revolution became an urgent search, however devious, to find methods of involving the proletariat in questions of environmental policy – despite the fact that trade unionists have not always agreed that 'good environment' is necessarily also good for ensuring jobs for the workers! Nevertheless, it is precisely this search which has produced a more comprehensive view of the scope and purpose of environmental education whereby, to the Rousseau tradition of the educationist and the conservationist tradition of the ecologist, has been added a new urban-proletariat influence having its origins in the thinking of Kropotkin, Geddes and Marx.

Environmental education as a world movement

By 1970 demands for school curricula orientated towards environmental education objectives had sprung up in many countries throughout the world, inspired mainly by ecological considerations. The term 'environmental education' was in any case first used in the United States. As Mark Terry reminds us, 'Environmental Education, whether termed "ecology", "nature study" or another name, was championed at nearly all the life science curriculum meetings in this country [the USA] since the turn of the century.'[26] It is no surprise, therefore, that when other countries were just beginning the development of environmental education programmes, the USA became the first nation to pass an Environmental Education Act in 1970.[27]

The work of the IUCN (International Union for the Conservation of Nature and Natural Resources), under the leadership of Dr Jan Cerovsky, provided the impetus towards what the IUCN term 'environmental conservation education'. Indeed, the most popularly used, but by no means universally subscribed to, definition of environmental education was agreed to at the IUCN Nevada Conference of 1970. This definition is discussed in the next chapter, but it is interesting to note, however, that the definition did not include the word 'environment' because the participants sought in vain for an explicit and clear definition of the noun to which they could all subscribe.

The United Nations Conference on the Human Environment held in Stockholm in September 1972 focused world attention not only on international ecological problems, but also on the problems of human settlement as well. Here controversy broke out between the representatives of the developing countries and the affluent industrialized countries. The latter were accused of wanting to limit the further progress of the poorer nations by using the excuse of environmental pollution as a means of preventing competition arising from industrialization in those less fortunate parts of the world. In addition, breakaway groups sprang up which ignored conference proceedings in order to develop ideas of their own which they considered more relevant than those being canvassed by official government representatives. Finally, agreement was sought in the publication of a Declaration on the Human Environment giving broad guidelines for governments to follow, and a World Action Plan for the Environment was approved. In particular, the conference recommended that an international programme in environmental education should be established, 'with a view to educating the ordinary citizen as to the simple steps he might take within his means to manage and control his environment'.[28]

Education for environmental participation

The next important educational development in Britain occurred when the Town and Country Planning Association, spurred on by numerous requests for information received from schools, established an Education Unit. The Association felt that 'planning had become so pervasive in its effects and influences that the Association base should be broadened to cover fields hitherto neglected – including education'.[29] In early 1971, Colin Ward, a former architect and teacher, and Anthony Fyson, geographer and planner, were appointed Education Officers. To this task they have brought a panache for propagandizing ideas concerning urban environmental education which complements the powerful ecological and conservation groups campaigning also for environmental education. The TCPA Education Unit has set out to do three things: to publish a monthly *Bulletin of Environmental Education* (*BEE*); to establish town trails in urban areas;[30] and to campaign for the setting up of Urban Study Centres.[31] The Unit has taken much of its inspiration from the work of Patrick Geddes, emphasizing and up-dating his concept of education for citizenship and modelling the idea of the Urban Study Centre on the prototype of the Outlook Tower. In addition, the educational strategy advocated in the pages of *BEE* derives much from the radical educational philosophy of thinkers like Paul Goodman and the de-schoolers such as Ivan Illich. The emphasis of this approach is contained within the term 'streetwork' coined by Anthony Fyson, and explained by him thus: 'The emotional contact with poverty, unhappiness and general dissatisfaction with which urban studies pupils are inevitably confronted seems barely represented by the bland and curious phrase "urban fieldwork", and I propose "streetwork" in its place – suggestive I hope of the kind of community involvement already aimed at in the *avante-garde* theatrical world through "street theatre".[32]

The first issue of *BEE,* May 1971, carried an article by Michael Storm entitled, ' "School and Community", an issue-based approach', which provided the TCPA Education Unit with a 'manifesto' based on the educational recommendations of the Skeffington Report and urging the adoption of a conflict-centred curriculum for environmental studies orientated towards understanding community issues in an urban context. Such a curriculum, Storm argued, 'would bear relatively little resemblance to present courses bearing this label; pupils might be more concerned with pressure groups and the mechanism of environmental decision-making than with the mere recording of existing land use. A crucial stage of political sophistication would be reached once it was realized that opposing interests are not necessarily physically distinct as are the adequately housed preservationists, and the inadequately housed militant.'

Since that original issue *BEE* has provided the main vehicle of ideas for introducing planning education into the school curriculum. In addition, it has campaigned for the introduction of architectural education,[33] and in this endeavour it is supported by the current (1974) preparations for European Architectural Heritage Year, 1975. In many ways, too, the views and trends expressed in the columns of *BEE* were endorsed by the Government report on the human habitat, *How Do You Want to Live?,* brought out as a contribution to the 1972 Stockholm Conference, which proposed as a prime recommendation that 'Environmental education and the exercise of citizenship go hand in hand; the opening up of opportunities for public participation in decision-making is the most important of all means to environmental education, which should aim at developing a critical, moral and aesthetic awareness of our surroundings.'

Conclusion

Despite well-publicized efforts to develop issue-based environmental education with an urban component, it is still possible for environmental education to be mistaken for a synonym of ecological conservation education, and for its impact to be dissipated in a multitude of overlapping approaches. This gives rise to a dilemma of identity as was reflected once again in a recent survey which discovered that environmental education was being 'taught partially and incoherently, with virtually no overall thought or organization'.[34] Undoubtedly the plurality of environmental education is both its strength and its weakness; but many questions concerning its definition and its curriculum objectives have to be answered if progress is to be made towards devising coherent and relevant programmes encompassing all age groups and ability levels. Hopefully, the task of resolving these internal dilemmas may be accomplished by the recently formed Sussex University Environmental Education Research Project, funded by the Leverhulme Trust.[35] Ultimately, too, hope rests in the fact that environmental education is one important manifestation of the new idea of environment that contemporary man is seeking to formulate in a dangerously threatened habitat.

References

1. WATTS, D. G., 1969, *Environmental Studies*, Routledge & Kegan Paul, London.
2. FLETCHER, R., 1969, 'Frederick Le Play' in T. Raison (ed.) *The Founding Fathers of Social Science*, Penguin, Harmondsworth.
3. NORDENSKIOLD, E., 1946, *The History of Biology*, Knopf, New York.
4. WHEELER, K. S., 1970, 'The Outlook Tower: Birthplace of Environmental Education', *SEE—Bulletin of the Society for Environmental Education*, **2**, No. 2.
5. WATTS, *op. cit.*
6. CLACKEN, J., 1956, 'Changing Ideas of the Habitable World' in W. L. Thomas *et al.* (eds.), *Man's Role in Changing the Face of the Earth*, The University of Chicago Press, Chicago.
7. NICHOLSON, M., 1970, *The Environmental Revolution*, Hodder & Stoughton, London.
8. WILLIAMS-ELLIS, C. (ed.), 1937, *Britain and the Beast*, Dent, London.
9. CHRISTIAN, G., 1966, 'Education for the Environment', *The Quarterly Review*, April.
10. NICHOLSON, *op. cit.*
11. *REED: Review of Environmental Education Developments*, quarterly newsletter of the Council of Environmental Education, Reading.
12. Editorial, *SEE: Bulletin of the Society for Environmental Education*, **1**, No. 1, 1968.
13. ROLLS, I. F., 1969, 'Environmental Studies, a new Synthesis?', *Education for Teaching*, Spring.
14. MARTIN, G. C., 1969, 'Across the Disciplines', *The Times Educational Supplement*, 28 March.
15. CARSON, S. McB. (compiler), 1971, *Environmental Studies: the construction of an 'A' Level Syllabus*, National Foundation for Educational Research in England and Wales, Slough.
16. Centre for Educational Research and Innovation (CERI), 1973, *Environmental Education at University Level: trends and data*, Organisation for Economic Co-operation & Development, London.
17. Association for Science Education (see list of addresses at the back of this book).
18. Institute of Environmental Sciences (see list of addresses at the back of this book).

19. PARKER, T. M. & MELDRUM, K. I., 1973, *Outdoor Education*, Dent, London.
20. NICHOLSON, *op. cit.*
21. STAPLEDON, G., 1964, *Human Ecology*, Faber, London.
22. (a) EHRLICH, P. & A., 1970, *Population, Resources, and Environment*, W. H. Freeman, San Francisco.
    (b) COMMONER, B., 1970, *Science and Survival*, Ballantine Books, New York.
23. GOLDSMITH, A., 1972, *Blueprint for Survival*, Tom Stacey, London.
24. MEADOWS, D. H. *et al.*, 1972, *The Limits to Growth*, Earth Island, London.
25. Skeffington Report, 1969, *People and Planning: Report of the Committee on Public Participation in Planning*, HMSO, London.
26. TERRY, M., 1971, *Teaching for Survival: a Handbook for Environmental Education*, Ballantine Books, New York.
27. HAWKINS, D. E. & VINTON, D. A., 1973, *The Environmental Classroom*, Prentice-Hall, Englewood Cliffs, N.J.
28. Recommendations for Action of the United Nations Conference on the Human Environment, Stockholm, 5–16 June 1972.
29. Report of meeting on environmental education held at the Planning Centre, Town and Country Planning Association, 6 November 1969.
30. (a) WHEELER, K. & WAITES, B., 1972, 'Leicester Town Trail', *Bulletin of Environmental Education*, September.
    (b) GOODEY, B., 1974, *Urban Trails: a preliminary list of trails and sources*, Centre for Urban and Regional Studies, University of Birmingham.
31. (a) Council for Urban Study Centres, 1974, *First Report*, The Town & Country Planning Association.
    (b) FYSON, A., 1974, 'What happens at an Urban Study Centre', *Bulletin of Environmental Education*, April.
32. WARD, C. & FYSON, A., 1973, *Streetwork: the exploding school*, Routledge & Kegan Paul, London.
33. WARD, C. & MACEWEN, M., 1973, 'Architecture in Schools', *Bulletin of Environmental Education*, June.
34. BERRY, P. S., 1974, *National Survey into Environmental Education in Secondary Schools* (Report and Recommendations), The Conservation Society, Chertsey.
35. Further information from: The Director, Environmental Education Research Project, University of Sussex (see the list of addresses at the back of this book).

2 A review of objectives for environmental education

George C. Martin

The objectives for environmental education vary according to the values and interests held by those advocating the necessity to teach about the environment. Those advocates holding conservationists' ideals want a form of environmental education that sets its objectives firmly on the promulgation of the wise use of natural resources. The educationists who urge the implementation of environmental education curricula in schools and colleges vary in their objectives according to their respective emphasis upon environment as a concept; or on education as a process stimulated or hindered by environmental experiences. Much discussion has also taken place on the definition of 'environment'. Is the 'natural environment', or the 'built environment' the one to be considered? Does the term 'human environment' cover the total environmental setting for human beings including natural and social phenomena? In dealing with the objectives for environmental education the efforts of the nature conservationists and the educationists will be reviewed and placed within the context of educating about the human environment.

Conservationists

As has been explained in the preceding chapter, the use of the term 'environmental education' was introduced to Britain at the Countryside in 1970 Conference held in 1965. In 1967, Robert Arvill indicated a need for a form of environmental education requiring a new approach in schools.[1] He wanted children to learn respect for other forms of life and suggested that caring for their environment is essential to a child's own personal status as well as to a proper enjoyment of that heritage. Arvill's aim for environmental education was the stimulation of enquiry into the factors governing environment and the interactions between it and man. He considered that man's powers and responsibilities, and his capacity to alter and recreate society should be explained to pupils.

At the same time the movement towards environmental education was under way in America. In 1969 Stapp, writing in the American *Journal of Environmental Education,* claimed that environmental education was aimed at producing citizens who were knowledgeable about the bio-physical environment and its associated problems, aware of how to help solve those problems, and motivated to work towards their solution.[2] In addition, an international working meeting was held in Nevada in 1970 by the International Union for the Conservation of Nature and Natural Resources (IUCN). The following definition was proposed at that conference: 'Environmental education is the process of recognizing values and clarifying concepts in order to develop skills and attitudes necessary to understand and appreciate the inter-relatedness among man, his culture and his bio-physical surroundings. Environmental education also entails practice in decision-making and self-formulation of a code of behaviour about issues concerning environmental quality.'[3] The conference further agreed that environmental education was a science-orientated, multi-disciplinary subject where most, if not all, school subjects could, and should be, incorporated.

Mark Terry, on the other hand, stressed that the process could occur in all educational situations, scientific and humanistic. Nevertheless, he is concerned essentially with conservation education based on a sense of urgency deriving from the threat of an ecological crisis.[4] In this country, Charles Mellowes gave his overall objective for environmental education as the progressive development of a sense of concern for the environment based on a full and sensitive understanding of the relation of man to his surroundings. Mellowes was satisfied that all aspects of environment came within that objective – rural as well as urban – and that the bounds of the environment expand as age and experience widen an individual's horizons.[5] Colin Selby, more specifically, asked teachers to cause their students to 'think conservation' as he saw environmental education concerned more with fostering an attitude rather than teaching a subject. That kind of attitude to environment and resources should be second nature to every citizen, claimed Selby.[6]

In fact, conservation education was equated with environmental education until about 1970 when as a complete objective for that process it was first questioned at a Society for Environmental Education Leicester Conference held at the end of that year. Phillips pointed out that conservation interpreted as by, for and on behalf of the middle classes made a poor motto for a movement which was supposed to be of urgent concern to the whole of mankind.[7] Carthy also argued that considerable danger lurked in the suggestion that everything should be subservient to conservation. Just as natural selection produced a compromise between all the needs of an organism so also conservation should aim to be a compromise between social and aesthetic needs as well as the needs of the future environment. Therefore, he suggested, it was time to emphasize that environmental education is not the same as conservation education.[8] Instead of being mainly concerned with the management of resources such as soil, water, forests, wild life and air, environmental education should be equally concerned with all aspects of the social environment of man, with man-made environments and their effects on man, as well as the natural environment.

We have seen that the advocates of environmental education with a bias towards conservation conceive of it also including the development of an 'environmental ethic'.[9] They want the moral relationship of people towards the natural environment taught as part of the curriculum, for such an ethic determines the way people use the land, air and other resources which in turn determines the quality of the human environment. The search for the quality of environment is, therefore, linked to the quest for an environmental ethic. Vivian suggests that any ethic for environmental quality must include three basic beliefs:

1. A reverence for all life;
2. A respect for the right to existence of all life;
3. A recognition given to placing the highest priority on achieving environmental quality.[10]

Ron Colton, the Director of the Schools Council Project Environment, stressed that a conservation ethic, meaning a deep sense of responsibility towards the earth and all its inhabitants, was the ultimate goal for environmental education.[11] His deputy, R. F. Morgan, put forward the idea that the aim of environmental education is to develop attitudes and levels of understanding leading to a personal environmental ethic. Further, he wanted to see pupils educated so that their actions and influence upon collective decisions would be positively for the benefit of the environment.[12]

The Conservation Society recently prepared a statement on educational priorities. The first priority is seen as the need to make sure that young people have an appreciation of man's place in history, and particularly of the critical nature of his present phase. Second, they place the promotion of the study of ecology, both for its own sake and as a help in understanding the nature of man's present predicament based on enquiry, into the three inter-related areas of population, resources and environment. Third, they wish to maintain a debate on the social conditions required to effect a smooth transition to a sustainable society, and fourthly to consider what such a future society might be like. The Conservation Society, therefore, wishes to encourage schools, colleges and universities to become more closely involved with the life of the community they serve in order to achieve the objectives implied in these educational priorities.[13]

Educationists

The conservationists may have led the way in proposing environmental education programmes, but educationists, as indicated in Chapter 1, were also developing ideas concerning environmental education employing teaching methods using the direct impact of the environment, as in environmental studies, or for teaching about the environment, as with the fieldwork methods developed by subjects like biology and geography.[14] The International Bureau of Education, a UNESCO organization, carried out an international inquiry into the educational use of the environment as practised by schools in the mid-1960s.[15] The Bureau's questionnaire brought replies from seventy-nine countries, and these showed general agreement that the study of environment by schoolchildren provided rich educational opportunities for training in observation and the encouragement to think, compare, analyse, synthesize and research. It was claimed also that in this way pupils developed a love and respect for nature and adjusted better to their surroundings. Those, of course, are similar objectives to the ones argued for by the conservationists. But the enquiry revealed another benefit, which was that such studies contributed to social and civic education as well as fostering international understanding. In order to accomplish this global awareness of environment the report suggested that this study should start with immediate surroundings and move out to consider more distant forms of environment.

Similar pleas have been heard in the development of curriculum work within environmental studies in this country. Environmental studies, as noted in Chapter 1, is a term which has become well accepted in primary and secondary schools in Britain.[16] The Schools Council (Welsh) Environmental Studies Project aided that acceptance for the middle years of schooling. The broad objectives for environmental studies, as advanced by the project, are the development of confident, enquiring children aware of the nature, variety and beauty in the world around them, and having the skills to order and communicate their awareness in a variety of forms. Skills that could be developed by environmental studies, and thereby form part of environmental education, were placed into three groups by the Project team:

1. Study skills such as mapping, collecting and classifying materials; experimenting, preparing interviews and questionnaires, and the reading of photographs and documents;
2. Basic skills of literacy and numeracy developed to support the study skills;
3. Social skills – including attitudes shown to people and respect for the quality of the environment.[17]

As suggested already, educationists distinguish between learning *from* an environment and learning *about* an environment. Both aspects of environmental studies use the environment as a medium for education. This was noted, for example, by the Council for Environmental Education in their *Report No. 9* where they further considered that some educationists viewed environment as a medium for education by advancing the educational value of using man's biological and physical environment as a basis for studies at first hand.[18] George Watts has called learning *from* an environment 'applied' environmental studies. It can occur throughout the range of subjects contained within a school curriculum where the aim is to select learning situations using the environment to bring about the achievement of purely educational objectives. On the other hand, learning *about* an environment has been labelled by Watts as 'pure' environmental studies because it has as its central objective the acquisition of knowledge about that environment. In this case the environment provides the learning situations in which a range of skills can be developed to achieve the desired knowledge as in geographical or biological field studies. Watts offered four objectives for a pupil undertaking pure environmental studies. These are:

1. The ability to identify the main features of any local environment in which he finds himself (knowledge);
2. The ability to explain how these features interrelate, contributing to the character of the neighbourhood (analysis);
3. The ability to perceive where modifications to the environment might be made (synthesis);

4. The ability to evaluate the various interpretations which have already been made of the environment (evaluation).[19]

Lines and Bolwell added a further dimension to this version of environmental studies when they asked that students be given opportunities to do more than observe, record and analyse the environment. They want them made aware of the need to be involved in the active conservation of what is valuable in the environment, and in the improvement of the quality of the environment in which they live, by taking an active interest in local planning problems and, where possible, taking part in surveys on which planning decisions are based.[20] The arousal of concern about these same kinds of environmental matters has also been emphasized by educationists, Colin and Mog Ball,[21] and identified as the essence of environmental education which they described as being 'two steps forward' from the geography usually taught in schools – step one being environmental studies and rural studies which stress that learning about the environment should take place in the environment rather than in the classroom. It is environmental education which takes the next step by urging that learning about the environment must encourage a felt concern for it. Martin has pointed out a third step for environmental education which is the move from concern for the environment to the stage of taking action to improve it.[22]

The IUCN definition for environmental education, already quoted, was accepted by the working party for an 'A' level syllabus for environmental studies, and from that definition the working party agreed on the following educational objectives:

1. To make clear the concept of the ecological inter-relationship of the physical and biological factors that make up the environment;
2. To develop skills and attitudes necessary to appreciate the place of Man in the environment and the impact of human society on his biophysical surroundings;
3. To study the ways in which Man may control his environmental impact and to recognize the values by which such control may be guided.[23]

The working party suggested that these objectives would be better advanced by placing students in situations of personal involvement, contributing to their studies through extensive field and laboratory work rather than too much authoritative teaching.

The IUCN definition was also adopted by the Joint Working Party on Environmental Education, which identified the objectives in primary school teaching as assistance to acquire and progressively develop basic skills and concepts, to provide a source and stimulus for creative work and to give opportunities for making discoveries at first hand. This approach should lead in turn to the development of an awareness of personal environmental responsibilities. In secondary schools, the working party urged there should be a continuation of learning from the environment by direct experience so that a concern for the environment may be developed. The working party further agreed that most subjects could make their own contributions to environmental education.[24]

Such a view that environmental education could be implemented in diverse ways has been frequently cited by the Society for Environmental Education. The Society fully recognizes the value of education proceeding from experience of the environment as well as the necessity to educate about the environment. This in turn ensures that the implementation of objectives is firmly based in the area of child development. These convictions are further reflected in the aim of SEE to provide opportunities for the discussion and interchange of ideas on the role of the environment in education. Thus the Society sets its own objectives as the encouragement of:

1. The recognition of the usefulness of the environment in providing a stimulus for learning and creativity, and
2. The recognition of the importance within a general education of developing both an understanding and appreciation of environment.

In supporting both educationists and environmentalists in these two objectives SEE plays an important part in the development of environmental education in this country.

Similarly, the need for an 'environmental ethic' expressed originally by conservationists and ecologists was recognized also by the Council for Environmental Education when it reported that some people considered there was a need to promote a sense of personal responsibility for the state of the environment, and that teaching for such an ethic could be regarded as an important aim for environmental education agreed by environmentalists and educationists alike.

In its report the Council reflected on its experience based on the findings of its separate sub-committees for Higher Education, Schools and Resources. Already, by European Conservation Year 1970, the Council sensed an uncertainty about environmental education in this country, with different people meaning different things by the term, and even some quite unsure what they meant by

26

its use. Some of this confusion still comes from a tendency for the followers of various disciplines to appropriate the word 'environmental' to their own subject – whether it be ecology, geography, history, archaeology, architecture, planning, sociology or rural studies. It is interesting to note, for example, that the National Rural Studies Association became the National Rural and Environmental Association about that time, and then changed its name again within a short time to the National Association for Environmental Education.

Charles Mellowes, then Secretary of CEE, spelled out the different objectives required to meet the overall aim of progressively developing a sense of concern for the environment.[25] At the primary stage, Mellowes felt, the objective should be to introduce a child to the elements of school and home environments, and only towards the end of that stage should a scientific approach to the child's surroundings be introduced into the curriculum. For secondary school work Mellowes defined four objectives for environmental education. One was to use the environment as a medium for teaching a subject. Another was to ensure the implications of the application to environmental developments of scientific discoveries. A third objective was to introduce pupils to an understanding of the conflicts of environmental interests within a community, while his final objective was to encourage pupils to participate in local conservation schemes. In addition, Mellowes wanted the development of a social conscience fostered in further education students by working within a framework of environmental education as, for example, examining the current problems of pollution and conservation; looking objectively at the conflict of interests in the problems affecting the student's own neighbourhood.

Martin further proposed the long-term objectives for environmental education as sensitivity towards the environment and Man's status therein.[26] His medium-term objectives included environmental awareness, which he explained as the ability to perceive the range and quality of factors, elements or variables in an environmental situation. The other medium-term objective he labelled 'environmental thinking' which he explained as the ability to:

1. Obtain significant meaning from environmental facts;
2. Apply environmental facts and generalizations to the solution of new problems;
3. Respond critically and discriminately to ideas and arguments about environmental matters.

Within his short-term objectives, Martin placed environmental information, study skills and action skills. For environmental information a student should develop a familiarity with facts and generalizations relevant to significant environmental problems. The study skills are similar to those already identified by the Schools Council (Welsh) Project for Environmental Studies; but action skills call for a knowledge of the social processes which bring about environmental changes.

George Watts has stressed that a consensus of agreement about the role of environmental education in the school curriculum will be found in the area of child development.[27] The real difference, therefore, between environmentalists and educationists is, as Martin points out, that the former are concerned with the quality of the environment whereas the latter are concerned to improve the quality of life.[28] A compromise between these two extremes is needed if further progress is to be made towards implementing environmental education objectives in the school curriculum. Perhaps this can be achieved by considering what is meant by the human environment.

Human environment

The question as to what environmental education *is*, and therefore what educational objectives it should set out to achieve, involves also defining the meaning of the word environment. In fact, a satisfactory definition of environment is notoriously difficult to achieve. It may be useful, for example, to think of environment as the total complex of inter-relationships making up the physical, biological and social surroundings. On the other hand, Britain's Department of Environment, a government ministry, is responsible for the whole range of functions affecting peoples' living environments.[29] Furthermore, within the United States Senate Report explaining the 1970 Environmental Education Act there is a definition of environmental education, and an explanation of what could be termed environmental.[30] It stresses that environmental education is an integrated process which deals with man's inter-relationship with his natural and man-made surroundings. Environmental education is seen as a study of the factors influencing ecosystems, mental and physical growth, living conditions, the decay of cities and population problems. Environmental education, the report claimed, was

intended to promote among citizens the awareness and understanding of environment, our relationship to it and the responsible
action necessary to assure our survival while improving the quality
of life. Continuously occurring in the debate about the spirit and
purpose of environmental education are the terms 'natural environment', 'living environment' and 'total environment'.

In 1972 the term 'human environment' was first used in this conec-
tion at the United Nations Stockholm Conference. The report,
published as a British contribution to this conference and entitled
How do you want to live?,[31] considered that environmental education was concerned with teaching about a human habitat which is
not merely a world of objects, but also a world of values. The moral
purpose of environmental education, therefore, is to enable citizens
to understand these values. The report linked this to a form of civic
education leading to a more advanced environmental consciousness
which could be expressed through using the political processes
governing the creation of the human environment. The need for
awareness and participation in environmental decision-making by
the public is, therefore, an important aim for an environmental
education concerned with improving the quality of the human
environment aesthetically, culturally and physically.

Perhaps the most important educational method for developing
education about the human environment is through 'streetwork' as
advocated by Colin Ward and Anthony Fyson of the Town and
Country Planning Association Education Unit.[32] Importantly, they
see society moving from a formal democracy to a fully participatory
one in which people cherish their environment because it is theirs to
take part in creating and conserving. This approach has been
summed up by Jean Forbes in a recent article in the *Bulletin of
Environmental Education* where she offers the following definition
of environmental education: 'the study of the activities of people in
relation to the physical world around them, and the study of the
socio-political institutions (e.g. the statutory planning system) which
regulates this relationship in the interests of society as a whole.'[33] In
other words, as Michael Storm and other commentators have noted,
environmental education does not ultimately have validity unless it
also involves educating to change the human environment for the
better by understanding on the one hand the political processes by
which this can be done as 'participating citizens'; and on the other
hand, as noted by the conservationists and other environmentalists,
by acquiring an environmental ethic and a knowledge of the ecological basis of all life, on which value judgements about the en-

vironment can be based. Thus any definition of environment must take into account human and natural aspects of the surroundings we inhabit.

Conclusion

As yet no unifying environmental or educational philosophy underlies the diverse ramifications of the environmental education move-

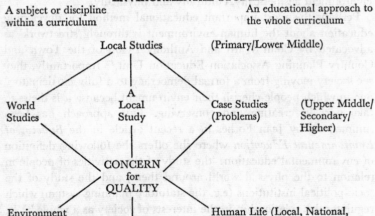

ENVIRONMENTAL EDUCATION

| Environmentalists (concern for environment) | | | Educationists (concern for education) |

METHODOLOGIES

Segmentalists	Inter-discip.	Multi-discip.	Holists
within separate subjects	within a few linked subjects	across a wide range of subjects	undifferentiated approach (Who cares which subject areas we use to understand the whole?)

ENVIRONMENTAL STUDIES

A subject or discipline within a curriculum

An educational approach to the whole curriculum

Local Studies (Primary/Lower Middle)

World Studies — A Local Study — Case Studies (Problems) (Upper Middle/ Secondary/ Higher)

CONCERN for QUALITY

Environment (Conservation)

Human Life (Local, National, International)

INFORMED CONCERN AND ACTION THROUGH PARTICIPATION IN THE PLANNING PROCESS

Figure 1

ment, which extends right across the educational spectrum from its earliest stages up to higher education. The complexity of the various approaches to environmental education reviewed in this chapter is summed up in Figure 1. The rest of this book gives the student some insight into environmental curricula being introduced into schools, colleges and institutes of higher education both in this country and abroad, on which a fuller consideration of the objectives of environmental education may be based.

References
1. ARVILL, R., 1971, *Man and Environment*, Penguin, Harmondsworth.
2. STAPP, W. B. *et al.*, 1969, 'The Concept of Environmental Education', *The Journal of Environmental Education*, **1**, No. 1.
3. International Working Meeting on Environmental Education in the School Curriculum, 1970, *Final Report*, International Union for Conservation of Nature and Natural Resources, September.
4. TERRY, M., 1971, *Teaching for Survival*, Pan Books, London.
5. MELLOWES, C., 1972, 'Environmental Education and the Search for Objectives' in *Environmental Education: the Present and Future Trends*, *Occasional Paper No. 6*, Society for Environmental Education, Portsmouth.
6. SELBY, G., 1970, 'Think Conservation', *Dialogue*, Schools' Council Newsletter No. 6 August.
7. PHILLIPS, A. A. C., 1972, 'The Countryside Commission's research and implications for environmental education', *Occasional Paper No. 6*, Society for Environmental Education, Portsmouth.
8. CARTHY, J. D., 1972, 'Environmental Education and the Adult', *Occasional Paper No. 6*, Society for Environmental Education, Portsmouth.
9. VIVIAN, V. E., 1973, *Sourcebook for Environmental Education*, C. V. Mosby, St. Louis, Mo.
10. VIVIAN, *op. cit.*
11. COLTON, R. W., 1972, 'Environmental Education in Secondary Schools: a new role for rural studies', *Occasional Paper No. 6*, Society for Environmental Education, Portsmouth.
12. MORGAN, R. F., 1972, 'An Exploration of Objectives and Approaches in Environmental Education', *Occasional Paper No. 7*, Society for Environmental Education, Portsmouth.
13. Conservation Society, 1973, *Education for Our Future*, Conservation Trust, Chertsey.
14. MARTIN, G. C., 1969, 'Towards a Definition', *SEE*, **1**, No. 2.
15. UNESCO Report, 1968, *The Study of Environment in School*, Geneva.
16. MARTIN, C. G., 1969, 'Across the Disciplines', *The Times Educational Supplement*, 28 March.
17. HARRIS, M. I., 1972, 'The Nature and Value of Environmental Studies', *Occasional Paper No. 6*, Society for Environmental Education, Portsmouth.
18. Council for Environmental Education, 1970, *Report No. 9*, Reading.
19. WATTS, D. G., 1969, *Environmental Studies*, Routledge & Kegan Paul, London.
20. LINES, C. J. & BOLWELL, L. H., 1971, *Teaching Environmental Studies*, Ginn, Aylesbury.
21. BALL, C. & M., 1973, *Education for a Change*, Penguin, Harmondsworth.
22. MARTIN, G. C., 1974, 'Chairman's Remarks', *SEE* 6, No. 1.
23. CARSON, S. McB. (compiler), 1971, *Environmental Studies: the construction of an 'A' Level Syllabus*, National Foundation for Education Research, Slough.
24. Joint Working Party on Environmental Education, 1972, *Report*, Conservation Society, Chertsey.
25. MELLOWES, *op. cit.*

26. MARTIN, G. C., *Environmental Education and its Objectives*, Council for Environmental Education Discussion Papers, Reading (no date).
27. WATTS, D. G., 1973, 'Environmental Studies: some afterthoughts in an exploration of objectives and approaches in environmental education', *Occasional Paper No. 7*, Society for Environmental Education, Portsmouth.
28. MARTIN, G. C., 1973, 'Environmental Education: an exploration of objectives and approaches', *BEE* (Town and Country Planning Association), May.
29. Department of Environment, 1970, *White Paper Cmnd*. 4506, HMSO, London.
30. United States Office of Environmental Education, 1970, *The Environmental Handbook*, Washington, D.C.
31. HMSO, 1972, *How Do You Want to Live? (A Report on the Human Habitat)*, HMSO, London.
32. WARD, C. & FYSON, A., 1973, *Streetwork: the exploding school*, Routledge & Kegan Paul, London.
33. FORBES, J., 1974, 'Towards a co-ordinating framework for environmental education—a planner's view', *BEE* (Town and Country Planning Association), March.

Section 2

Insights into environmental curricula in school and higher education

The chapters in this section are arranged to provide a progression from an examination of the problems and possibilities occasioned by the introduction of environmental curricula into secondary schools to examples of courses, such as planning or human ecology, which are emerging in higher education and which could provide a basis for similar developments in schools. The reader is thus given a range of current interdisciplinary ideas to follow up; ideas which are intended to stimulate thought about the nature and role of environmental education, as well as to provide suggestions for curriculum development in the school and college.

3 Establishing environmental education in a secondary school

Tom Shaw

Ten years ago teachers meeting in order to plan courses in environmental education saw themselves as pioneers planning new enquiry-based pupil-centred courses. Since then there has been a rapid advance of environmental studies of many kinds. Much pioneering work has by now been done, and environmental courses have proliferated all over the country. One has only to glance through the advertisement section of the *Times Educational Supplement* to see that 'environmentalists' are often required. This might mean a geographer or a biologist who wishes to place a different emphasis on the nature of his teaching; but one also notices how there has appeared a whole new range of integrated courses involving some sort of environmental enquiry work, often taking place under the umbrella of a new environmental studies department with a separate head of department who often finds himself vying with the head of English for the key role of developing the curriculum on the Arts side. The same advertisements also generally require that the applicants have experience in, or be willing to undertake the assessment of, the course at CSE, or even 'O' level by Mode III methods; or else to prepare pupils for one of the new Mode I Environmental Studies 'O' levels offered by several boards. This is a good indicator of the extent to which environmental studies has spread to upper schools, and has become part of the examination framework.

Obviously, a great many teachers do favour this new emphasis on the objectives of environmental education which they feel can be best served by the organization of such courses, otherwise the demand for environmental studies would not have grown to its present proportions. But this does involve considerable changes in the organization and teaching of a school if it has been structured around traditional subject disciplines, and any group of teachers establishing a course of environmental studies will come up against problems which do not occur with more traditional subjects. The appreciation and solution of these problems is a powerful force for educational change. Chapter 2 of this book deals with the object-

34

ives of environmental education and there are many books describing work done in schools under the title of environmental studies – as is shown in the select list at the end of this chapter.[1] Therefore, this chapter will consider some of the problems confronting the teacher who is asked to help establish environmental studies in a secondary school.

The problem of integration

Teachers with all sorts of training are asked to involve themselves, or wish to participate, in teaching environmental studies. Because of their training in fieldwork geographers are involved more than others, but biologists, historians, sociologists, religious educationalists and English teachers are commonly involved in secondary schools. It is far more frequent for a team of such varied specialists to be asked to initiate an environmental course than for a single department to organize it. For success it is essential that the teachers sink any jealousies that may exist and learn from each other. If the teachers are forced to join an environmental studies team by threats to their security they will not be likely to help the children much and will probably do harm in planning meetings by destructively pointing out what is being omitted from the course rather than constructively suggesting stimulating materials, books or visits. Since one of the main aims of environmental education is to show children how to be involved in the quality of their environment and constructive in improving it, it is essential that the teachers share the same positive view and plan the work with keenness and imagination. Assuming, however, that staff cohesion can be engendered, any plans for the development of the course will depend for their implementation upon the structures established within the school. Each of the pre-requisites could be written upon at length, but the key ones are: the support of the Headmaster; a sufficient allocation of finances to cover the rising but necessary costs of transport, film hire and stationery; a flexible timetable with at least one morning or afternoon block of time for fieldwork; some open-plan area where several groups can share the same experience together; the acceptance of movement and activity not only inside the building, but in and out of school; and the establishment of good community relations. The acceptance of these may raise problems regarding the integration of the environmental studies teachers within the framework and philosophy of the school, and this needs to be discussed by the whole staff. In discussing the relationship of the course to the total curriculum it would be important to ensure that environmental studies is seen not so much as a subject, but as an educative method. Emphasis on the drawing up of agendas for such meetings, and also for basic planning meetings of the team, should be upon the objectives of environmental education (see Chapter 2) and on the processes of learning involved rather than upon the content.

Many teachers who have experience of planning environmental studies within the context of a humanities department report problems of integration with English teachers who wish to develop language work and literature appreciation through a concern for the environment. Borrowing ideas from taxonomists such as Bloom, teachers often devise a taxonomy of objectives for environmental education and then find it difficult to involve English teachers in the team because of the impossibility of categorizing the uses of language and literature under a hierarchy of skills. Obviously English teachers should work in the team if they wish to since English is both the medium of pursuing, and the means of enriching, environmental studies. There are various models for language development which can usefully be adopted, of which perhaps the best is that devised by J. E. Merritt in his *Perspective on Reading* (an Open University publication). This can be adapted to many kinds of written stimulus and does emphasize the need for purposes to be defined and plans used before writing, and then developing and reviewing the work presented. Also, the development of English skills in conjunction with the broad categories of knowledge, comprehension and application can lead to some useful discussion of the different uses of language to suit different kinds of purposes. However, the relationship of language-use to the development of an understanding and appreciation of the environment is a complex one, and teachers should study the books on language teaching given in the references to this chapter.[2]

The problem of organizing techniques of environmental enquiry

The discussion of objectives almost invariably wanders into excited talk about the first-hand experiences the team could provide for the students. The problems then become very real and practical because to get the children out of school is essential, but this involves increasing costs as petrol prices soar. Some schools own mini-buses, but they only take half sets. Should pupils be made to pay some or all of the costs of what to them is ordinary schoolwork? If a great many pupils are involved in fieldwork then the task of organizing travel out of school for hundreds of pupils on the same day can be formidable. Some teams appoint a road manager to cope, but even if he can order and pay for buses he will come up against the problem of over-use of the favourite sites by numerous schools in the area developing environmental courses. Factories, town centres, villages of special beauty or interest, sewage works, farms, churches will all be saturated by the invasions of energetic adolescents, not all of whom will treat the environment with the concern that the teacher is trying to instill into them. It is of vital importance to maintain good relations with each community, to make detailed prior preparations to seek permission for any invasion of privacy, to send off the children with scaled maps, questionnaires, equipment and worksheets giving adequate guidance, without putting off the pupil who responds best by being left with an open-ended situation where he can give flow to his own responses. Museums can provide very valuable help and guidance – some may even set up classrooms in the museum and allow pupils to work there on old maps and documents. Failing this, archivists may be willing to come to school with documents or allow photocopies to be made, or lend microfilm copies. A whole range of visitors: industrialists, town and country planners, outdoor activity or leisure centre organizers, social workers, politicians, local councillors, etc., can come to talk to the children. If numbers create a problem then closed-circuit television can be of great assistance, and the tape kept for later occasions.

The use and development of resources for learning about the environment provide many challenges to the teacher. There are many books on the market now, but they are not always of value because it is important to develop resources related to the school's locality. If the school has no resources department then one of the team of teachers should be in charge of resources concerning the environment. *Resources for Learning* by L. C. Taylor (Penguin Educational) is a useful reference book for teachers. Various materials, maps, lists, small sets of books, photographs, slides, film-strips, overhead transparencies, historical document tapes, VTR tapes, etc., should be stored and indexed along with relevant worksheets. One of the team should be asked to organize the early booking of films; the waiting list for the popular ones is now often a year in length. The school librarian should be encouraged to develop a taste for local documents, histories, old maps, etc., and could perhaps be prevailed upon to organize the reviewing of current newspaper and magazine articles to be cut up and indexed under environmental topic headings. If the course extends through to the sixth form this would be valuable work for a group of well motivated students. If the team is a large one and takes up an important part of the school's curriculum, then the teachers should push for a typing and reprographic assistant so that they can have the essential services of clerical and technical aid. This has been established as necessary in both the science and design areas of the curriculum, and the need is just as strong in the development of environmental education.

To cope with such a wide range of learning situations and materials teamwork is required. *Team Teaching* by David Warwick (University of London Press) would be helpful reading. One experienced teacher should be co-ordinator to see that meetings occur regularly, that materials are available in sufficient numbers and that visits are properly prepared. Obviously, if the team is a large one then members can specialize in different types of preparation. Team preparation will often lead to team teaching, but this may depend more upon the school layout and classroom size than the willingness of the teachers to teach together. If there is no large area then the team may pursue a method of inter-disciplinary enquiry on a theme rotating the classes around a series of teachers who each present their particular view of the theme. If it is considered important for the children to stay with one teacher then the materials related to the theme may be rotated – this method may have to be used anyway because of the shortage of resources. In the upper school pupils value the opportunity to exercise choice in their study of urban or rural themes. For example in an urban study they may wish to choose a study of industrial or canal pollution; to make a comparison of an old terraced housing area and a new housing development or a leisure centre; to analyse transport problems concerned with roads or railways. However, it should be possible for the team to offer such a range of studies that students can become involved in a subject which interests or excites them. Initial stimulus could be given in a lead lecture with a film or audio-visual aids to create enthusiasm and acquaint the students with the range of urban issues.

Whichever method of teaching is used, it must be borne in mind that the teachers' convenience should not predominate over the learning needs of the child. Environmental studies can become so involved with content and method that contact between child and teacher can be lost. The aims of environmental education to develop attitudes to one's surroundings and to make qualitative judgements on the environment can best be fostered if personal knowledge and contact is maintained with each child. Although by the time that the students leave school it is to be hoped they will be able to motivate themselves in their fieldwork and continue to be concerned with man's uses of the environment, while they are in the process of learning at school a personal contact with a teacher is invaluable for a structured learning of the skills of fieldwork enquiry; and the lasting enthusiasms for the quality of the environment are perhaps 'caught' from teachers rather than taught by them.

The problem of the course content

Everything can be said to be in the environment. How is one to choose which aspects to include in the syllabus? Who chooses? Does the head of the department, the co-ordinator or the whole team of teachers? Is the content to be written out in detail? Can it be left to be written out anew each year by different combinations of teachers? How far will examination boards insist on full coverage of a statement of content? Can opportunities be created for the children to exercise some choice? There is a great deal to be decided, and there will doubtless be differences of opinion among the team of teachers, so it is essential that flexibility of content is preserved. There should be freedom within a framework of content headings for individual teachers to develop their interests, for current issues to be studied, for students to choose between a variety of work suggestions and for them to have an opportunity to work for an extended period of time upon a project or theme of their own choice and organizing.

Teams planning the content would be advised to study the current 'O' level syllabuses published by the AEB, London and Oxford Boards. These show a concern for studying earth sciences, landscape formation, ecology, the social environment, production systems, rural and urban sociology, principles of conservation, and influences changing and developing the environment. All of these are seen as integrated courses, but the emphasis tends to be upon eco-systems, and the London examination is hardly environmental studies for the urban child and would attract the rural biologist rather than the humanities teacher. Some CSE syllabuses provide a more variable content, a popular one being a spiral of awareness of the environment starting from those things close to the experience of the child and extending out into the wider world – from the individual to the local, to the regional, to the national and, eventually, to the international. This structure can allow a recurring study of concepts and attitudes at different levels.

One problem that may arise could be differences of opinion over the extent to which man should be missed out of the content out of fears that the course will develop too great a bias towards sociology or overlap too much with English. However much the emphasis may be on scientific enquiry, the course must not deteriorate into just counting pylons or endless trips around the gasworks, with the human element overlooked. Generally speaking, it is best to avoid too great a bias in any subject specialist direction. The course should have elements of history and geography because comparisons in time and space are both important; ingredients of sociology are also inevitable because it is not desirable to omit some studies of group organization within the environment. Whatever the bias of the content, areas of study should be chosen which allow children to come to well considered moral and aesthetic judgements on Man's effects upon his future and that of his planet.

The problem of assessment

Assessment procedures may have to be an early consideration in planning a course in the upper age range of secondary school. There are only three 'O' level Mode I courses, and it takes two years before a course is accepted by examination boards as a Mode III examination. The AEB and London 'O' levels do allow some course work assessment, and London have even developed a Mode III 'A' level for Hertfordshire which allows 30% teacher assessment. A booklet on this syllabus has been published by the National Foundation for Educational Research called *The Construction of an 'A' level syllabus,* compiled by S. Carson.

Teachers must be willing to give considerable time to pondering assessment criteria, to devising means of recording marks and moderating varying internal standards. If a syllabus is accepted as a Mode III examination by a CSE or 'O' level board the team must accept the assessment procedures because they cannot be radically changed from year to year. A terminal examination will raise the issue of the suitability of testing factual recall, and it may be possible to devise an examination testing cognitive and comprehension skills using documents, maps, diagrams or statistics. Essays could be set at 'O' level to test open-ended imaginative responses. Course work may well predominate in a Mode III assessment, and for this folders will have to be preserved for presentation at the end of the course. In some schools double certification has been allowed for an integrated course, and this has raised the problem of separating out the criteria for marking the skills of environmental enquiry from those of English writing. Criteria must also be agreed upon for marking projects of a widely differing nature if students are allowed a range of choice. Projects can all too easily deteriorate into a mindless copying out of information and teachers will need to emphasize the need for a developed sense of purpose and involvement, and some originality of treatment. Some schools also value some element of oral assessment. Environmental education need not to be too book-orientated, and the use of tapes and orals can lead to a more valid assessment of pupil involvement.

Having outlined these four problem areas facing teachers of environmental studies in secondary schools, it is to be emphasized that the problems are readily soluble with a keen staff and sufficient finances. A carefully prepared course does lead to a higher degree of involvement by both staff and pupils. If we are to preserve the quality of our environment it is surely desirable that children should be taught how to appreciate it throughout the whole of their secondary education.

Bibliography
1. *Environmental Studies in the Secondary School*
BERRY, P. S., 1974, *Source Book for Environmental Studies*, George Philip, London.
CARSON, S. McB. (compiler), 1971, *The Construction of an 'A' Level Syllabus*, National Foundation for Educational Research, Slough.
Council for Environmental Education, 1972, *DELTA* (*Directory of Environmental Literature and Teaching Aids*), Reading.
Council for Environmental Education, 1973, *Directory of Centres for Outdoor Studies*, Reading.
CROSBY, T., 1973, *How to Play the Environmental Game*, Penguin, Harmondsworth.
HAMMERSLEY, A. *et al.*, 1968, *Approaches to Environmental Studies: teachers' handbook*, Blandford, London.
HMSO, 1974, *Environmental Education: a report by HM Inspectors of Schools*, HMSO, London.

MARTIN, G. C. & TURNER, E., 1972, *Environmental Studies*, Blond Educational, London.

TAYLOR, L. S., 1971, *Resources for Learning*, Penguin, Harmondsworth.

WARWICK, D., 1969, *Team Teaching*, University of London Press, London.

WATTS, D. G., 1969, *Environmental Studies*, Routledge & Kegan Paul, London.

WHEELER, K. & WAITES, B., 1974, *Environmental Geography*, Rupert Hart Davies, St. Albans.

2. *English Teaching and Environmental Education*

BARNES, D., BRITTEN, J. & ROSEN, H., 1969, *Language, the Learner and the School*, Penguin, Harmondsworth.

BRITTEN, J., 1970, *Language and Learning*, (Pelican) Penguin, Harmondsworth.

CREBER, P., 1968, *Sense and Sensitivity*, University of London Press, London.

CREBER, P., 1970, *Lost for Words*, Penguin, Harmondsworth.

DOUGHTY, P., PEACE, J. & THORNTON, G., 1971, *Language in Use*, Arnold, Leeds.

HINDLE, A., 1973, 'The Relationship of English Studies to Environmental Education', in *An Exploration of Objectives and Approaches in Environmental Education, Occasional Paper No. 8*, Society for Environmental Education, Portsmouth.

4 Education for the conservation of natural resources

John Burton

The need

Education is, or ought to be, a way of equipping people for the future. Unfortunately, we are unable accurately to predict what kind of a world our pupils will inherit. There are some certainties, however: world population will double within the next thirty years or so unless some catastrophe intervenes; resources are going to become increasingly scarce; and the countries of the Third World, learning from the example of OPEC, will charge more and more for the raw materials needed by the industrialized nations. To advocate conservation used to be somehow unpatriotic, one was trying to erect obstacles on the motorway to the new affluent Jerusalem; or, worse, it was a middle class conspiracy to prevent the less fortunate benefiting from the general rise in consumption of the world's riches. Now conservation is becoming respectable. Soon it will be essential!

Unfortunately, most people do not yet see the connection between inflation and resource depletion. Even those who do so do not feel an obligation to limit the size of their families or to adopt a less extravagant style of living. This is hardly surprising since for the last twenty years we have all been conditioned by advertising, salesmen, politicians and the media to indulge in conspicuous consumption, and for the last twenty thousand years man has regarded the Earth's bounty as a gift from the gods to be exploited. It is only now that we are beginning to realize that it is a heritage that must be conserved.

What exactly is meant by conservation? There are a number of definitions. Max Nicholson defines it as 'all that man thinks and does to soften his impact upon his natural environment and to satisfy his true needs while enabling that environment to continue in healthy working order' (*The Environmental Revolution*, 1970). Conservation is the management of the environment for the benefit of the community as a whole to provide life of a high quality. The word 'community' is here used in the ecological sense meaning all

43

populations in the biosphere. It is important to emphasize that the environment is not to be managed solely for the benefit of man alone, although if man is regarded as part of the natural order (which he surely is) and not distinct from it, he will benefit from safeguarding the working of the natural environment.

The question of environmental ethics has been discussed from the Christian viewpoint by a number of writers including the Bishop of Kingston (Montefiore, 1973) and, in more general terms, Bruce Allsopp, who used the analogy of the garden to clarify man's role as husbandman or steward of the Earth (Allsopp, 1972). The term 'geobiotic ethic' has been used to express this concept (Shoman, 1964). Perhaps this is the new creed that the world is searching for, perhaps in time it could supplant or supplement the old religious faiths that have tended to divide us and perhaps the geobiotic ethic could serve as a basis to unite mankind.

In his seminal work, *Environment, Power and Society*, H. T. Odum has listed 'Ten Commandments of the Energy Ethic for Survival of Man in Nature'. He also states that 'If God is defined as the source of revealed truth and if such truth is defined by the complex network of man and nature in terms of its own survival, God becomes identifiable with the networks of which individuals are mere parts'; his penultimate sentence is 'A new and more powerful morality may emerge through the dedication of the millions of men who have faith in the new networks and endeavour zealously for them' (Odum, H. T., 1971).

That the Earth is finite is a truism, but it is easily ignored. 'There are plenty more fish in the sea' and the ocean seems vast. 'The resources of air, land and water must be husbanded . . . and the biosphere contains many delicate biological processes which have taken many centuries to evolve . . . there is a natural equilibrium for life-sustaining processes dependent on relatively slow rates of recycling and . . . these rates have been greatly exceeded by man' (Open University, *Maintaining the Environment*, 1972). These facts are by no means obvious and can only become known to people by education. The main concern of environmental education is, therefore, to establish an environmental ethic (*Project Environment*, 1972), but for this environmental awareness and understanding are essential. Conservation education, then, is not a subject, it cannot exist in isolation, it must form part of, surely the kernel of, a general environmental education.

But what exactly should this kernel consist of?

Environmental issues

What aspects of the environment must all our pupils understand? What are the main issues of environmental concern? They must understand that for hundreds of millions of years life continued in incredible and ever increasing richness and diversification. Numerous species evolved and became extinct, to be succeeded by even more species. Life was self-perpetuating and maintained by complex biogeochemical cycles. This self-regulating system has now been threatened by our success as the dominant species. It is our population growth and our technology that now menace the Earth's and our own life-support system. If we reduce the time-scale of the Earth's existence to a twenty-four hour day our industrialized technology occupies the last 1/250th of a second, and in this brief period we have destroyed vast forests, built huge cities, polluted the rivers and the seas and begun to use up the raw materials on which our modern way of life depends.

SURVIVAL?

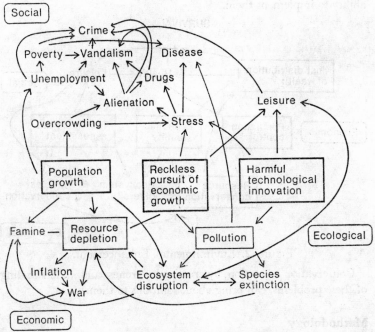

Figure 1. Environmental Degradation.

The main issues of environmental concern, then, are the exponential growth of the world population, pollution, the depletion of resources, the need to conserve wildlife and the question of environmental quality. All children should be aware of these problems by the time they leave school. The root causes of these problems are the population explosion, the reckless pursuit of economic growth and harmful technological innovation. A stable economy, so essential to conserve resources, can only be achieved within a just society where wealth is fairly distributed. The interaction of these issues can be diagramatically expressed as in Figure 1. Here the inter-relationships of population growth, the reckless pursuit of economic growth and harmful technological innovations are shown with their possible social (top of diagram), economic (bottom left) and ecological (bottom right) effects. In Figure 2 the effects of controlling the population, establishing a steady economy with a fairer wealth distribution and a system of technological assessment to prevent harmful technological practices from being implemented are shown with their probable social (top), economic (left) and ecological (bottom) results.

We know the solutions to the problems but lack the will and/or ability to implement them.

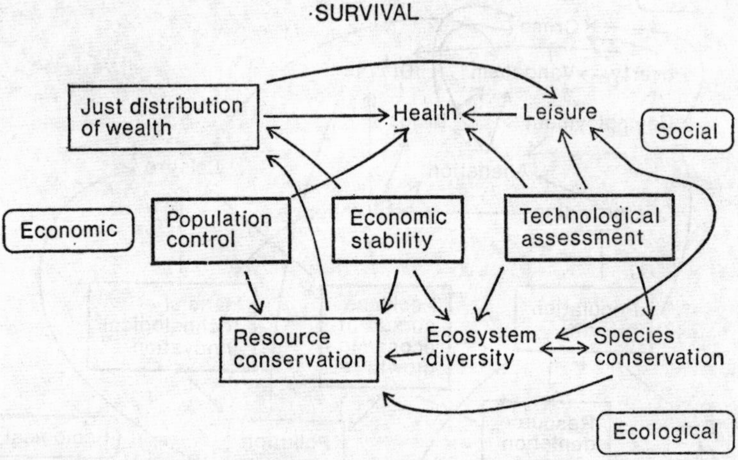

Figure 2. Environmental Enhancement.

Conservation education, by creating awareness and understanding of these problems, can bring about solutions to them.

Methodology

But if we are going to cover these vital areas of global concern, can we do so by using the teaching methods that have been widely used in environmental studies: field studies (including urban studies), discovery methods and, above all, the use of local environment? Of course we can (Burton 1974) and very effectively. In fact, since education for the environment has very definite objectives, motivation will be much greater than in the type of field study approach that the child will too often remember merely as 'when we did that transect' or 'when we counted the traffic'. What is the point of the usual dreary traffic census? Let us examine instead some of the investigations that can be carried out in a traffic survey which could be part of a study of resources or environmental quality, or used as a bridge between the two.

Environmental quality, of course, is determined by a wide range of factors, including healthy living conditions, good food, pleasant homes, clean air and water, modern medical treatment, political freedom, entertainment, beautiful surroundings, satisfying work. Many of these factors relate specifically to the built or to the social environment, which because of the terms of reference are not covered by this chapter.

Traffic and resource consumption

1. What proportion of the town (or smaller area) is devoted solely to traffic? (In Los Angeles it is 60% of 5 000 square miles!)
2. What is the area of the car parks? According to the Road Research Laboratory the number of cars will double in the next 30 years. How many houses will have to be bulldozed to cater for the cars? Where will we put the parking spaces, if the Road Research Laboratory is correct?
3. Measure a bridge over a motorway. Consult a map to find its length. What area of land does it use up? How much food could be grown on this land using average yields of (say) wheat? How much did the motorway cost at £1½ million per mile? How many homes could have been built with this money?
4. Ask older people, parents or grandparents, for instance, how far they travel to work and how far they travelled 20 years ago. Average the results. Estimate time and energy wasted by dispersal of population.
5. A car census. Yes, but wait for it! Count the number of occupants. How many buses per hour would be needed to carry them? How much fuel would thus be saved? Ask local people how many would use public transport if it were (a) cheaper, (b) more frequent, (c) more reliable.
6. Simulation. Spring Green Motorway. (See Bibliography.)

The contribution of the motor car to the resource depletion problem could also be dealt with. Each car requires 20 000 kilowatt hours (the equivalent of $2\frac{1}{2}$ tonnes coal) in its manufacture, and $\frac{1}{4}$ million cars are dumped in Britain every year, a loss of 190 000 tonnes of iron and steel, 2 200 tonnes of copper, 3 300 tonnes of zinc and 3 300 tonnes of aluminium (*Drive*, Summer, 1974). According to the AA it cost £16 a week to run a car in 1974, and the average wage was then £40.90. Hence the average person in Britain worked 16 hours a week to pay for this car. According to Illich the average American 'puts in 1 600 hours to get 7 500 miles: less than five miles per hour' (Illich, 1974). Pupils could check the figures for Britain and decide whether the benefit obtained from the car in providing personal mobility can compensate for its demerits in causing death and injury, noise and air pollution, resource depletion and, according to Illich, social disintegration (*op. cit.* 1974).

Resources

This traffic survey could be part of a study of resources, and a large proportion of this topic could be dealt with in the same way. One could begin by considering what the most important components are of our environment. These are the air we breathe, the water we drink, the food we eat. Next come the clothes we wear, the homes that shelter us and the energy resources that provide us with warmth and power, our transport and industries.

The children we teach must understand the role in the biosphere played by plants which provide us with all our oxygen and all our food. As we become increasingly urbanized there is less and less understanding of this role. They should also understand how food is produced and what happens to it on its way to our kitchens.

By comparing the prices in the shops of vegetable and animal food products, the cheapest ways of obtaining proteins and calories can be discovered. This can lead to a consideration of food chains, trophic levels, flow of energy, and can be linked to Third World food problems to show why most people never eat meat.

No study of food can be complete without the children growing some themselves. If a plot within the school grounds is used for this purpose the children will learn how difficult it is. They can work out the productivity of the particular crop grown, examine the pests that attack the crop and, by leaving a section unweeded, come to understand an important type of environmental control. This could be followed up by farm visits to show how modern agriculture copes with these problems. For senior pupils a consideration of fertilizers, fuel, equipment and feeding stuffs bought by the farmer will lead them to understand why it has been stated that modern farming practice is inefficient in terms of energy and why for each inhabitant of Denmark, a food exporting country, over 100 kilograms of protein are imported each year, mainly from the Third World (Borgstrom 1973, Odum, H. T. 1971).

At this point, too, *soil studies* and *land use studies* would be undertaken. The importance of *water* to life and the hydrological cycle must also be understood, and this should be accompanied by *meterological studies* and studies on the supply of water and disposal of sewage.

In fact every resource can be dealt with by seeking answers to two or three questions. Where does it come from, where does it go and what environmental impact does it have? For example, consider the wall of the classroom: how are the bricks and the mortar made? Visit clay, sand and limestone quarries to see the environmental impact, or use visual aids. This can be linked to *population studies*, since the rate of the population increase in this country necessitates the building of a new school every day. Similarly the paper used in school comes from trees, and 1 tonne of paper uses 17 fully grown trees, 125 kg sulphur, 160 kg limestone, 250 000 litres of water and 260 kilowatt hours of electricity. Where does the old paper go? We throw away 20 million paper bags daily. This can usefully lead on to *pollution studies*, perhaps beginning with a visit to the local rubbish dump.

Nature conservation

To many, conservation is synonymous with nature conservation, but since most wild life will inevitably disappear if our population continues to double every thirty years or so, nature conservation can only properly be considered within the whole environmental education framework.

The obvious response of the young urban sophisticate to a plea for wild life is to ask why. Why indeed should we worry about cowslips and tigers, whales and bee orchids? The approach must be through their importance to man. An approach through religious or moral considerations is only likely to appeal to the pre-adolescent or to sensitive and idealistic older pupils (who may nevertheless be more plentiful than many adults suppose).

If we stress the importance of wild life to man, the starting point must be that of inter-relationships, and to understand these a simple ecological study will be necessary. Here the concept of the ecosystem is useful, and perhaps for an introductory study a wood or a pond would be most suitable. A pond can easily be made in the school grounds using butyl rubber, or, if vandalism is expected, concrete. It can be used to examine food chains and food webs, habitats and niches, the function of producers, consumers and decomposers and the importance of each organism in the ecosystem. Biogeochemical cycles must also be understood, although a detailed study is not necessary.

This study of a natural ecosystem with its diversity, its checks and balances and its avoidance of waste by recycling can then be compared with traditional mixed farming, with its emphasis on soil conservation, and with monoculture and intensive livestock rearing. Inputs for the latter come from far afield and it may be necessary to consider the earth as an ecosystem.

Species, once extinct, cannot be recreated, and everyone should be aware of the importance of gene conservation. The dangers of relying on a limited number of breeds or cultivars, can be stressed. The threat to species of habitat destruction and of pesticide build-up in food chains should also be known. A comparison can be made between control by chemicals and by natural predators, with the possibilities for biological and integrated controls.

The importance of wildlife for research, for beauty, for interest and for recreation can also be covered.

But perhaps the most successful method of nature conservation teaching is by involvement. Let the children take responsibility for part of the school grounds where there is space to do so, or for a local scheme of environmental conservation or improvement. Let them raise trees from seed, preferably in a Dunemann bed, let them plant them out in a nursery plot and when large enough into their permanent positions. As transport becomes more expensive the role of the *school grounds as a teaching resource,* at present ignored, will grow increasingly important. One of the problems facing field study centres is overuse of the local area. It is absurd to visit a field study centre to examine features that are present in the immediate surroundings of the school or to study techniques that could be practised in the school grounds. Another problem is the depletion of species by collection. Primary school teachers have sometimes been guilty of encouraging children to collect wild flowers, insects and frog-spawn; biology teachers and biological suppliers have been blamed for the virtual extinction of frogs from some areas. Too much emphasis is placed by examiners on dissection and not enough on ecological techniques. But many of these problems could be solved by the intelligent use of the school grounds. For example, wild flowers can be grown from seed and planted in a wild flower plot, frogs can be reared in the pond mentioned above, insects and birds can be encouraged by planting suitable food plants and establishing suitable habitats.

The school grounds as an educational resource

In addition to the uses of the school grounds outlined above, the following features could be developed:

1. Managed grassland compared with unmanaged.
2. Habitats, including areas for growing hydrophytes, xerophytes, calcifuges, calcicoles and for showing the influence of micro-climates including north and south facing slopes.
3. A conservation trail, to show dependence of plants on soil and water, plant adaptation to habitat, evidence of decay, effects of scavengers and decomposers, the failure of plastics and man-made fibres to decompose, man's dependence on plants and animals.
4. A weather station.
5. Conservation plots, for growing rare wild plants and to feed insects and birds.
6. Production systems comparisons.
7. Man-environment problems, e.g. spoil heaps, soil erosion, pollution of soil and water.
8. A water table monitor.
9. Soil profiles.
10 Agricultural crops.
11. Other plants of importance to man.
12. Systematic beds.
13. Investigation.
14. Livestock.

Conservation of the Countryside

According to the Office of Population Censuses and Surveys the average daily increase in the population of England and Wales from mid-1972 to mid-1973 was 373 persons, and latest projection (1974) for England and Wales for 2001 is 54 855 500, an increase of more than five million over the 1973 figure of 49 174 600. Hence we will have to find room for five Birminghams in the next twenty-five years.

There is an enormous pressure on the countryside which is so important for food production, recreation and wild life. The Town and Country Planning Acts are internationally admired and should be understood by everybody. In particular, the designated areas that do so much to protect our heritage, National Parks, Country Parks, Areas of Outstanding Natural Beauty, Green Belts, Nature Reserves and Sites of Special Scientfic Interest are all worthy of study. The work of voluntary bodies such as the National Trust, CPRE, the Conservation Society and the Friends of the Earth should also be understood.

An integrated approach

An integrated approach is obviously needed for this type of education. All subject disciplines have a part to play. Unfortunately, educational specialists erect barricades around their specialisms at the drop of a hat. What our society desperately needs are generalists: people who *can* see the wood for the trees.

Other obstacles that must be overcome are the examination system, an overloaded curriculum, conservatism and, of course, ignorance of environmental matters.

Both the IUCN (IUCN 1970, 1972) and the Conservation Society (Conservation Society 1973, 1974) have suggested ways in which conservation education could become part of every person's education.

The current disregard for posterity is without historical precedent. The children in school are the first wave of posterity. Let us equip them through conservation education to protect the world of the future they will inherit.

Bibliography
A. Education Publications
CARSON, S. McB., 1971, *Environmental Studies: the Construction of an 'A' Level Syllabus*, National Foundation for Educational Research, Slough.

The Conservation Society, 1973, *Education for our Future*, Conservation Trust, Reading.

The Conservation Society, 1974, *National Survey into Environmental Education in Secondary Schools*, Conservation Trust, Reading.

IUCN, 1970, *Final Report on International Working Meeting on Environmental Education in the School Curriculum*, International Union for the Conservation of Nature and Natural Resources, Morges, Switzerland.

IUCN, 1972, *Final Report of European Working Conference on Environmental Conservation Education*, International Union for the Conservation of Nature and Natural Resources, Morges, Switzerland.

Schools Council, 1972, *Project Environment* (Report No. 3), Schools Council, London.

SHOMON, J. J., 1964, *Manual of Outdoor Conservation Education*, National Audubon Society, New York.

TERRY, M., 1971, *Teaching for Survival*, Ballantine Books, New York.

B. School Text Books

ALLSOP, K., 1971, *Fit to Live In* (English Countryside), *Connexions*, Penguin, Harmondsworth (age 14+).

BAINBRIDGE, J., 1972, *Conservation*, Evans, London (age 9 to 14).

BURTON, J. H., 1974, *Man and His World:* 1. *Population;* 2. *Conservation of Wild Life;* 3. *Pollution;* 4. *Resources;* 5. *How would you like to live?* (Environmental quality), Blackie, Glasgow (age 13+).

JACKSON, O., 1971, *Conservation and Pollution*, Batsford, London (age 11 to 15).

KELLY, P. (ed.), 1974, *People and Resources*, Evans, London (age 14+).

MASON, J. E., 1971, *Interdependence of Living Things*, *Nuffield Secondary Science* (Theme 1), Longman, Harlow (age 13 to 15).

SEARLE, G., 1972, *Project Earth*, Wolfe, London (age 13 to 16).

C. Simulations and Games

BASSEY, M., *European Environment 1975–2000*, Conservation Trust, Walton-on-Thames (age 17+).

Coca Cola Export Corporation, *Man and Environment*, London (age 8+).

Community Service Volunteers, *Spring Green Motorway*, London (age 11+).

Intercom, *Teaching about Spaceship Earth* (A Role-Playing Experience for the Middle Grades), New York (age 9 to 14).

Royal Society for the Protection of Birds, *Conservation*, Sandy, Beds. (age 11+)

WADDINGTON, I., *The Star River Project*, CRAC, Cambridge (age 17+).

D. Environmental Issues—Teachers' Reference, and for VI forms

ARVILL, R., 1973, *Man and Environment*, 2nd Edition, Penguin, Harmondsworth.

BARR, J., 1969, *Derelict Britain*, Penguin, Harmondsworth.

BARR, J., 1970, *The Assaults on our Senses*, Methuen, London (Sphere, 1971).

BORGSTROM, G., 1969, *Too Many*, Macmillan, London.

BORGSTROM, G., 1973, *World Food Resources*, Intertext Books, London.

Committee on Resources and Man, National Academy of Science, U.S. National Research Council, 1969, *Resources and Man*, W. H. Freeman, San Francisco.

Department of the Environment, 1972, *Sinews for Survival*, HMSO, London.

Department of the Environment, 1972, *Pollution: Nuisance or Nemesis?* HMSO, London.

Ecologist, 1972, *A Blueprint for Survival*, Penguin, Harmondsworth.

EHRLICH, P. R. & A. H., 1973, *Population, Resources, Environment*, 2nd edition, Freeman, San Francisco.

HARTLEY. S. F., 1972, *Population, Quantity V. Quality*, Prentice-Hall, Englewood Cliffs, N.J.

HODGSON, H. V., 1972, *The Diseconomics of Growth*, Earth Island, London.

ILLICH, I. D., 1974, *Energy and Equity*, Calder and Boyars, London.

C

MEADOWS, D. (ed.), 1972, *The Limits to Growth*, Earth Island, London.

MELLANBY, K., 1967, *Pesticides and Pollution*, Collins, London (Fontana, 1971).

ODUM, E. P., 1971, *Fundamentals of Ecology*, 3rd edition, W. B. Saunders, London.

Open University, 1972, *Energy Conversion, Power and Society*, Open University Press, Bletchley.

Open University, 1972, *Maintaining the Environment*, Oxford University Press, London.

PARSON, J., 1972, *Population versus Liberty*, Pemberton, London.

RUSSELL, E. J., 1957, *The World of the Soil*, Collins, London.

STAMP, L. D., 1969, *Nature Conservation in Britain*, Collins, London.

WARD, B. & DUBOS, R., 1972, *Only One Earth*, Penguin, Harmondsworth.

E. Environmental Ethics

ALLSOPP, B., 1972, *Ecological Morality*, Frederick Muller, London.

MONTEFIORE, H., 1973, *Ethics and the Environment*, Council for Environmental Education, Reading.

ODUM, H. T., 1971, *Environment Power and Society*, Wiley-Interscience, Chichester.

5   Historic conservation education

Bryan Waites

What are the dangers?

An anonymous telephone call in November, 1972 to the Director of
the York Archaeological Trust alerted him to the threat of redevelopment hiding for all time the largest complete Roman sewer
system in the country under York. 'The dream of an archaeologist's
lifetime, like wandering in a lost city', said Mr P. V. Addyman, but
the developer's reaction was more realistic: 'It's very nice to find
these things. I just wish they were on other people's sites. We must
put full pressure on Mr Addyman to get in and out as quickly as
possible.' These contrasting views emphasize the crisis in urban
archaeology today.

'History makes way for city office block', 'Lincoln Cathedral
besieged' . . . typical headlines which each day can be read
throughout the land to the accompaniment of the busy rumble of
bulldozers actively engaged in the erosion of history. London's
Temple of Mithras was saved by public outcry; Leicester's hidden
under its new Holiday Inn. The danger to Palace Yard, West-
minster, site of Saxon and Norman palaces, medieval Exchequer
and Star Chamber, was no less despite its national importance, and
all for an MP's car park. The Northampton-Wellingborough
expressway, the North Wales Shell pipeline, the M40 motorway are
only a few threats to archaeology mentioned in recent issues of
Rescue. The Dorset County Magazine has attacked farmers for
ploughing hundreds of prehistoric sites. It has highlighted damage
to Eggardon Hill Fort and the Army's destruction of four Purbeck
round barrows. Most important of all, the bulldozing activities of
the Southern Electricity Board in the summer of 1974 threatened
Dorchester's famous Roman Christian cemetery, the earliest and
largest in Britain.

This is only part of the nationwide crisis in historic conservation.
With one of the richest archaeological and historic heritages on
earth this country is squandering its historical assets at a tragic rate.
One major archaeological site is destroyed for every half mile of

55

motorway built. Out of 640 scheduled sites in Wiltshire only 100 remained undamaged or undestroyed in 1970. Half of the historic county boroughs in England have already been destroyed for all archaeological purposes according to a recent report of the Council for British Archaeology. Of the remaining 229 historic towns, 224 are 'seriously threatened'.

'The physical evidence for the history of the British people is being destroyed on an immense scale, at an increasing pace and often without record. In town and country, by development and redevelopment, by extraction of sand and gravel, by mining, by farming and afforestation, the surviving remains of our past are being steadily eroded . . . the most important towns of all historical periods will be lost to archaeology in twenty years, if not before . . .' wrote Martin Biddle in his preface to the vitally important CBA report on the *Erosion of History*, but, as early as 1963, the *Buchanan Report* commented there is 'a great deal at stake: it is not a question of retaining a few old buildings but of conserving, in the face of the onslaught of motor traffic, a major part of the heritage of the English-speaking world, of which this country is the guardian.'

This, then, is the scale of the crisis. On land and sea; below and above the ground; in town and country; in suburb and in wilderness; at home and abroad; in the distant past and the imminent present; with the ugly as well as the beautiful, the crisis is to be found. People, too, as well as buildings, provide a continuous record from the past to be conserved.

The expansion of interest and activity in extra-terrestrial areas shows that here also is a new danger area. The *Vasa*, the *Mary Rose*, the Dutch East Indiaman in the Thames, the *Ascension* off the Scillies, the excavation of the submerged Port Royal in the West Indies, and the underwater Roman villages of Holderness Bay, all these are dramatic and exciting but how far will the increasing exploitation of off-shore zones by gravel diggers, marina constructors, oil pipelines, rigs and so on compete here also?

Some people think historic conservation applies only to standing buildings and to towns but although these are critically important, as we have seen, below the ground there is an archaeological crisis. One area ignored by archaeologists and historians is the twilight world of caves. Yet here too, as the fungoid growth obscuring the famous paintings of Lascaux shows, there is great risk, increased as tourists and others penetrate further underground. It is, however, the landscape features above ground in the country areas which are now receiving almost as much attention as the conservation of towns. 'Historic landscapes in danger' ran the headlines describing the recently published report of the Historic Buildings Council which calls attention to the need to protect the landscape, especially around buildings: 'the landscape itself is of outstanding interest in its own right.' Of course, Professor W. G. Hoskins and others have long been proclaiming that 'the English landscape is the richest historical record we possess'.

A recent booklet produced by the Essex Planning Office (*Essex Landscape No. 1: Historic Features*) lists the major features of the historic landscape in danger as ancient woodlands, boundaries and field patterns, hedges, greenways and footpaths, trees, especially pollards, gravestones and churchyards, walls, commons, greens, heaths and fens, medieval deer parks, moated sites, deserted medieval villages, castle sites, ridge and furrow, earthworks, windmill and mill sites, ponds, pits, markstones, disused sea walls, marsh lanes and sheepwalks, pill boxes and airfields. To this list might be added crosses, mazes, topiaries, monastic sites, disused railways and stations plus all the impedimenta of industrial archaeology, and this would still not cover all the landscape features to be safeguarded.

In wilderness areas, too, increasing tourism and industrial exploitation can endanger the archaeological and historic environment. Paul Johnson, writing in the *Daily Telegraph*, calls the Scottish Highlands and the mountain fringes of the Celtic Sea a 'doomed landscape! . . . for not just people but the very physical structure of the land and sea will be recast . . . the speed of historical change increases with every year.' He identifies the threat as coming from the gigantic vision of wealth to be found from oil and other minerals. Certainly, indiscriminate destruction of crofters' cottages, potential archaeological sites and the like would make even more necessary 'modern' recreations of past landscapes, lost landscapes, such as currently being done at Landmark, Inverness, and Cregneish, IOM.

Perhaps most attention has focussed on the conservation of historic towns, however, since the Civic Amenities Act (1967) and the publication of the outstanding conservation reports on Bath, Chester, Chichester and York in 1968 (HMSO). Since 80% of the population live in urban areas and since such areas may be said to be at greatest risk such bias can be understood. It should not, however, obscure other important needs. Nor should conservation deal exclusively with *historic* towns. The ugly as well as the beautiful may need conserving. For example, Batley and Birstall Civic Society has shown that 'the shoddy past is worth saving' by fighting for the conservation of the industrial hamlet of Kilpin Hill (*Daily Telegraph*, 16.12.72). Huddersfield and Darlington have their merits, which recent town trails have demonstrated, whilst the attraction of industrial landscapes such as Coalbrookdale is testified by the vast increase in visitors, particularly schoolchildren.

Historic conservation should be studied abroad as well as at home, especially with the impetus from European Architectural Heritage Year (1975). Outstanding examples such as Venice can be supported by study of pilot projects in places like Bruges, Middleburg, Namur, Rouen, Salzburg, Berlin, Trujillo and Engelberg's Ironworks, Sweden, all referred to in the current series of *European Heritage* (Council of Europe, 1974–75). Attention to Continental attitudes to conservation is useful too. Throughout Scandinavia developers can be prosecuted if they 'forget' to alert experts. In Germany planning permission for a new building depends on an 'all-clear' from a qualified archaeologist. Norway, Denmark, Sweden, Holland, Belgium, France, all the provinces of West Germany have a state archaeological service with a qualified archaeologist in charge.

Another important attitude is the awareness that historic conservation does not only relate to the distant past. Most people know Stonehenge is a valuable monument though some would still vandalize it, but few realize that the site of the battle of Naseby or Bosworth is also of intrinsic value. In Vietnam, shell holes are being conserved as tourist attractions; in Flanders, Vimy Ridge and elsewhere trenches are preserved as part of the past. A 1914–18 Trail links up viewpoints, trenches and cemeteries in the Ypres area. At Waterloo, however garish it may be, models, dioramas and films supplement the visual battlefield and form a reconstruction. Interest in Bedford Park, London, the pioneer garden suburb celebrating its centenary in 1975, illustrates the renewed fascination for the nineteenth century, but we and our children should consider our own century, too, and the likely monuments we ourselves will leave for the future. Which of these will remain?

Why bother?

It may be argued by children and adults alike – so what? Why bother about historic conservation at all? One answer is that the Civic Amenities Act (1967) *required* conservation policies to be formulated and conservation areas to be delineated in towns and villages throughout the country. The legal position is summarized well in *Cambridge Townscapes* and *Chester: a study in conservation*. Action on historic conservation is therefore occurring around us all in our environment. We can hardly ignore it. Another answer is that historical assets in landscape and townscape represent income for the region and the nation, mainly through tourism. The English Tourist Board survey, *A Study of Tourism in York* (1972), shows that 2 595 000 visitors to the city in 1971 spent £3 920 000. The stately homes of England and Scotland, set in beautiful landscaped parkland, had a turnover of more than seven million paying customers from home and abroad in 1973 with gross returns of £2 500 000 (*Daily Telegraph,* 22.10.73), so legal and financial reasons provide some answer to doubters.

Some of the objectives stated in conservation reports give more detailed 'official' reasons for bothering. Here is a small selection:

York
1. The commercial heart should remain alive and able to compete on level terms with its neighbour cities, new or old.
2. The environment should be so improved by the elimination of decay, congestion and noise that the centre will become highly attractive as a place to live.
3. Land uses which conflict with these purposes should be progressively removed from the walled city.
4. The historic character should be so enhanced and the best of its buildings of all ages so secured that they become economically self-conserving.
5. Within the walled city the erection of new buildings of anything but the highest architectural standard should cease.

Shrewsbury
1. To preserve the medieval street plan and spaces and maintain existing building lines.
2. To conserve specific areas and groups of buildings essential to the character of Shrewsbury.
3. To effect environmental improvements which will benefit the pedestrian.
4. To safeguard the landscape setting of the town centre and the open spaces within and surrounding it; and to enhance and extend public use and enjoyment of the riverside.

Banbury
1. The presence of old buildings lends to their surroundings a sense of the sequence of time.

2. An old building is often a work of art and its very existence enriches the environment.

Newark

1. To restore and improve the total environment of the core ... particularly where traffic has destroyed, or threatens to destroy, buildings and street pattern, or substantially reduces the enjoyment of these features by its excessive intrusion.
2. The realization of the full tourist and recreational potential inherent in Newark's history, character and location.

Basically, conservationists will argue that they are concerned with, on the whole, unique features and unique character in town and country which once gone cannot be recaptured or replaced; 'Britain's historic towns are the nation's greatest legacy; they must not decay by default or neglect.' But why should all this agitation come now? The pace of urban change, the transitory nature and value of individual life in the shadow of two world wars and nuclear catastrophe contributes a psychological need for stability in general terms. Consequently, the explosion of environmental concern during the last few years has arisen. Historic conservation is emerging as one important part of this. Ultimately, then, the reason for bothering is to achieve an improvement in our living environment. *How do you want to live?* is the evocative title of the Government Report on the Human Habitat for the Stockholm Conference on Human Environment (June, 1972). The whole *raison d'être* is focussed here:

> While we pummel our schoolchildren with endless instruction in the history of painting and sculpture, arts which many of them find alien and to which most of them will never return, we tell them virtually nothing of the art of architecture which they are seeing about them every hour of the day. It is in failures such as this that the real danger to the future identity of London lies.

You will find other quotations in the report equally telling.

We aim, then, for our children to develop a critical, moral and aesthetic awareness of their surroundings. We encourage their participation in decision-making by practical activities and projects both in rural and urban environments. We hope to promote their judgement and evaluation of what is good so that 'the qualities we inherited from the past can become a discipline for change today' (Worskett, 1969).

In terms of conservation of towns, this means consideration of setting, skylines, views in and out, the boundary between town and country, focal points, space and layout, street patterns, street names, street furniture, frontages, façades, roofscape, the scale, character and condition of individual buildings and groups of buildings, trees, urban texture, particularly of building materials, archaeological features such as walls, river crossings and earthworks, riverside conservation, site values, environmental improvements and current planning projects, noise, pedestrian and traffic movement. Conservation cannot be seen in isolation. It must be seen within the framework of general planning policy.

Curriculum innovation resulting from historic conservation will demand, among other changes, allowance for how to assess and appraise townscape, opinions of what to conserve and, most important of all, perceptions of the past for, as Kevin Lynch has rightly written, 'In the development of the image, education in seeing will be quite as important as the re-shaping of what is seen.' As Professor Philippe Wolff writes, 'Tomorrow's urban textures run a great risk of losing in charm and in human value what they gain in expansion. Our children run a great risk of growing-up joylessly in soulless cities.' If bothering about historic conservation prevents this alone then it will be justified.

The role of historic conservation in schools: advantages for teachers

The resources available for the study of historic conservation are already profuse. The bibliography at the end of this chapter lists some of the excellent conservation reports produced by planning departments or private consultants. These are supported by an increasing number of background books. Newspaper and magazine references occur almost daily and, with the advent of EAHY in 1975, they are likely to increase. The activities and publications of local groups, civic societies and the like provide further material. One excellent example is *The Medieval Buildings of Stamford* produced by the Stamford Survey Group and published by the Extra-Mural Department of Nottingham University. The introduction of illustrated town trails has created a new approach and material for environmental awareness (for instance, *Leicester Town Trail*). Periodicals such as the *Bulletin of Environmental Education* (*BEE*), *Rescue, Interim* and *Watchword* are doing a great deal to encourage the interest and activities of schoolchildren, especially in urban conservation. Campaigns such as 'Save the Village Pond' stimulate landscape conservation whilst national organizations such as the Countryside Commission (with, for example, *The Changing Countryside Project: a Report*, 1971) and the Royal Commission on Historical Monuments (see their volumes on York) also provide excellent detailed resources. *An Environmental Directory* listing national and regional organizations concerned with amenity and the environment has been issued by the Civic Trust (whose address is listed at the back of this book).

Such resources give the teacher an excellent start. The fact that they are varied and often largely visual also helps. It will be shown later how they contain many new ideas and approaches which can bring a freshness to lessons.

The need for historic conservation can be seen everywhere, in town as well as country, and so wherever your school may be there will always be a relevant connection. Maybe the school itself is an ancient monument; some village schools are. Perhaps, as at Oakham School in Rutland, the original school building (1584) has been converted to other uses such as, in this example, a Shakespearean Theatre. Hamilton High School, Leicester, lies almost on top of the deserted medieval village of Hamilton and its associated ridge and furrow. In many towns and cities the school may be an old Board School or Wesleyan Day School. Since most schools have an urban situation where conservation problems are usually dramatically displayed, there is ample scope for study.

The controversial issues involved in historic conservation often lead to emotional involvement of pupils and teachers. There is surely a great need for this in our lessons. Personal concern will encourage individuals and the class to do something active, perhaps helping the local civic society to clean out the canal or assisting the Planning Officer in conservation investigations related to a new county structure plan. *Rescue,* Advisory Centre for Education, the Deserted Medieval Village Research Group and the Moated Sites Research Group all encourage active participation by young people.

The contemporary significance of conservation gives it an urgency and relevance. It brings past, present and future together well and naturally. It integrates disciplines such as art, architecture, archaeology, history, geography, environmental studies and planning by its holistic approach. This leads to curriculum innovation in which a sequence of problems to be solved by a team of teachers and pupils replaces a conventional syllabus. Often, working in association with local adult groups, perhaps at weekends, may also demand a new approach. The all-embracing requirement of documentary analysis, library work, fieldwork, photography, sketching, mapwork and so on also integrates techniques of study in an active and purposeful way. The problems of historic conservation themselves cut across time and place thus obviating the purely historical and geographical bias. Instead of interminable June crocodiles of children making straight for the obvious Castle Museum, Clifford's Tower and the Minster in York, the set pieces of history – perhaps they might turn their attention in more discrete groups to the old warehouses along Queen's Straith, the need for conservation in Aldwark, the redeveloped old railway station site on Toft Green and the possible future of All Saints, North Street. Maybe, in 1975, they will start their studies in the proposed architectural interpretation centre in the redundant St Mary's church, Castlegate, to get on the right wavelength. In Portsmouth, perhaps children should examine Old Portsmouth instead of rushing as usual to HMS *Victory*, and maybe the conservation of Greenwich is just as important as the famous maritime museum.

Another teaching advantage is that historic conservation is not purely local though it may start there. It can be developed thematically from the home base to the region and then to national and international levels. The curriculum should be designed to allow for this. Conservation in Spalding may lead outwards to similar considerations in Bruges and Amsterdam, to the problems of Venice and the situation of Stockholm.

Especially valuable and relevant is the current interest in industrial archaeology. Children are fascinated by the visual attraction of machinery, especially when moving. The open-air museum at Blist's Hill, Coalbrookdale, with its gigantic machines, its canal, inclined plane and tar tunnel has all the spectacular attraction that only industry, notably old industry, can provide. It has acquired a romantic appeal too, and, best of all it can be touched, climbed on and gone into! The complicated machines and the associated technical words are, oddly enough, intrinsically attractive and memorable. The recency of it all, the present concern with the nineteenth and twentieth centuries, the fact that documents about it are understandable and in 'modern' English, the personal connections through family memory, anecdotes and times of hardship recalled, all these reinforce the interest. Why not, then, start alongside your own canal or railway, then think about and visit Coalbrookdale, Abbeydale (Sheffield) or Cromford to investigate the conservation of the industrial landscape so successfully achieved in these places? Move on to consider the conservation problems of the Ruhr and later the

American and Australian ghost towns left after the collapse of mining.

Best of all, historic conservation should involve children and teachers in the exercise of opinion, appraisal and judgement in varying degrees: 'You should make up *your* own mind and don't let anyone else make it up for you and that means finding out something about what is really going on and something about the problems we face in town, country, at home and on holiday' (ACE letter to members of Watch). It gives opportunities for these qualities to develop through open discussion with other people who care and feel deeply about their homes and their environment.

How can historical conservation be developed in schools: some examples of what can be done

Children should assist in public projects on a local and national basis. The success of ACE's hedgerow, river pollution and noise survey testifies to this. Already 'Young Rescue' involves children as do the DMV and Moated Sites Research Groups. Where cooperation is undertaken with civic societies and local groups it should be on the basis of a continuing programme. For example, the Rutland Field Research Group for Archaeology and History have produced an *Inventory of Projects* to which schools and colleges can contribute assistance in a systematic and progressive way. Children assist at digs already, many working with great enthusiasm along the Roman Wall, for instance, at Vindolandia. In Stamford a primary school recently completed an important churchyard survey. The recently established Iron Age Farm at Butser Hill, near Petersfield, Hampshire, to be run as it would have been in 300 BC, will enlist the help of students and schoolchildren. Teachers can extend their classroom work by means of competitions and holiday projects to give additional appeal. In many areas these might fit into local contributions towards EAHY.

Your class should keep a *public watch* on local and national conservation events, especially through newspapers. Building up a classified cutting collection could be one way of organizing this watch (see Anthony Fyson, 'Newspapers as a Resource', *Times Educational Supplement*, 28.6.74). 'Will Venice become just another city?', 'Lucky Ludlow keeps its head', 'When tidy minds go to the country' . . . all these and more contain useful up-to-date information and ideas. In some instances the class may want to write to their newspaper. Watch should be kept especially on large engineering projects such as reservoirs or motorways. Collective walks over these areas often reveal surface finds.

Adoption of a city street, square or row of houses, a greenway, churchyard, wall or pond can be a useful way of pinpointing and personalizing interest in conservation. It can be studied, worked on and defended together. A city dictionary of conservation and/or an environmental vocabulary might be compiled in association with this. The future of your chosen item would be investigated in the planning office just as the past would be in the record office. Children are using archives and air photographs now in ways that were never thought possible before.

Conservation trails, town trails and tourist trails can be attempted, perhaps in liaison with the local council, teachers' centre (as with the *Loughborough Trail*) or regional tourist board. Eyesores as well as attractions should be shown. *Watchword*, No. 2, Summer, 1973 (ACE) suggests useful holiday activities in 'What a way to see a town' (the noise jig-saw is a good idea). Use of a noisemeter and pocket tape-recorder can extend your scope and contribute to better townscape appraisal.

Conservation fieldwork activities are almost unlimited and include items such as recording buildings, ridge and furrow, hedge studies, investigation of redundant churches, following city walls, comparative skyline and map studies. A full discussion of such activities can be found in 'Historical Geography in the Field' in *Geography in the Field*, 'The Past Environment' in *Handbook of Environmental Studies* and 'The Conservation of Historic Towns' in *Environmental Geography*. It should be noted that all fieldwork depends on classroom preparation which includes understanding large-scale maps, looking at relevant documents, perhaps tithe and enclosure maps, knowing how to identify architectural styles, classifying vernacular buildings, reading aerial photos, developing interviewing techniques and becoming familiar with most of the published sources. This may sound a daunting task but since some of it goes on alongside actual fieldwork it usually becomes more meaningful. Teachers should note other school projects which may be going on as this often gives a stimulating idea for your own work. Ready links with natural conservation can be made, too, since woodland, deer parks, hedges, commons, enclosure verges, graveyards, walls, ponds, pits and so on have strong botanical connections which should not be ignored. In fact, the changing biogeographical patterns in an area represent a good combined approach for history, geography and biology (see K. Messenger, *The Flora of Rutland*).

In the classroom role-playing might be developed where an enquiry is set up into a particular threat. A model example might be the proposed inner ring road for York using the book *York 2000,* with children taking on the roles and vested interests of car drivers, archaeologists, civic society and so on. The sequence and procedure for this type of activity could be based on that suggested in the appendix to *Chester: a study in conservation.* Eventually, the pupils could design their own conservation policy and an associated conservation game based on *Monopoly* could be formulated.

The best and most accessible sources for work are the town and country conservation reports themselves, produced by planning departments (see bibliography). Sometimes these can be obtained in multiple copies quite cheaply. They contain large-scale base maps not easily obtainable elsewhere, which give streets, buildings and areas in detail. Usually a series of old maps and skylines show the evolution of the town (see *Cambridge Townscapes*). Sometimes street gazeteers are included with detailed architectural descriptions of buildings (see *York: a study in conservation*). *Shrewsbury: the challenge of conservation* has an unusual and excellent section on street names and also on shuts, passages and loads in the town. *Conservation Study No. 2 Banbury* contains excellent sketches which can form the basis of classwork if duplicated and might be associated with 'make your own façade', a possible activity stimulated by the many façade sketches to be found in most of the reports (see Micklegate in RCHM volume, *York South-West of the Ouse*). Detailed descriptions of individual buildings and groups, often with map and illustrations also provide a basis for comparative work. *The Medieval Buildings of Stamford* is excellent in this respect and can be used in conjunction with *Stamford: Buildings of Special Architectural and Historic Interest* (1963), *Stamford Town Centre Historic Areas Policy* (1966), *The Making of Stamford* (A. Rogers, 1965), N. Pevsner's *Buildings of England: Lincolnshire* and local civic society reports. The Royal Commission on Historic Monuments (RCHM) volumes are excellent for York and Cambridge whilst the visual analysis of a typical Rows Building on p. 86 of *Chester: a study in conservation* is of specific value and might form the basis for a 'conserve your own house' exercise.

Photographs both old and new, together with reproductions of old engravings occur frequently in conservation reports. Information and sketches of building materials and styles can start off enquiries into CPRE recommendations, regional character of building materials, origins and so on. The *Thaxted Report* has excellent data on building materials and uses in house construction. A host of background books, such as A. Clifton-Taylor's *Pattern of English Building*, provide a good context for this work. *The Criteria for Study Areas* (p. 99 *Chester*) could be used as a basis for classifying your own town buildings.

Other topics which arise from conservation reports are city walls and redundant churches. Several useful sources are mentioned in the bibliography for both York and Norwich in this field. There is a special publication on *Norwich City Walls*, and *York: the Defences* deals exclusively with its walls. The recent CBA report on the *Archaeology of Churches* was presented to the conference on this topic held in Norwich in April, 1973, and it introduces the problems of redundancy outlining a programme for action.

A collection of conservation reports such as those mentioned above would provide a very good and unorthodox foundation for classwork. Further class activities could be the production of a series of case studies of towns like Ludlow, Cambridge, Stamford and also European towns; tourism and its effect on historic conservation; the future city; the 'city of our dreams'; whose city; what do *you* want; *your* mental map of the conserved city . . . make an identi-kit picture of it.

The scope for school work in and out of the classroom is increasing and will continue to do so. The development of streetwork centres through the Council for Urban Study Centres (CUSC) will help to focus actively the need to study historic conservation and it should provide greater facilities to do so. It should contribute 'to halting the loss of irreplaceable buildings and the erosion of character in historic European towns' – the aims of EAHY – or at least make children aware of the danger. Local projects at CSE and 'A' level will encourage greater interest in conservation studies; team-teaching and integrated studies, already well developed, will allow expansion of conservation into the curriculum, and even within conventional history and geography syllabuses it can be introduced to give a new look and new dimension. At the same time, general encouragement from public, press and extra-mural groups ensures a strong community interest.

Ultimately, historical conservation must be seen as part of the individual, regional and urban crisis that besets us all. The former has been well-charted and, in fact, 'Education and the Urban Crisis' was the subject of the Ditchley Park Conference in 1973 (*Times Educational Supplement*, 16.2.73). Creative conservation rather than lame and passive preservation aims to renew values for young and old. There is a relationship between social behaviour and visual quality, as yet little researched, but intuitively there. 'Perhaps in a fast-moving world there is some deep-felt social reassurance in the historical continuity of ancient towns' comments the *Chester* report: 'the old deserves to be saved not merely because it is old but because it possesses qualities of *permanent value to humanity*' echoes the CBA in 1966. The individual in town and country seeks his identity, he seeks 'the reoccupation and replenishment of the landscape as a source of essential values in a balanced life' (Lewis Mumford). It is hoped historic conservation may encourage this, but, in school and out, it will also have to pay greater attention to the conservation of the past *within* the individual, for physical appearance, speech, hereditary traits and behaviour are all a summary of the past. They form individual character and contribute to regional distinctiveness. As F. Ratzel said, more than a hundred years ago, 'a people expresses itself through its landscape just as it does through its towns and houses'. This expression through landscape and towns is now realized and attempts are being made to conserve it. The next dimension is the understanding and conservation of the past in the hearts, minds and behaviour of people. This will be the challenge for the future and it should begin in the schools.

Bibliography
Council of Europe, 1974/75, *European Heritage* (5 issues), Phoebus Publishing Company, London.
CULLEN, G., 1961, *Townscape*, Architectural Press, London.
Department of the Environment, 1971, *Aspects of Conservation: No. 1, New Life for Old Buildings*, HMSO, London.
HEIGHWAY, C. M. (ed.), 1972, *The Erosion of History*, Council for British Archaeology, London.
HOSKINS, W. G., 1973, *English Landscapes*, BBC Publications, London.
JESSON, M., 1973, *The Archaeology of Churches*, Council for British Archaeology, London.
JOHNS, E., 1965, *British Townscapes*, Arnold, London.
LOBEL, M. D. (ed.), 1969, *Historic Towns*, vol. 1, Lovell Johns-Cook Hammond & Kell, London & Oxford.
LYNCH, K., 1960, *The Image of the City*, MIT Press, Cambridge, Mass.
MARTIN, G. C. (ed.), 1972, *Handbook of Environmental Studies*, Blond, London.
SHARP, T., 1968, *Towns and Landscape*, John Murray, London.
WARD, P., 1968, *Conservation and Development in Historic Towns and Cities*, Oriel Press, Newcastle-upon-Tyne.
WHEELER, K. S., 1971, *Geography in the Field*, Blond, London.
WHEELER, K. S. & WAITES, B. (eds.), 1975, *Environmental Geography*, Rupert Hart-Davis Educational, St. Albans.

WORSKETT, R., 1969, *The Character of Towns*, Architectural Press, London.
  See also: *Rescue News* (Trust for British Archaeology, Worcester), *Interim* (York Archaeological Trust) and *Watchword* (ACE, Cambridge).

Regional References

Banbury: Oxfordshire CC, 1968, *Conservation Study No. 2 Banbury.*
Bath: HMSO, 1968, *Bath: a study in conservation.*
Cambridge: PURDY, I. M., 1971, *Cambridge Townscape: an Analysis*, Department of Architecture & Planning, Cambridge.
  Royal Commission on Historic Monuments, 1959, *Survey & Inventory of the City of Cambridge*, HMSO, London.
Cheshire: Civic Trust for the North West, 1969, *An Environmental Vocabulary: Cheshire Villages.*
Chester: HMSO, 1968, *Chester: a study in conservation.*
Chichester: HMSO, 1968, *Chichester: a study in conservation*
Darlington: WINDERS, R. & GRAY, L. S., 1974, *The Urban Trail*, Learning Resources Unit, Regional Management Centre, Sheffield Polytechnic.
Essex: Essex CC, 1966, *Thaxted: an historical and architectural survey.*
  Essex CC, 1972, *The Essex Countryside: a landscape in decline?*
  Essex CC, 1974, *Essex Landscapes No. 1: Historic Features.*
  Essex CC, 1974, *Conservation in Essex No. 4: Historic Buildings.*
Huddersfield: *Local Information Papers: a town trail*, 1974, Huddersfield Polytechnic.
Leicester: WHEELER, K. S. & WAITES, B., 1972, *The Leicester Town Trail*, Bulletin of Environmental Education, Town & Country Planning Association, London.
Lincoln: HILL, J. W. F., 1948, *Medieval Lincoln*, Cambridge University Press, Cambridge.
  HILL, J. W. F., 1956, *Tudor and Stuart Lincoln*, Cambridge University Press, Cambridge.
  HILL, J. W. F., 1966, *Georgian Lincoln*, Cambridge University Press, Cambridge.
  JACKSON, P., 1968, *City of Lincoln Conservation Area No. 1: The Historic Core*, City Plannning Department, Lincoln.
London: BIDDLE, M. & HUDSON, D. (eds), 1973, *The Future of London's Past*, Rescue, London.
Loughborough: Teachers' Centre, 1973, *Loughborough Town Trail*, Loughborough.
Ludlow: Salop CC 1971, *Towards a plan for Ludlow: Survey Report.*
Newark: 1968, Nottinghamshire County Planning Department, *Newark: action for conservation.*
Norwich: GREEN, B. & YOUNG, R. M. R., 1968, *Norwich, the growth of a city*, Norwich Museums.
  Norwich Society River Group, 1969, *A Journey Along the Waterways of Norwich*, Jarrold, Norwich.
  PEVSNER, N., 1962, *The Buildings of England: N.E. Norfolk and Norwich*, Penguin, Harmondsworth.
  SPENCER, W. & KENT, A., 1970, *The Old Churches of Norwich*, Jarrold, Norwich.
  WOOD, A. A., 1967, *Norwich Draft Urban Plan*, Norwich City Council.
  WOOD, A. A., 1969, *Conservation in Norwich*, Norwich City Council.
  WOOD, A. A., 1970, *Norwich City Walls*, Norwich City Council.
  See also *Official Guide*, Information Bureau, Norwich.
Rutland: MESSENGER, K., 1972, *The Flora of Rutland*, Leicester Museums, Leicester.

Shrewsbury: Borough Council, 1970, *Shrewsbury: the challenge of conservation.*
Stamford: Kesteven CC, 1963, *Preservation of Buildings of Special Architectural and Historic Interest in Central Stamford.*
    Kesteven CC, 1966, *Stamford Town Centre Historic Areas Policy.*
    Kesteven CC, 1970/71, *Stamford Town Centre Scheme.*
    ROGERS, A. (ed.), *The Making of Stamford*, Leicester University Press, Leicester.
    ROGERS, A. (ed.), 1970, *The Medieval Buildings of Stamford*, Department of Adult Education, University of Nottingham.
    Stamford Civic Society, 1972, *Stamford and Leisure.* (See also other annual reports of the Society.)
York: CUMMIN, D., *York 2000 People in Protest,* from York 2000 Offices, Micklegate, York.
    HMSO, 1968, *York: a study in conservation.*
    Information Bureau, 1975, *York Official Guide and Miniguide.*
    PEVSNER, N., 1972, *Buildings of England. Yorkshire: York and the East Riding,* Penguin, Harmondsworth.
    Royal Commission on Historic Monuments, *City of York:* 1962, Vol. 1 *Eburacum: Roman York*; 1972, Vol. 2 *The Defences*; 1972, Vol. 3 *South West of the Ouse*, HMSO, London.
    WARD, W. R., 1971, *The Walls of York*, Dalesman Publishing Co., Clapham, Yorks.
    York Group for the Promotion of Planning, 1968, *The Strays and Ways of York*, Sessions Book Trust, York.
N.B. the general value of the *Victoria County Histories*, especially for York and Cambridge, also N. Pevsner's series, *The Buildings of England*, published by Penguin.

6 Urban studies

Ivor Goodson

Urban studies have grown out of the efforts to establish environmental education in schools which really began in earnest in the late 1960s.[1] The progress of these early efforts is important because the evolution of urban studies is thereby placed in perspective and because many of the problems encountered in establishing environmental studies in schools will undoubtedly be inherited by urban studies.

The emergence and evolution of environmental studies

The environmental studies courses which emerged in schools in the late 1960s were a combination of new approaches: a newly packaged body of content, a new way of looking at (and across) the disciplines, a new methodology of learning. Work was to focus on, and often take place in, the rural environment outside the school classroom. Early advocates felt that all students would benefit from the approach, especially the non-involved minority who would be motivated to learn.

In many ways what the early advocates postulated was indeed true. Certainly the approach offered the kinds of intrinsic motivation which suited the new epistemologies of curriculum theorists, such as Bruner. Environmental studies offered a new approach to learning with special emphasis on new kinds of motivational material. This offer was validly intended for pupils of all abilities. The tragedy of environmental studies has been that in secondary schools the approach has come to be centred on, and available to, only the 'less-able' or 'non-academic'. This has happened in spite of the efforts, most notably in Hertfordshire and Wiltshire, to give the approach 'respectability' in terms of 'O' and 'A' level status. In most secondary schools at the present time, while environmental studies are undertaken by the less able, the able continue to study the traditional academic disciplines. Environmental studies have become the preserve of those whom the school cannot traditionally involve – the overwhelming motivational capacity of environmental work is being squandered as a means of social control over the school's deviant population.

A second problem has become evident in the environmental studies courses that have been established. As well as limiting the audience, the potential of environmental work has been further confined by the highly rural bias of the early advocates. This rural bias is present in very nearly all of the environmental studies courses found in contemporary English secondary schools, as any survey of current CSE, 'O' level and 'A' level syllabuses will confirm.

The need for change: new directions for environmental education

Since the twin problems of environmental studies – their non-academic and rural bias – have been found at their most pernicious in the secondary school, where they have traditionally been buttressed by ability groupings and examination syllabuses, it is in the secondary school that the need for change is most acute. A strategy for change must be worked out with the secondary school, therefore, mainly in mind.

Fortunately, this is already a period of significant change in English secondary schools. Increasingly the able and less able are found within the same school and, as streaming begins to disappear, even within the same classroom. Moreover, the less able (now known more politely as 'young school leavers' in some quarters) are staying on for an extra year until they are sixteen. Comprehensivization, unstreaming and ROSLA are combining to persuade schools to seek new methods of motivating students and to provide new syntheses of knowledge to match the new strategies.[2]

The changes in English secondary schools are opening up the possibilities for a major extension in the scope of environmental education towards a consideration of the urban environment. The case for this extension is twofold:

(1) Eighty per cent of our children live in urban surroundings, and over ninety per cent go to urban schools. Urban studies, therefore, fully answer the progressive educationist's demand to 'begin where the child is'. More importantly, urban studies might hope to offer the child that sense of relevance and involvement which is the key to motivation and learning.

(2) Urban studies would aim to train children to participate in their *own* environment. As Ward and Fyson state, this aim is valid for all children: 'we are concerned here with the education of active *citizens,* and where else can this be undertaken if not in the city.'[3] The need for such involvement is possibly greatest in the Priority Areas. As one of the pioneers of Priority Education, Eric Midwinter, says: 'Through a closer investigation of their social environment the children might be that much readier to understand their own needs with more clarity.'[4]

Urban studies offer the possibility of unifying the academic and social elements in education and of presenting this new synthesis in a way that motivates pupils of all ages and abilities.

Urban studies: a review of progress so far

Urban studies can be defined as that part of the school curriculum using, directly or indirectly, the urban environment as the resource for learning. Urban studies are not the preserve of any particular academic discipline; but are simply that part of the curriculum staffed by specialists enthusiastic to teach about the urban environment.

The sheer variety of urban study work is well illustrated in Colin Ward and Anthony Fyson's book *Streetwork* subtitled somewhat provocatively *The Exploding School.* The authors in their roles of Education Officers at the Town and Country Planning Association have been extremely active in pioneering a new concept of environmental education based on urban 'streetwork' (as opposed to rural fieldwork). They see this work being often directed ultimately from Urban Study Centres. A Council for Urban Study Centres has consequently been set up and a number of centres are about to be opened. A recent advertisement for the post of director of the Notting Dale Urban Study Centre mentioned the uses of the building as ranging from 'school courses through adult illiteracy work to an advice centre and base for local planning displays'.

The concept of streetwork has been explored in the pages of the journal *BEE* (Bulletin of Environmental Education) edited by Ward and Fyson for the Town and Country Planning Association. The discussion of town trails in *BEE* by Keith Wheeler and Bryan Waites captures the 'feel' of urban studies:

The length of the Town Trail depends on the number and variety of visual experiences to be included. Contrast, juxtapositions and surprises are essential to the success of the Trail. Do not lead the Trail along the obvious route, but deviate; find out unusual pathways; do not stick to the 'beaten track'; go through controversial areas where the planner or developer may be in conflict with the public over the use of a particular site. Take the Trail through environmentally 'negative' as well as environmentally 'positive' parts of the city because what might be soothing to one eye might be an eyesore to another.[5]

As the authors summarize: 'The Town Trail is intended to be an open-ended exercise in informal environmental education which leads the tracker to ask questions and evaluate experiences without having the answers fed to him.'[6]

Wheeler and Waites (and indeed Fyson) are geographers, similarly *BEE* is mainly taken by geographers. There is, however, ample evidence that other specialists are following the geographers' lead and are beginning to use the urban environment as a central resource for learning. Bernard Aylward in his book *Design Education in Schools* shows how design work can focus on the urban community;[7] Ken Baynes in his 'Front Door' project based in London shows how architectural education in schools can centre on the urban environment and can use architects and planners;[8] G. A. Chinnery, the Leicester City Archivist, has recently produced a pamphlet for the Historical Association on *Urban History in Schools*[9] showing how the historian can concentrate his lessons on the urban scene: similarly Ken Worpole's *Hackney Pack*, a collection of local social and historical documents, helps the history teachers of East London to look at local urban and community life in their classes.[10] There are also efforts to explore within schools the possibilities of urban activities such as street theatre, conservation studies, urban sociology, ecology and industrial archeology.

Nor is the change of emphasis confined to secondary specialists. Midwinter's 'Priority' project in Liverpool has concentrated on getting primary school children out investigating the streets that surround their schools – recording interviews, digging up deserted housing areas, writing stories, drawing real and imaginary streets and measuring street noise with transistor radios in terms of the distance from which a radio can be heard. This change in curriculum has often been echoed by a change in the school ethos, and the schools have become open and responsive to the urban communities surrounding them.[11]

The changing emphasis in the curriculum towards a use of the urban environment has been reinforced by a range of educational agencies, most notably the Schools Council and certain educational publishers. Several recent Schools Council projects have embodied the urban approach. Indeed it was 'Project Environment' which first spoke of 'the exploding school' and the Schools Council's 'Geography for the Less Able' project contains much urban material whilst continuing to warn of the divisiveness of a curriculum aimed only at the non-academic. Educational publishers have similarly responded to the changing emphasis: *Jackdaws* (Cape) include a collection of documents on the theme *Man and Towns* dealing mainly with the financing of city planning, and Penguin have produced a set of splendidly visual books on the theme *Human Space* in which Brian Goodey's *Where You're At* and Colin Ward's *Utopia* suggest new and interesting themes for urban study work.[12]

Urban studies cover a whole range of subject disciplines and a whole spectrum of educational activities from a one-page essay on 'The street I live in' to something like the Parkway Education Programme in Philadelphia. Parkway, instead of using a school building, uses the city as a vast educational resource and all teaching goes on in the urban community: 'art students study at the Art Museum, biology students at the zoo, business and vocational courses at on-the-job sites . . .'[13] But Parkway is some distance away from English secondary education and here urban studies have to be seen as agent of more specific change. Within the secondary school curriculum urban studies could serve to establish environmental learning based mainly on the child's own (urban) environment and available to children of all abilities.

A strategy for change

The strategies for establishing urban studies as a part of the curriculum that is available to children of all abilities need to be very carefully considered. The fate of environmental studies points out many of the dangers which might await any new initiative in the field of environmental learning. Three considerations would seem paramount:

1. The method of introducing urban studies as an area of study, which is of interest and value both to the able and the less able, and of establishing that urban studies can be taught successfully to such a mixed-ability grouping;

2. The need for careful definition of the relationship between urban studies and the traditional disciplines both at the professional and pedagogic levels;

3. The process of exploration and definition of urban studies as a potentially new synthesis of knowledge must be undertaken through the schools and examining boards.

A teacher introducing urban studies to a mixed-ability group at the present moment will be doing so with the current examination subjects in mind. His students will probably be taking geography, history, social studies or biology at 'O' level and CSE. Although in the short run urban studies must work within these frameworks a good deal can be achieved by devising strategies which take account of these constraints.

As an example I want to describe some work I undertook with a class of fourth year students of mixed ability at Countesthorpe Upper School in Leicestershire. The possibilities for such work are particularly good at the school for two reasons: the school has a very flexible timetable which encourages interdisciplinary work and examinations in English, social studies and history, both 'O' level (the school takes the examinations set by the Associated Examining Board) and CSE, allow about a third of total marks for project work.

From the beginning of the school in August 1970, individuals and pairs of students had expressed interest in, and carried out, studies of the urban environment in social studies periods. The work, which began in September 1971, from the first promised to involve a large group of students of mixed abilities. The work started when the City Archivist visited the school to talk to the social studies staff. Some of the students heard about this and came along to talk to him themselves. They arranged to visit the archives and, after this visit, we decided to undertake some sort of urban study. The archives group was made up of highly motivated students taking 'O' levels in English, social studies and history. Although I was not able to accompany the students in class time, since at this time only a minority of the class (about a dozen) were involved, the archivist and I spent a great deal of time after school sorting out relevant documents and maps and discussing subjects and activities that might interest the students.

After several sessions at the archives searching through the maps and documents, the students decided to concentrate on one area of Leicester: the Saint Matthew's parish, an area of slum clearance and re-development. At this stage students, individually or in pairs, began to select aspects of the area that they wished to investigate – health and housing, education, religion, entertainments and social life, and so on. As would be expected with a group that chose to work in archives, most of their work initially was historical. But soon their projects began to broaden and throw up demands for information that was not historical and hence not available to them in the archives. In turn this led to requests from some of the students for help in acquiring more information, especially about the area as it stands today.

The requests for help sometimes came to me but were also passed on directly to students in the social studies class still working at school. Members of this latter group now began to ask if they could join in the work going on in Saint Matthew's. As a result I decided to take this group on a visit to the Saint Matthew's area. The feature which most interested them was how much the area was visibly changing, the commonest question was: 'What was it like before?' In the course of the visit and in the following lesson at school students came up with a variety of activities that they wanted to undertake. Some were interested in the industrial archaeology of the area, others wanted to do practical sociological work, such as interviews, visits and surveys, others wanted to try mapwork and photography.

At first the work of the second group remained separate from the work at the archives. But there was a clear basis for interaction since both groups were seeking to know how and why an urban area changes. Consequently the two groups began to merge. Within a month all of the second group had visited and worked in the archives to find out what work had already been completed on the area. New groups were formed and projects redefined and broadened. For instance, the two students who had listed the pubs currently in the area and had interviewed some of the publicans joined the student at the archives who was defining the entertainments of nineteenth century Leicester and were soon as involved in music halls as they had been with pubs. The merging of groups ensured that over a period of time each student tried both archives work and work in the area and became aware of the difficulties and rewards of both methods.

For the moment all students in the class had found an activity they wanted to pursue. The constraint they now complained about was that one afternoon a week was too short a time for the work and made it seem disjointed. Consequently the English department was approached and agreed to use the urban study as a way of developing English skills. This co-operation meant two things. Firstly, the students could now use the whole of Wednesday for their studies.

Secondly, one teacher could always be available in school to help those who wanted to work there for writing up their work, drawing maps or developing films. Thus on Wednesdays the students might be working at the archives, or in the Saint Matthew's area, or in school.

A report of this kind seems almost inevitably to read as if everything went smoothly; this was certainly not always the case. The first few weeks did run smoothly as a result of excitement at working out of school and interest aroused in discovering a new area (all the students lived outside urban Leicester in suburban or rural surroundings). After this honeymoon period problems began. Some students said they felt that they had begun projects that were not leading anywhere. Normally this was a result of their inability to work out a 'plan of campaign' with which to attack their chosen topic. With advice and encouragement, all the students but one were able to pass through this crucial stage. Other problems were posed by students who got on to a project which led them outside the Saint Matthew's area and hence to the point where they had to consider abandoning their original plans. For instance, a group of girls became so interested in visiting schools, as part of their study of education in Saint Matthew's, that this became their overriding concern. We decided that they should abandon the original plan and begin visiting schools elsewhere in Leicester. After this survey of schools had been conducted they finally settled on a primary school in the main immigrant area of Leicester and for several months each attached herself to one of the classes in the school. Each student kept a detailed journal of events in the school.

In general, visiting the Saint Matthew's area seemed to offer so many possibilities for the student that even those who, like these girls, found their interest in the original urban study waning discovered other projects they wanted to do. The only exceptions were two boys who 'skived off' on several afternoons and one boy who decided after looking at Saint Matthew's that he would now do the theme work on urbanization at school.

After the first month, apart from the few who re-directed their work, most students had so much work and interest involved in their projects that the main problem was in locating sufficient sources to provide the answers they sought. One student, for example, wrote over fifty letters, made twelve telephone calls and carried out ten interviews. His project emerged as a fascinating microcosmic study of one of the main streets in the area. Other students visited private homes, Evergreen Clubs, old folk's homes, local factories, the vicarage, the Town Hall, Radio Leicester and the local community centre in search of information. Sample surveys were carried out on traffic, health, housing and religion.

For all the students involved, work which began with the urban study lasted throughout the fourth year. In the summer term most students organized their work into some sort of finished product, comprising extended essays, maps and photographs, cassettes of interviews, reports and surveys. This final organization was determined partly by their own desire to have a finished product to show people, partly by the demands of the examinations for project work and partly because they had agreed with the people who helped them at the museum to set up a small exhibition of their work.

The work at Countesthorpe offers an illustration of one sort of strategy for introducing urban studies to a mixed ability class. From the methodological standpoint, starting with an interested and motivated group paradoxically proved the best way of involving the whole class. The group working at the archives to begin with provided a historical information base from which to launch a broad interdisciplinary urban study. As the study progressed, the archive group, now somewhat changed in composition, served to initiate and direct activities undertaken in the Saint Matthew's area. This function was especially helpful for those students who had difficulty in sustaining and directing their own studies. Throughout the study the work at the archives helped to provide ideas and strategies for the more practical work being completed in the area, and this points to the value of having a nucleus of students, working with existing, concrete resources, for directing and sustaining a large urban study.[14]

The relationship between urban studies and the traditional disciplines has to be carefully defined at two levels :

1. *Professional* – because any teachers of 'traditional' disciplines planning to undertake urban study work need to know precisely how their subject can best contribute to such work. Geographers especially have been undertaking urban study work for decades and without close definition might rightly be tempted into thinking that geographical urban study work *was* urban studies.
2. *Pedagogical.* The tradional disciplines contain and train pupils to handle some of the skills, techniques and content which urban studies draw upon. Rigorous definition of the relationship between the disciplines and urban studies is crucial at this level.

In recently attempting to define the relationship between my own subject, history, and urban studies, I concluded this way:

> An urban study is not just an historical exercise. To define it thus not only excludes the possibilities offered for literary, sociological and geographical work, but in doing so narrows the possibilities for historical work. Ideally within each project there is an almost endless self-feeding process. Historical work can lead to a geographical investigation with some possibilities for sociological survey work which suggests more historical research and so on. To limit an urban study to historical research alone denies the student entry to this interaction of disciplines and in the process limits the possibilities for historical study.

If this is true about history it would seem to me to be similarly apposite for other traditional disciplines in their relationship to urban studies but the definition of that relationship clearly needs to be undertaken in detail by other subject specialists.

The need for a third stage in the strategy for establishing urban studies as part of the curriculum for all students lies in the nature of the present examination system. Of course, urban study work can go on satisfactorily in any number of subject areas. 'O' level syllabuses, however, are traditionally packed with factual content that is difficult to learn in the time allotted and which is formally examined. Hence the kind of flexibility in time and form of assessment needed for urban study work is not normally available. In this situation urban studies would inevitably be offered only to the non-academic pupils if one were to work through the established subjects.

A broad-based campaign to persuade examining boards to accept urban studies for 'O' and 'A' level examinations is obviously necessary. Already there are hopeful signs: a growing number of Mode 3 CSE and 'O' level urban studies are now in operation. The Associated Examining Board has recently accepted as special Mode 3 'O' levels a number of urban/community studies syllabuses and, as a result, a group of schools in Leicestershire are teaching the subject at 'O' level. My own school, Stantonbury in Milton Keynes, has also submitted an urban/community studies Mode 3 'O' level to the Associated Examining Board.

With environmental studies the campaign for examinations was never broad-based enough and the first two stages in the strategy suggested here were given scant attention. If 'O' and 'A' level urban studies courses were widely established as the culmination to the three-phased strategy I have outlined, there is a real possibility that the potential of environmental work for motivating and involving children of all abilities in learning situations could be finally fulfilled.

References

1. MARTIN, G. C., 1973, 'Environmental Education: Objectives and Approaches', *BEE*, May.
2. BOON, G. S., 1973, 'Urban Studies and the Young School Leaver', *BEE*, March.
3. WARD, C. & FYSON, A., 1973, *Streetwork: The Exploding School*, Routlege & Kegan Paul, London.
4. MIDWINTER, E., 1972, *Priority Education*, Penguin Education, Harmondsworth.
5. WHEELER, K. S. & WAITES, B., 1972, 'How to Make a Town Trail', *BEE*, Nos 16–17, August–September.
6. *Ibid.*
7. AYLWARD, B., 1974, *Design Education in Schools*, Evans, London.
8. Ken Baynes is a member of the Royal College of Art Design Research Department.
9. CHINNERY, G. A., 1971, *Urban History in Schools*, Historical Association, London.
10. *If It wasn't for the Houses In Between*, N.U.T. (undated).
11. MIDWINTER, *Op. cit.*
12. GOODEY, B., 1974, *Where You're At* and WARD, C., 1974, *Utopia*, Penguin Education, Harmondsworth.
13. WARD & FYSON, *Op. cit.*
14. GOODSON, I., 1972, 'Urban Studies at Countesthorpe College', *BEE*, December.

Bibliography

GOODEY, B., 1974, 'A Framework for Urban Environmental Education', in SPENCER, D. & LLOYD, J. (eds.), *A Child's Eye View of Small Heath, Birmingham: Perception studies for Environmental Education. Research Memoranda No. 34*, Centre for Urban and Regional Studies, The University of Birmingham.

7 Community studies

Colin and Mog Ball

Whatever we call home, comely cottage or high-rise flat, we live these days in a man-made environment. Yet although the fields, streets, buildings where we live and work, even increasingly the very air we breathe, are all made by men, they have an ironic grip on the actions of men. They are the imperatives which define the scope of our lives. Maybe we are just kidding ourselves when we say that we make and shape our environment: for most of us it is the environment which shapes us.

Part of 'community studies' is concerned with the creation of an awareness of these imperatives which limit our lives and the lives of other people, both within the small community round about as well as within the more general context of 'suburban life', 'urban life' and so on. This kind of study has always formed a part of geography courses, though it concentrated on the effect of the physical, as opposed to the man-made, environment on communities and examined the life-styles they assumed as a response to physical imperatives. Every geography course included those Hopi Indians, jungle fruit-gatherers and nomads. 'Geography,' said the master in the first term at secondary school, 'is about places and the people who live in them.' Now community studies is about the places people have made, and the way they and others respond to them.

This awareness is merely the starting point. The study of a community from the point of view of the student must be complemented by an examination of the point of view of other people, for otherwise the personal understanding will be narrow and the response selfish. It must be complemented, also, by an experience or, ideally, a set of experiences, of response to other environments, both man-made and physical, and the responses of other people to both 'our' and 'their' environments. All of this constitutes a kind of community studies fieldwork, direct descendant of those groups of geographers who swarm over Malham Cove or study tomato-growing techniques in the Po valley. This fieldwork takes students from rural Cambridgeshire to Sparkbrook for a week or two, and vice versa, to

82

find out their own response to the new environment and try to understand the response of longer term residents.

The aim is a depth of understanding and awareness in the student essentially on a personal, and probably emotional, level which is set in a broad context.

This is only part of the community studies story, however. The success of the study is allied to the amount of involvement on the part of the student; that is, the sort of involvement which illustrates that the man-made environment must and can be continually re-shaped by all men, provided only they are aware, confident and competent enough to do it. It is a failure of our schools that young people emerge from them unaware of the imperatives, let alone the possibility of changing them; most, therefore, have no confidence in their own ability to change these imperatives, for the benefit of themselves or others.

The result of this is the paradox with which we began: man controlled, dominated and harassed by the very environment he has created for himself. The involvement is not just a necessary part of community studies for its value as a means of encouraging helping relationships between people, but also because it enables young people, growing up into a man-made world, to see that it is neces-sary and possible to change that world.

Let us examine the methods of community studies, then, begin-ning with ways which create awareness of those factors which govern our lives and the lives of other people. The awareness must begin with some sort of 'total' view of the community in which one lives. That means looking at every aspect of community life, from how the Parish, District and County Councils work and what aspect of the individual's life they 'control', to how easy it is to cross the road, how often the buses run, whether there are playgroups, where there is playspace, what kind of shops and what you can buy there, what the places where people live are like, how many people own these places, how many rent them, what they pay and whether it's worth it. It means finding out where people work, how industrial activity affects the community, not just through employment, but also through noise, smell and ugliness. To begin with, the discover-ing answers the question: 'How does all this affect me – what controls me, what liberates me?' We can hardly set out here all the facts and issues to be discovered. Inevitably they will be focussed on the key issues in any one community. But from that focus a multi-plicity of views and angles are possible, where a straightforward course or syllabus would prove much less fertile.

Inevitably this kind of enquiry, undertaken at first from an individual standpoint, will extend to the feelings and knowledge which other people in the community have about life there. This will give the student's feelings some perspective and will certainly throw up issues which, being young and healthy, he had not considered. Time spent with elderly people (in their own homes, or in school, as a result of invitations) has a double value: it enables students to learn the elderly's view of the current environment and it balances the present with a view of the past – 'there used to be. . . .' Using old people as a valued *resource* in this way, instead of as an often unwilling target for community service by young people, might just do a little to encourage some mutual respect. Too often the young see the old as another imperative which limits their activities, and the old look at the young in the same way.

Particularly worth investigating are the lives of handicapped people and their view of the community. A young person is often surprised by the number of limitations which too often completely destroy the quality of life for the mentally and physically disabled. For the former the limitations may be obvious: whole lives spent institutionalized. For the latter the limitations may not be so clear, until the student realizes that kerbstones are cliffs to a wheelchair user; flights of steps are barriers, and narrow doors, like those on telephone booths, might just as well be locked. There are many others whose opinions about community life and facilities should be sought, starting with young children and their mothers, who face considerable limitations.

Work experience must feature as one of the most important ways of putting oneself in someone else's shoes. Working with, for or instead of a person reveals many of his problems. We have pointed out that one important defining imperative is work. Working with a man helps us not only to understand how his work environment affects him, but also how it shapes his attitudes, opinions and actions. This kind of work experience is not uncommon in schools, but it is arranged to enable a young person to decide whether he wants to take up that sort of work. Our emphasis is quite different. If we are to understand people and what governs their actions then we must get out of the sterility and security of the classroom. No amount of books and films and discussion will ever convey what it is really like to be digging a trench on a cold, wet day; to be performing the same simple manual operation 500 times a day, five days a week; to stand behind a counter selling sweets; to stand up in front of a class of thirty, bored children. But, to repeat, the idea is not to see if you like, or can do, the job, it is to see what the job does to you; how it limits you, how much it tires you, how much it bores or excites you.

In certain areas, the student can also discover the effect of the welfare industry on a community. This would be most likely to occur with work experience for someone who looks after community problems: teacher, nurse, social worker, policeman. Work with these people gives insight not only into their problems, but into the imperatives they bring into the lives of those they are serving.

These imperatives say you must go to school to learn; you must see a social worker rather than a neighbour if you've got problems; you must call the police if noisy motorbikes annoy you, not sort things out yourself. In some ways these lessons are the most important ones to be gained from work experience. They indicate how many people in the community are rendered impotent by those who 'serve' them. The student may judge this division of labour right, inevitable, economical, valuable, or whatever. Any judgement based on work experience will provide a useful insight into this powerful and influential segment of community life.

Alongside an examination of the community using these methods, there must be experiences which give bases for comparison. Of course, any experience of life in other communities is necessarily going to be less complete, as any fieldwork is, but it is important, though one must remember that the 'community next-door' may be just as valuable a basis for comparison as any other. Naturally there may be some students who have had experience of life in other communities. Such experience will be useful, particularly if it is of life in India, Africa, Cyprus or the West Indies.

It would be as well to mention at this point another, quite different, form of experience which must play an integral part in the community studies course. At a period when individuals in many communities find themselves isolated from even their friends and neighbours (such isolation is, indeed, one of the imperatives which students of the community will probably discover early in their investigations), it does seem important to create a situation where people can live close together and, particularly, where they can depend on one another. In this lies a chance to examine the comparative satisfactions of a community life based on interaction and interdependence and one comprised of isolated individuals. Within the school itself young people are brought together, but they are in no way dependent on one another. Out of school, placed in what may be a harsh and difficult environment, they have the chance to

85

learn that their very survival may depend on co-operation, on the creation of some kinds of imperatives for themselves, and on some kind of division of labour.

This hair-raising approach can be seen in practice at the Pacifica High On Location School in California. This is a 'school within a school' as it is part of an ordinary high school. It operates in unusual ways and includes work experience, along the lines we have described, community work and living together in hazardous physical circumstances. The students hike through the high Sierra Nevada and camp in Death Valley. In school, 'government' means learning about Senate and White House; on location, it means that the students form laws with which to govern themselves. Interdependence, division of labour, become necessary, yet nobody is isolated for that means loneliness, hunger and misery. Perhaps there are lessons in the response to the physical environment which apply to the responses of men to their man-made environment?

Up to now we have been looking at ways in which a young person can be enabled to examine his community through his own eyes, through the eyes of others, with the long term objective of realizing how his and other people's lives are limited by the community environment. He will find that it is by no means as simple in its effects upon man as the physical environment, for it comprises not just man-made controls like roads and houses and industries, but the very controls which men impose upon one another. This is not just another way of saying it's all a question of 'them' and 'us', though that's a part of it; it is about how we affect, and are affected by all people around us. What comes next is active involvement. Not the least reason for this is the realization that a passive response to the community and the environment is dangerous. That passivity has been at the root of much of the less pleasant developments in the environment and the community. And the very method of investigating the community, the need to go out from the school to follow up leads into the most unlikely parts of the community and, above all, to communicate with people while he is doing it, provides the student with a confidence and a relevant knowledge which militates against the passive role. The alternative is an active stance to combat imperatives and the inadequacies they produce in individual and community life.

Should this be a concern of young people? Yes. Firstly because the inadequacies of community life will only be overcome by the community itself. There is no doubt that any community has the skills to do this. But first it must recognize certain facts: that it bows to imperatives which can be changed, and that each individual contribution to the community brings satisfaction to the individual as well as well-being to the community. If everyone is to have that role, then youth must be admitted to that role, for like everybody else, young people need the confidence in themselves which will let them realize their particular skills. Not insignificant among these are initiative, enterprise, energy and ingenuity, all of which can be realized in the service of the community. And like everybody else, young people need the confidence to assert that they do not need constant ministration, only an opportunity to assert their value within the community.

Now we've claimed all that, it's important to typify the involvement. From the point of view of students and their teachers, two things need to be known. Firstly, where can the involvement take place? In the past this has often meant securing a list of local old people. It is clear that the involvement will take place in those areas of limitation which the students have previously discovered affect people's lives. No play space? Then involvement to try to secure it, or something to overcome the lack of it. Interestingly, even the response in situations like this may be limited by imperatives. Street theatre is one kind of 'involved' response – it can be no other kind of theatre if all you have to play on are streets. Kerbs and steps are barriers to the handicapped? Do something about it – in the beginning by conducting a thorough survey of access for the disabled in every part of the community. Then you start building ramps, having a go at whoever it is who provides public toilets (who that is the students will know by now), producing a guide-book for the disabled. Who will do these things if young people don't? So many old, mentally handicapped and even young people are institutionalized. They will continue to be so until people feel at ease and able to enter institutions and become involved in them.

But is is not just a question of where, it is a matter of how. There is a world of difference between this kind of involvement and the work experience described earlier, though both are valuable and necessary. One can see, for example, that a student would gain by working in a hospital geriatric ward or with a group of mothers running a play group. The young person would work alongside the staff, as we have said earlier, to see their methods, to see how their work affects them and those they work for. Now we are suggesting a different kind of involvement based on an acknowledgement of inadequacies rather than an attempt to perceive them. This involvement enables the young to contribute in their own way the skills which they have. In the hospital ward this would not mean simply making tea, talking to patients and doing traditional service tasks, but taking in plays, art classes, gymnastic displays, running a radio station for the whole hospital, brightening the decor – the list is as long as the skills and interests of young people.

On the question of involvement, then, the second thing that needs to be discovered is the student's answer to the questions 'What are my skills?' 'What have we to offer in our group?' 'How we can apply what we know, the facilities within the school at our disposal and the interests we have for the benefit of others in the solution of problems and the overcoming of inadequacies and limitations faced by people in our community.'

There is not space to detail the things young people can offer. It is enough to repeat that these things include individual skills and the use of school-based resources.

Our concern in community studies, then, is people, for they are a pretty important feature of the environment. Our concern is to enable young people to be aware of those around them; and the teacher must be, above all, an enabler. He must also be highly determined on two essentials. The first is that community studies has a flexible place on the curriculum. We remember the teacher who asked if there was a playgroup operating in the community at 10.30 am on Wednesdays, since that was his community studies period. The community does not revolve around the school's demands. In community studies the very opposite must be the case.

The teacher's second obsession must be to ensure that community studies does not continue to be just one of several oddments and discontinued educational lines thrust upon the non-academics and early leavers. The community studies exercise is as rigorous an academic course as any. And it would be very wrong to confine the understanding of people and the opportunity to contribute to community life to any one small group of young people. All need the awareness and confidence that will come from the opportunity for positive action.

Reference
BALL, C. & M., 1973, *Education for a Change: Community Action and the School*, Penguin Education, Harmondsworth.

8 Architecture in environmental education

Frank Chippindale and Colin Ward

It is nobody's business to teach about architecture in schools, and this is one of the reasons why it is so seldom attempted. It depends on the enthusiasm and insight of individual teachers, and their wisdom and sensibility is more important than their subject. Every teacher with a feeling for the built environment is involved in the business of architectural interpretation. They have undertaken the task of opening their pupils' eyes to the visual aspects of their habitat in order to make it comprehensible. In this sense the interpretation of the built environment is no different from that of the natural environment. Freeman Tilden, the pioneer of interpretive methods in the American national parks, defined the art as 'an educational activity which aims to reveal meanings and relationships through the use of original objects, by firsthand experiences and by illustrative media, rather than simply to communicate factual information.'[1]

Who are the teachers who have undertaken this task? We might assume that it is the art teacher's business, but in fact not many of them are concerned with the buildings that surround our daily lives. When the art teacher does manage to get his class out of the art room and into the street, it is not usually to interpret, evaluate, assess and enjoy *the thing itself*, but to gather raw material to be worked up later in the studio, so that the drawing or painting becomes the important thing. This does not mean that the exercise is valueless. It is useful for the same reason that geography teachers find field sketching valuable: knowledge and insight are gained by the act of recording, since this depends on the art of seeing. In the formal structure of art education virtually every GCE syllabus includes an architectural option – usually a purely historical one – but if we are enquiring what enlightenment about architecture occurs in the formal education of most schoolchildren we have to remember that a majority of them do not reach GCE level, that art is not a particularly popular examination subject (8th at 'O' level and 9th at 'A' level) and that, in any case, it is only a small proportion of art candidates who prepare for and sit for the architectural options.

The built environment, however, does creep in to a variety of other school subjects. The study of houses, for example, often has a place in home economics courses, the teacher of religious education may seek to interest his class in the history of churches and cathedrals (there is even today among the English a tendency to equate architecture with ecclesiology), the English teacher may be interested in the built environment as the basis for descriptive or creative writing, just as the art teacher sees it as a source for graphic work. More than one sixth former has been drawn to the profession of architecture by the introduction to the theory of structures provided in the Nuffield 'A' level physics course, while one of the teaching packages in the Schools Council 'Mathematics for the Majority Continuation Project' approaches its subject very imaginatively through architectural calculations.[2]

Architecture *may*, of course, feature in such amorphous school subjects as social studies, general studies, liberal studies, community studies (or, in Scotland, modern studies). But the likeliest encounters with the built environment *in a school context* (for obviously we encounter it every minute of our lives simply through living in it) are not even under the label of environmental studies, which as a school subject is still often interpreted as relating only to the rural or natural environment, though this bias is rapidly giving way to a broader interpretation. Those school children who are exposed to some kind of teaching about architecture or are incited to some form of investigation of it, are most likely to have encountered it in history or geography. This, once more, is the study of architecture as a means to something else. The historian and the geographer are interested in architecture as *evidence*. In both subjects there is a growing emphasis on fieldwork and on urban and local studies,[3] with a corresponding growth of interest in the techniques of recording, identifying and dating buildings.

From the point of view which regards buildings as things in themselves, to be studied and cherished for their own sake, the collecting and classifying approach is more important than it might seem. For many people a lifetime of architectural interest and concern has been kindled by just such an effort to 'read the street'. It is also a valuable corrective to the common approach to architecture in which excessive emphasis is placed on isolated gems – bits of the jewellery of the building trade – in a sea of workaday buildings which are deemed to be unworthy of consideration. Here there are several current growth-points, dependent once again much more on individual teachers and on the interest they are able to arouse in their classes, than on the boundaries of subjects. One is the increasing interest at school level in industrial archaeology which brings with it the urge to investigate the rich heritage of industrial buildings. Another is the very new field of housing history. Aided by the recent flow of academic works on this theme, we are recognizing that every city is a living museum of housing, and that our present dilemmas which we would like our pupils to understand, grow out of past policy which is displayed all round us in bricks and mortar.[4] A third new enthusiasm of this kind is vernacular architecture, those anonymous unpedigreed buildings with marked regional and local characteristics: the folksongs of architecture. Dr Ronald Brunskill of Manchester University School of Architecture has developed a system of notation and classification for vernacular buildings which provides an admirable framework for school activities in this field.[5]

Again it is undeniably true that, since most schools are in suburbs, really local studies will in very many instances, be suburban studies. There is a growing literature on the suburb, sociological, geographical and architectural, and there is room for genuinely pioneering work by schools on the architectural morphology of the suburb.[6]

All these potentialities for injecting some kind of architectural awareness into the school curriculum are simply in the margins of established subjects. Some would say that they are also in the margins of architecture. Is there any hope for some consideration of the visual aspects of the built environment in its own right? Should visual education not find a firm and universally acknowledged place within the spectrum of art education? This is a reasonable question, but it is one which launches us into the deep end of the perennial debate on the function and purpose of education itself. A continuous line of educational philosophers from Rousseau, through Ruskin and Morris, to Herbert Read have urged that the education of the senses should be the central task of the school, instead of a peripheral, marginal or optional extra. They have sought to enhance and enlarge the role of the arts in education, and today there is a significant lobby within the world of art education itself which seeks to transform it into design education, by integrating it with the craft subjects and with home economics, joining together activities which a tradition stretching from William Morris to the Bauhaus has steadfastly maintained should never have been separated. The design lobby in art education has shown fruitful results and has had very persuasive advocacy.[7] Its critics amongst art and craft teachers have two misgivings about it: first, that pupils' energies may be dissipated over too wide a range of problem-solving design projects, so that no skills are developed beyond an elementary level, with the danger that ordinary graphic and manual skills are neglected; second, that the compilers of timetables may take advantage of the combination of craft and art subjects to allocate fewer pupil hours to it than to the total of its previously separate and distinct components.

The view that all of these are marginal to the *real* (that is, academic) functions of the school is still widespread. It must be admitted that the well-organized programmes for the teaching of the sciences, for example, have pushed aside the claims made for the teaching of aesthetic sensibility, with the result that the visually illiterate children of one generation become the arrogantly insensitive adults of the next. 'Isn't it extraordinary,' Jo Grimond once remarked, 'that the enormous expansion of higher education in the last two decades, has done nothing to improve the quality of life or the quality of the environment?'

Once a school has made the leap to a design education approach it is unlikely to reverse the procedure. For advocates of architectural studies in general education the design education movement offers many advantages. It makes a clean break with the antiquarianism that considers that 'architecture' stopped somewhere in the nineteenth century and that everything else is a 'concrete jungle' to be deplored automatically. Its problem-solving approach is likely to give more insight into the architectural *process* than one based on developing a passive 'good taste'. There is a parallel in musical education in the view that it is better to perform than to listen. At the same time, this point of view is not the whole of the truth. Just as there are performers, especially child performers, whose musical activities are compounded of motor skills and perseverance rather than of aesthetic experiences, so there are architects whose activities are technical rather than visually satisfying. It can be said, indeed, that this is the whole tragedy of the modern movement in architecture. The eye demands a richly worked surface texture and cannot be satisfied with a bland mechnical slab of curtain-walling. There is a need, as much in the old art department as in the new design department for active sensory exploration of the built environment in the same way as there is room in musical education for active listening.

We can claim indeed that there is a case for 'Hearing Architecture'. Steen Eiler Rasmussen devotes a chapter to this theme in his book *Experiencing Architecture* where he asks us to be still and listen: 'Can architecture be heard? Most people would probably say that as architecture does not produce sound, it cannot be heard. But neither does it radiate light and yet it can be seen. We see the light it reflects and thereby gain an impression of form and material. In the same way we hear the sounds it reflects and they, too, give us an impression of form and material. Differently shaped rooms and different materials reverberate differently.'[8]

He is, and we are, concerned here with the neglected affective aspect of environmental education: the domain of sentiments and feelings. At a time when it is evident that a proportion of the young are actively at war with their environment, precisely because they have no say in shaping it and no other influence on it, we are concerned with *topophilia* a word coined by Yi-Fu Tuan[9] for that love of place which it is surely our aim to generate. We want to incite our pupils to ask themselves the question: is this a good place? A value judgement. An aesthetic judgement. Geographers would rather talk about central place theory than make such a judgement. Planners would rather talk about cost benefit analysis, and even architects tend to shuffle off into sociological arguments. Leopold Kohr remarks that 'to talk aesthetics amongst theorists of industrial location nowadays is like raising the question of sex amongst pre-Freudian child educators. Half of them cannot grasp the connection and the other half are shocked. In their eyes nothing could be more frivolous that the injection of beauty into economic or other utilitarian debate.'[10] And yet, he points out, aesthetic considerations are, 'as every jeweller, car designer and musician knows, amongst the most outstanding determinants of economic forces such as consumer demand.' And he insists that they are also measurable: 'As aggregate utility finds its operating dimensions in the form of price, social beauty finds it in the form of elements such as the frequency and intensity with which the aggregate of citizens, the public, is drawn into worshipping it, enjoying it, beholding it and, in particular, staying close to it.'

To assess this kind of quality in an environment, we need to look beyond the characteristics of individual buildings. We have to assess nothing less than the *genius loci*, the spirit of the place. What sort of place is it, what is its personality and character? Does anyone love it, would anyone miss it, does it generate topophilia? Ralph Jeffrey HMI has kindly permitted us to quote the leading questions he has used for this kind of investigation.[11]

Space: the square, alley street; how is space enclosed bent, framed, deflected? How does it widen, narrow, lead on in sequence or not, provide variety, have a sense of direction or ambiguity? Spaces between houses, of houses, cf. with widths of streets, in plan, elevation; space enclosures — walls, fences, changes of level (vertical space).

Decoration: Pattern on walls, ground; architectural decoration; graphics, lettering, shop and road signs; decorative effect of trees, shrubs, railings, repetition, ornament.

Light: Cloud and sun; shadow patterns; night/day and dusk; water, reflections, glass; floodlight, neon, profiles, silhouettes, interaction of street and sky.

Building: Scale and proportion; architectural style, materials, colours, texture and their sequence, backs and fronts, street furniture.

Notice that what is conventionally called architecture plays a rather small part in his environmental checklist. *Style*, which most of the handbooks identify with architecture, is very low on his list. He asks us to identify what is good and bad about the habitat and why. What is missing from it, what is superfluous, what could be done to improve it, is it harsh, soft, hostile, friendly, man-scaled, dramatic, relevant to modern life-styles? What are the factors for change and stability?

We should notice too, that his visual enquiry can only be done through direct experience of *the thing itself*. Its context is that of streetwork[12] rather than that of the classroom. The enormous growth during the 1960s of nature trails as aids to environmental interpretation in the countryside has been paralleled in the 1970s by a burgeoning interest in town trails or guided urban walks. The pioneering Leicester Town Trail[13] has inspired teachers at all levels from primary school to university to develop local trails, while many of them have discovered that the act of preparing a trail, with the research and appraisal this implies, is in itself an educational activity of great value. A town trail may, of course, display themes which are historical, geographical or sociological rather than architectural, but when it is undertaken as a tool of environmental appraisal, it is essential that contemporary buildings and their contribution to the townscape should be given as much consideration as historical architecture. Brian Goodey of Birmingham University has provided a survey of existing trails which also attempts to assess the strengths and weaknesses of urban trail techniques.[14]

A further important potential aid to the interpretation of the built environment is the urban studies centre, and the associated notion of architectural interpretation centres. Here, again, is an extrapolation into the built environment of educational aids (in this instance field centres) which have been valuable to schools in the study of rural environments. A Council for Urban Studies Centres was set up in 1973 and the first of such centres are already in existence.[15] An urban studies centre is envisaged as a base for streetwork in the locality, equipped with reference materials and display equipment, and staffed by a tutor-warden familiar with both the place and the techniques of urban study. One of its incidental advantages would be that the teachers using the centre with a party of children would themselves be gaining insights into these techniques.

This is significant since the quickest way to improve the quality and quantity of architectural teaching and learning in schools is to improve, or in fact to introduce, the training of teachers in this field. One of us surveyed the scope of environmental teaching in colleges of education (noting the gap between the printed prospectus and what is actually done), and concluded that 'It is clear that whatever the title of the course offered, compulsory or optional, of short periods (half day in one term) or spread over three years, the majority of students in Colleges of Education are *not* introduced to everyday problems of the built environment.'[16] Current changes in the structure of teacher training in Britain could be exploited to improve this situation. For example, the presence of schools of architecture and schools of education in the same campus *ought* to produce some creative cross-fertilization, but experience shows that departmental isolationism is a built-in feature of the higher education system.

Many architects themselves would like to be involved in an informal way in environmental education, but often the best use is not made of this willingness. For an architect to go in and address a class which has had no prior preparation and which will have no effective follow-up may have no more value than the novelty of a new face behind the desk.[17] It might be sensible and, in the long term, more rewarding to exploit these local skills, whether those of architects, planners or landscape designers, to help groups of teachers rather than in isolated talks to small groups of pupils. The most useful thing by far that an architect can do with a school group is to take its members for a walk. Time and again teachers have said to us, 'Until Mr X took us down the street, I had never looked above the shopfronts.' The habit of informed observation is the most precious slice of expertise the architect can offer and that teachers and pupils can absorb from him.

In arguing the educational claims of the *look* of places we have to stress not the esoteric and specialist nature of architecture, but its ordinariness, and the fact that a concern for it is one of the normal attributes of citizenship. 'Architecture,' declares S. E. Rasmussen, 'is produced by ordinary people, for ordinary people; therefore it should be comprehensible to all. It is based on a number of human instincts, on discoveries and experiences common to us all.'

References
1. TILDEN, F., 1967, *Interpreting Our Heritage* (revised edition), University of North Carolina Press, Chapel Hill.
2. Published for the Schools Council by Schofield & Sims, Huddersfield.
3. In history, see *Studying Urban History in Schools* by G. A. Chinnery (Historical Association, London). In geography, apart from the attention to architecture in the various handbooks on urban studies, see the specifically architectural values in such class books as *Townlook 1* by Gordon Boon and *Townlook 2* by Kenneth Lindley (both Pergamon Press, Oxford, 1969) and Mr Boon's more recent class books like *Words in Towns* and *Rocks in Towns* (both Methuen, London, 1974).
4. For the teacher there are such books as TARN, J. N., 1974, *Five Per Cent Philanthropy: An Account of housing in urban areas between 1840 and 1914*, Cambridge University Press, Cambridge, and GAULDIE, E., 1974, *Cruel Habitations: a history of working class housing 1790–1918*, Allen & Unwin, London, and for pupils, HUGGET, F., 1974, *Housing the People 1700 to the Present Day*, Nelson, London.
5. See BRUNSKILL, R., 1970, *Illustrated Handbook of Vernacular Architecture*, Faber, London.
6. RICHARDS, J. M., 1973, *The Castles on the Ground* (2nd ed.), John Murray, London. TAYLOR, N., 1973, *The Village in the City*, Temple Smith, London. JACKSON, A. A., 1973, *Semi-Detached London*, Allen & Unwin, London. THORNS, D., 1974, *Suburbia*, Paladin, London. BARRETT, B., 1971, *The Inner Suburbs*, Melbourne University Press, Melbourne.
7. BAYNES, K., 1969, *Attitudes in Design Education*, Lund Humphries, London. AYLWARD, B. (ed.), 1973, *Design Education in Schools*, Evans, London. GREEN, P., 1974, *Design Education: Problem Solving and Visual Experience*, Batsford, London.
8. RASMUSSEN, S. E., 1959, *Experiencing Architecture*, Chapman & Hall, London (MIT Paperbacks, 1964).
9. TUAN, Y-F, 1974, *Topophilia*, Prentice-Hall, Englewood Cliffs, N.J.
10. KOHR, L., 1974, *The City as Convivial Centre* (Tract No. 12), The Gryphon Press, Llanon, Cardiganshire.
11. Mr. Jeffrey tells us he was inspired by DE WOLFE, I., 1964, *The Italian Townscape*, Architectural Press, London. Another book with a similar approach is CULLEN, G., 1971, *The Concise Townscape*, Architectural Press, London.
12. WARD, C. & FYSON, A., 1973, *Streetwork: The Exploding School*, Routledge & Kegan Paul, London.
13. WHEELER, K. & WAITES, B., 1972, 'Leicester Town Trail', *Bulletin of Environmental Education*, No. 16–17, Aug.–Sept.
14. GOODEY, B., 1975, *Urban Walks and Town Trails: Origins, Principles and Sources*, Research Memorandum No. 40, Centre for Urban and Regional Studies, University of Birmingham.
15. FYSON, A., 1974, *Council for Urban Studies Centres, First Report*, Town and Country Planning Association, London.

16. See CHIPPINDALE, F., 1973, 'The Street and its Surroundings', *Society for Environmental Education Journal*, **5**, No. 2, Summer.
17. See WARD, C. & MACEWEN, M., 1973, 'Architecture in School', *RIBA Journal*, May and *Bulletin of Environmental Education*, June.

9 Design education and the environment

Bernard Aylward

The object of this section is to describe developments in a practical sphere of education of great relevance in devising a new curriculum for environmental education, namely 'design education'. There is always a danger with any curriculum development of setting up a 'new' subject that, in cutting across subject boundaries, cuts also the roots that nourish the work of other teachers. Curriculum developers should seek to find how work, already valid in its own right, may be given greater relevance by relating it to their own particular area of interest.

Much must be forgiven the enthusiastic teacher but he must beware of seeing his interest as all important. Development is taking place in all areas of the curriculum and the real educator should be aware of this. He should look for natural links that can with advantage be exploited so that the work of teachers so linked is mutually enhanced. This is particularly vital when considering workshop activities. It is too easy to look on these as an easy way to illustrate other studies. There is much to be said for practical illustration and model making, if time can be found for it; to expect this to be done at the expense of work designed to exploit the unique educational advantages of the crafts does not lead to willing co-operation from practical teachers. There are plenty of activities already going on that can support environmental education and it is these which should be exploited.

There has been a strong movement over the last decade or so towards developing the design aspect of all practical work in schools. There is not space here to describe this development in detail except to say that it has been stimulated by the same social pressures that have led to the development of environmental education. All teachers have been concerned to make education relevant to the world their pupils inhabit and, by doing so, help them to cope with the problems to be found in society.

Teachers in workshops and studios are giving children some experience of designing so that they may realize some of the constraints within which a designer must work. They can become aware of the many pressures that determine the sort of clothes we wear, the food we eat, the houses we live in and the goods we buy. They can realize that rarely is a design decision a simple one: hardly ever is there one perfect solution to a design problem.

This is something that can be very confusing to the layman who tends to see everything in black and white and so makes rash and simplistic criticisms of decisions which affect his environment. Such uninformed criticism is easy to ignore and this leads to frustration on the part of both designer and critic: the designer because his efforts to find a satisfactory solution are not appreciated and the critic because he feels that his wishes are not considered. This is a major cause of friction in society. It can lead to alienation and – depending on temperament and background – to apathy or violence.

As the increasing complexity of society and industry widens the gap between governors and governed, between planners and ordinary citizens, so the need for some way of opening up a means of communication becomes ever more urgent. Informed criticism is the communication link. It is only by forging this link that ordinary citizens can communicate their needs and planners seek to explain their solutions to those needs.

Design teachers are trying to give children experiences that will enable them to communicate in this way. The only way really to understand any complex activity is to partake in that activity. This is quite possible in school since design problems can be found in all degrees of complexity; problems that can be tackled realistically by pupils using the skills they have, on the materials available and with equipment provided in all schools. It is not impossible to build on this experience to give a better understanding of the problems that, on a wider stage, face society. The end result hoped for is a more informed critical appraisal of the whole environment.

In order to appreciate this it might be well to explain a little the meaning of the word 'environment' to the designer. Often this is used as a blanket term to encompass the larger features of the natural and man-made world we inhabit. But every single little thing within that totality adds to – or detracts from – the total quality. Literally – although minimally – a pencil placed on a table in a room alters the environment for those within that room. It is easy to think in terms of a total plan in which individual items fit and that is, indeed, the world of the town or country planner. More often, in fact, the totality is a sum of all the parts; all of them made and placed by different people. This is the world of the designer where he has to produce something that fits into the totality, adds to the satisfaction of the whole and does not, in solving one problem, produce others.

It can be argued that this is a natural way for young people to come to terms with the larger concept. They really can assess the needs of themselves in designing something for a purpose of their own. They can consider the suitability of various ways of making the design of their choice and, having made it, can make some attempt at assessing the success with which it serves their needs. They may even consider the extent to which it adds to or detracts from the environment in which it will be used. Here then, in miniature, is the activity of fulfilling man's needs. Working from the small to the large and from the immediate and known, it is possible to lead children to consider the wider issues.

The sort of work resulting from such a philosophy is different from that which resulted from the idea that the chief educational aim of an art or crafts teacher was the learning of a skill. Yet the actual objects made may not be all that different since there is a natural limit to what can be made with limited skill, equipment and materials. What is so different is the approach.

In common with other teachers, those in the studios and work-shops are more concerned now to 'provide learning situations' than to 'teach' their pupils. When learning how to use hard materials there is much to be gained from tradition. Technique simply means the best way to gain one's ends. If children are going to learn, some help in reaching the easiest way to proceed can save valuable time. But this can be done without insisting on the exact end result.

With less resistant materials like clay, paper, card, plastics and, of course, with paint and pencil, where free experiment can lead to exciting results, work can be far less structured. It must also be remembered that not all work in studios and workshops should be strictly design education, there is room also for expressive work and for craftsmanship. What is described here is the sort of work that can be developed in those areas, that is design oriented and which, therefore, can make its own contribution to environmental education.

Much of the early work is aimed at helping children to come to terms with various materials and various visual and spatial qualities. Such an understanding is essential both to designing and to understanding the environment. It is quite impossible here to describe even a small proportion of all the exciting ways in which children can develop this understanding but a few must be given as examples, and are illustrated in the photographs accompanying this chapter.

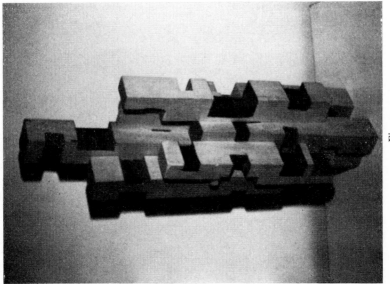

Fig. 2

Fig. 1

(Reprinted by permission of Bernard Aylward)

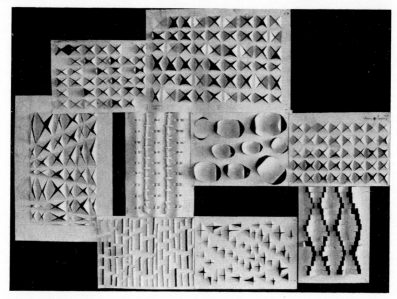

Fig. 3

Fig. 4

(Reprinted by permission of Alan Freeston)

Fig. 1 shows a piece of work in clay developed from units all made within overall limits. These can all be made by one pupil but more likely will be made individually by a class. The making of these units will give children an opportunity to find out how to handle clay and the discipline of trying to make them within limits is part of the learning process – particularly as, with clay, there is not too great a penalty for error. The assembling of these units would certainly be a group exercise arranged so as to stimulate a considerable degree of discussion. So the class can be led to consider ways in which variety can be obtained from units and the effect on the whole structure of the use of modules. This has obvious connections with the use of industrial components in building and hence the ability to criticize intelligently the large amount of building done today by this method. The connection would be brought home to the class by reference to local buildings produced in this way.

Fig. 2 shows a construction made of shaped pieces of wood. The grain of wood is one of its essential features and one way of coming to terms with this is to cut a clean groove across a piece of wood. This can best be done by means of an established technique which can be readily demonstrated and taught. The children are then left to cut grooves as wide as they like, as deep as they like and where they like. By doing so they will gain experience in a way that is free from the harsh penalties that invest a lack of accuracy when making a joint; yet which brings its own reward of a crisp finish as skill improves. The quality and beauty of a clean sharp line can be experienced and, by striving to achieve some balance and relationship between the cuts pupils can begin to gain some understanding of spatial relations, pattern, mass and void. Again, at the assembly stage discussion can be stimulated. And again, the relevance of spatial relations to architecture and the townscape can be demonstrated.

Fig. 3 shows samples of textures produced in paper with a knife. By means of actual examples and photographs children can be encouraged to appreciate texture and its importance in the environment.

As skill and understanding develop pupils will be given the opportunity to try designing something for themselves. This may be a very simple job and may be structured to restrain wilder flights of fancy, but it would be genuinely capable of different solutions. Unusual problems help children to avoid preconceived notions but many traditional jobs such as stools, boxes and small tables can be presented in a way that encourages fresh thinking.

Soon children can begin to tackle quite 'man-size' jobs. Fig. 4 shows the result of a third year project. Investigations carried out by the pupils into their own school environment showed that they considered that there was a lack of seating (or 'something') outside. Ways of overcoming this lack that were within their capacity lead to very lively thinking; as did consideration of the positioning of the units and the effect on both users and observers. This gave the children a total experience of environment including investigation, decision making and criticism of the agreed action.

Another brief used was: 'Produce something that will help visitors find their way to the school'. Note that a map is not specifically called for although this is an obvious answer. Put in this way it calls for analysis of all the ways there are of reaching the school, by all available transport; it also calls for consideration of the best means of communicating this information. Clearly it requires careful examination of transport systems in the locality and leads to a better knowledge of this aspect of the environment. Since it did result in something that was printed and used to send to intending visitors it was very real and not just an academic exercise.

Another series of briefs required groups of pupils to organize themselves into production units. Certain materials and equipment were made available and they were required to decide on something that they could make, package, advertise and sell to their fellow pupils. This proved a very realistic way of getting across a better understanding of some of the problems of industry in supplying man's needs.

Occasionally children can be asked to examine bought products and, by working backwards, decide the brief from which the designer worked. Examination of advertisements also plays a part in helping to clarify the complexity of commerce. The simple 'which is the best product?' can lead to the more accurate 'does this fulfil the brief?' It becomes apparent that rarely can a manufacturer indulge in producing the 'best' article. The most socially conscious of them can only hope to make the best that will sell. Often it is a question of producing that which will make the most profit.

In this way quite young children can be led to the stage when they are ready to consider some of the large issues facing mankind. Moreover, this is not a facile consideration remote from their own experience; it is something that arises out of their own work. Instead of thinking of pollution as something perpetrated by the wicked manufacturer, it can be seen as one factor in the whole process of producing goods that people need at a price they are willing to pay.

It is to be hoped that at least some of the pupils will begin really to accept that the responsibility for deciding on such matters as pollution is that of society as a whole and that society as a whole has the choice and must pay for its choice. This could well be the beginnings of social and political education.

The sort of work that is being done in 'design' at VIth form level is best illustrated by reference to the 'A' level syllabus in design of the Oxford Delegacy for Local Examinations. This was written some years ago by a few schools wanting to develop VIth form studies in design. Now, having passed a trial period required by the Schools Council it is generally on offer to schools wishing to use it.

The syllabus is set out in three sections: 'Man as an individual'; 'Man in society'; 'The designer and his resources'. Section one could be called ergonomics and requires the student to consider the nature of man and his needs, emotional as well as physical. The next section requires a knowledge of 'Environment, natural and man made; the social organizations, past and present, which help to reconcile man and the physical world he inhabits.' The final section looks at the materials from which man must satisfy his needs and requires the student to have some practical knowledge of how they can be used.

This amounts to a very heavy assignment for one 'A' level study and it could easily become a rather superficial and arid theoretical subject. What prevents this is that 60% of the marks given are for practical work, the major part of which consists of a design project. The quality of the candidate's thinking is assessed, not only by the success of his piece of hardware, but from a careful documentation (required by the examiner) as to how he arrived at his final solution; the sort of information he worked on; the decisions taken and the reasons for taking them. The theory papers then serve to put this thinking into the wider context and show that the candidate is capable of more than just the one project undertaken.

The syllabus is remarkable for a number of reasons. It is the first to demonstrate that practical work, far from being a soft option, can be the basis for a very demanding intellectual study. It shows that the work of the designer is an excellent basis on which to build a wide-ranging interdisciplinary study. It boldly tackles the problem of trying to assess 'creativity' and in doing so establishes new methods of examining at 'A' level. As a result of this it is one of the very few examinations of a practical nature that is accepted by university departments as an entry qualification.

Some of the projects tackled by students indicate the way in which this is developing in schools. An activity frame for an infant school gave one candidate the opportunity to find out from the children what their needs were: it resulted in a frame that encouraged imaginative play as well as physical exercise. Another candidate, in designing and making a chair for a handicapped child acquired a sympathy for the handicapped and some insight into the way society provides (or fails to provide) for the less fortunate. Research leading to the production of a range of table ware examined eating habits as well as marketing requirements.

The fact that a number of young people have been willing to take on such a heavy assignment demonstrates one of the important aspects of design as a basis for study; that of personal involvement. A leading professional designer said on one occasion that designers were paid to indulge themselves; they certainly know the meaning of self-expression. Although a designer works within strict constraints he is essentially creative and the act of creation gives great satisfaction and pleasure. Moreover, it is the whole man that is engaged; to design and make an original artefact makes demands on the physical, intellectual and emotional aspects of man's nature. It is the wholeness that gives the satisfaction and provides the drive sustaining a study which could otherwise be burdensome. It is appropriate that what is a study of the whole of mankind and his world should be through a medium which is equally complete.

Now it would be rash to suggest that all schools are doing the sort of work described, but an increasing number are and few are unaffected by the ideas recorded here – ideas which are pervading the whole of practical education. All schools are capable of this work and clearly it is educationally more valuable than making models of townscapes to illustrate other lessons. Moreover, the subject matter as well as the attitudes encouraged are relevant to the aims of environmental educationists.

Hence design education and environmental education are allies and should be concerned in supporting each other. The awareness of visual and structural qualities developed in design education will help pupils to be more aware of these qualities in the environment; comparing such qualities in the environment will reinforce an understanding of them. Experience of designing will make for a greater awareness of problems of environmental planning; the studying of environmental planning adds to an understanding of designing. Both, together better than apart, lead to a better understanding of society and its problems and, it is hoped, a greater willingness to 'opt in' to society and become thinking, concerned members of a community.

Bibliography

Periodicals

The Designer, Journal of the Society of Industrial Artists and Designers, London. (Monthly)

Look Out, Teachers' Notes, BBC TV Series: Design and Environment, BBC Publications, London.

Newsletter, National Association for Design Education, Leicester. Issued three times a year to members.

Studies in Design Education and Craft, College of Craft Education. (Twice yearly)

Books

AYLWARD, B., 1973, *Design Education in Schools*, Evans, London.

BANHAM, R., 1967, *Theory & Design in the First Machine Age*, Architectural Press, London.

BAYNES, K., 1965, *Industrial Design and the Community*, Lund Humphries, London.

BAYNES, K., 1967, *Attitudes in Design Education*, Lund Humphries, London.

CHERRY, G., 1968, *On Human Communication*, MIT Press, Cambridge, Mass.

GREEN, P., 1974, *Design Education: problem solving and visual experience*, Batsford, London.

JONES, C., 1971, *Design Methods*, J. Wiley. New York.

KEPES, G., 1945, *The Language of Vision*, Paul Theobald, New York.

KEPES, G., 1956, *New Landscape in Art and Science*, Paul Theobald, New York.

KEPES, G. (ed.), 1966, *The Education of Vision; The Man-made Object; Module, Symmetry and Proportion; The Nature and Art of Motion; Sign, Image and Symbol; Structure in Art and Science*, Studio Vista, London.

MAYALL, W. N., 1968, *Machines and Perception in Industrial Design*, Studio Vista, London.

PEVSNER, N., 1964, *Pioneers of Modern Design*, Penguin, Harmondsworth.

POTTER, N., 1969, *What is a Designer*, Studio Vista, London.

PYE, D., 1968, *The Nature and Art of Workmanship*, Cambridge University Press, Cambridge.

PYE, D., 1964, *The Nature of Design*, Studio Vista, London.

ZANKER, F. O., 1968, *Foundations of Design in Wood*, Dryad, Leicester.

ZANKER, F. O., 1972, *Design and Craft in Education*, Dryad, Leicester.

10   Third world studies and the environment

Michael Storm

It might seem surprising to discover a discussion of Third World studies in a book about environmental education. The environmental education movement surely poses enough definition problems without adding a *global* dimension? If we cannot even assume that environmental study is somehow basically local, is there anything left that cannot be labelled 'environmental'; will this omnivorous interdisciplinary cuckoo take over the entire curricular nest? It is, however, important to consider the place of 'exotic' or non-local studies within the curriculum. For if environmental work is seen as essentially local in content[1] and interdisciplinary in form, replacing archaic subject divisions, then what happens to those investigations of other civilizations, other physical and cultural environments, traditionally attempted within history and geography courses?

The study of distant parts of the world is sometimes held to be fundamentally less relevant and less practicable than projects based upon the local area and community. Time spent on the study of West Africa – even if such work somehow avoids the dreary amassing of 'useless information' – would be more sensibly used, it is argued, in investigating local problems in the 'real' world beyond the school gates. Such activities, involving the learner in direct inquiry, are more effective than Third World projects which inevitably must use 'second-hand' information. Local issues, it is maintained, will be more likely to motivate reluctant learners than well-meaning but futile attempts to stimulate concern for the landless peasantry of Bolivia. A programme of local study can hope to equip the school-leaver to understand his own area and to participate in its protection or development.[2] Finally, it is sometimes implied that global studies, being part of the content of the traditional grammar school curriculum (as regional geography) may be regarded, together with the Wars of the Roses and *Paradise Lost*, as part of an obsolescent and elitist style of education.[3]

Third world studies—an undistinguished record

Misgivings about the practicability of Third World studies are often intensified by the more euphoric vapourings of those dedicated to education for world understanding, who sometimes seem to suggest that a plate of curry and a few folk dances can usher in the millenium so far as international relations are concerned. Such enthusiasts rarely recognize the constraints of child development; for example, the slow growth of the concept of nationality, and the even slower sorting-out of the abstract entities of the political map. Similarly, the concept of 'reciprocity' evolves slowly; many eight-year-olds would agree that a French child visiting this country would be a foreigner, but cannot accept that they themselves could ever be 'foreign', even when travelling abroad. Since an objective commonly claimed for Third World studies is to enable the pupil to 'put himself in the place of' an Indian farmer or a Chilean copper-miner, these conceptual constraints cannot easily be disregarded.[4] It might appear that the investigation of the problems of world poverty necessarily involves a hazardously high input of generaliz-ation – GNP *per capita*, population density, subsistence cultivation, urbanization, terms of trade. To take one specific skill, the study of vast distant regions such as South East Asia or West Africa tends to involve the use of small-scale maps; though the pupil may happily copy and colour them, the level of abstraction is high – that blue squiggle is the Mekong, that red dot must stand for Accra's hotels and shanties. Whereas, in local studies, map-using skills can be systematically developed through large-scale representations of familiar terrain, where the shapes and lines on the map at least correspond to familiar streets and buildings.

Any review of the problems of teaching about the wider world has to consider the rather poor record of such teaching, which has almost always exhibited one of two equally serious flaws. Often, there has been a heavy emphasis upon the colourful, the bizarre, the tourist's-eye view, in which the 'non-Western' regions of the globe are roughly apportioned between picturesque peasants, fierce nomads and jungle hunters. This preoccupation with the culturally – as well as geographically – remote produces a situation in which people know about the plight of Brazil's Amazonian Indians but not about their desperate compatriots in the problem region of the dry north-east; or where some acquaintance with the life-style of the Kalahari Bushmen is a fairly common item of mental furniture, whilst awareness of the problems generated by Botswana's export of most of its male labour force to South Africa is less commonly found.

If the quest for exotic colour is one attribute of traditional global studies, another is the common degeneration of such work into various forms of encyclopaedism; the tracing and colouring of maps, the copying of swathes of reference material, the listing of towns, products, population data. If the 'picturesque' approach produces a dangerously static, unrepresentative and patronizing picture, the amassing of gazetteer-type information produces no picture of any sort. Though the project folders may be very neat and the wall-displays admirable, information-collecting alone is quite incapable of stimulating intellectual and imaginative involvement in another environment. Unfortunately, altering the *form* of study rarely guarantees more purposive *content*; most of the attributes of the drabbest kind of traditional regional geography may be observed today under the banner of humanities, or general studies, or, perhaps, Third World Studies.

Whatever the taxonomy adopted, school work which involves the recognition and discussion of the major spatial variations in levels of human welfare invariably encounters – in addition to the hazards of exoticism and encyclopaedism – the problems of *diagnosis*. It seems almost impossible to teach about development without involving, or implying, some sort of explanatory model. For example, much geographical material at the primary school level presents poverty as *simple environmental adaptation;* a passage about an African home with its flimsy mud walls, one dim window, and thatched roof concludes 'we should think this a very poor house, but it is all that Bombo needs'. In other words, poverty does not really exist, the 'poor' are merely sensibly adapting to climatic requirements. Equally common are implications that those who enjoy higher living standards do so because of a greater input of *physical effort*. This emphasis upon hard work as a major factor in the geography of living standards is commonly found in middle school material; 'in these environments, if a man works hard, he can build up a fine civilization, but if he gives up the struggle, if he is content to take things as they are, he will be weakened by malaria, and get a poor living from poor soil and uncertain water supply'. The moral flavour here – the same series talks about 'the world's naturally energetic peoples' – can lead imperceptibly into a basically *ethnic* diagnosis. Other common models include *natural resources* and *'overpopulation'*. Generally, these diagnoses are implicit rather than explicit, but any survey of teaching materials on the Third World

leads to the conclusion that, however we present foreign environments, we are going to be involved in the formation of *attitudes*; it
would be quite hard for the pupil to avoid forming the impression
that the world's richer peoples deserve to be so, since they are basically more intelligent and industrious, whilst the poorer peoples, living in unpleasant and unhelpful environments, can hardly hope for
better things.[5]

The fact that many schools operate in what is loosely termed a
'multicultural' context is often cited by advocates of Third World
studies. Yet this can produce additional hazards, especially if the
approach is 'pathological', with developing countries seen as
specializing in catastrophes. As a contributor to the 1974 Geographical Association Third World conference observed, 'it is
instructive to contrast the kind of image thus projected by schools
with the image the countries themselves project at a place such as
the Commonwealth Institute in London.'[6] An excess of evangelical
enthusiasm may even persuade teachers that 'immigrant' pupils
(almost certainly British-born) will be able and willing to serve as
experts and/or visual aids for a project on the Caribbean or India.

Environmental awareness and environmental autonomy

In view of all these difficulties – the constraints imposed by the
child's conceptual development, the dismal record of over-exotic or
totally encyclopaedic approaches, the hazards of crudely-articulated
diagnostic models with their effects on attitudes, and of employing
'immigrant' pupils as representatives of the Third World – it is
hardly surprising that even those environmental teachers who con-
cede that development studies are feasible in schools, might argue
that, given limited time and resources, priority should be given to
work on the locality and on contrasting regions within Britain.

Yet this view rests upon a curiously limited interpretation of
'environment' – one which excludes the ideological and imaginative
environment in which we operate, and which affects our attitudes
and actions at least as powerfully as our physical surroundings.
Local attitudes towards, say, Asian factory workers are not wholly,
or even mainly derived from local events and observations. They are
substantially affected by the sort of image of India that we possess,
and our grasp of processes operating in that part of the world.
Simple investigations using word-association and pictorial tests seem

to reveal that most older juniors already possess a 'mental map' of the Third World.[7] The phrase, loosely associating Fiji with Brazil, India with Costa Rica, would be unfamiliar, meaning even less than it does to adults bemused by rival categorizations recognizing Fourth, Fifth or Sixth Worlds (under-developed oil-producing states, the emergent major nuclear powers of China and India, the group of poorest poor states identified at the last UNCTAD conference). Nevertheless, children appear to be aware, very early, of the basic rich/poor polarity in the world. And the images they possess – derived from television, parental comments, the efforts of advertisers (selling peanuts, coffee, exotic holidays, or raising funds to help the undernourished, the drought victims, the refugees), comics, magazines, newspapers, and school work – probably in that order? – are strongly associated with attitudes and preferences. The Third World, in fact, is emphatically part of the environment in which our children grow up.

The fact that *awareness* of massive global disparities in levels of human welfare develops too early to be fitted into any neat progression reserving the study of the tropical world until the upper school, may be linked with another key theme; the absence of *environmental autonomy*, whether we are studying the local area or distant regions. Just as in curriculum design it is difficult to draw a boundary around certain types of knowledge as distinctively 'environmental', so the actual spatial limits of 'locality' dissolve once investigations start. In Britain, changes in rural land use patterns, urban expansion and industrial location are generally the landscape expression of decisions taken elsewhere, by distant individuals, firms, or government bodies, in London, Brussels or New York. One of the principal objectives of any environmental study should be to make this absence of autonomy evident, to demonstrate the linkages which exist between the area being examined and the wider world. If we add to this concern for linkages a recognition of the early development of awareness of the Third World and its problems, a basis for Third World studies emerges.

Links between Britain and the Third World have not been neglected in conventional regional studies, which have tended to portray the developing countries almost exclusively in terms of the primary commodities they contribute. Projects on Malaya, Ceylon or Ghana are almost unthinkable without the assistance of Dunlop, Brooke Bond and Cadbury. But it is up to the teacher to add other dimensions to the picture; the vulnerability of economies heavily dependent upon one or two non-mineral primary products, the wildly-fluctuating prices of such products compared with the steadily rising costs of imported manufactures. In any Third World study, the pupil's existing perceptions should afford a starting point *only*; the work must then involve material *not* widely evident in the media. Any commodity study developed in this way should, for instance, generate second thoughts about the 'hard work' diagnosis which pupils customarily express; if a Ghanaian cocoa-farmer works hard to produce twice as much, he may well end up with a smaller income. The widespread view that Third World states exist entirely on aid generously supplied by the rich nations might also be modi-fied by the realization that stablization of commodity prices would be of considerably greater value to most exporting countries.

Tourism is an increasingly important area of rich-poor linkage in regions such as the Caribbean. It should be a major component in any Third World studies programme, since here we have a large industry dealing in image-building and the exploitation of other primary resources of climate and culture. A review of tourist material for India, Jamaica or Egypt forms an excellent starting-point for the consideration of other aspects of these environments, and the highly controversial contribution of tourism to the develop-ment process.[8] The travel industry, understandably, stresses the uniqueness of cultures, the autonomy of environments; development economists and geographers, on the other hand, identify many themes common to all developing states – urbanization, unemploy-ment, rural fragmentation, regional economic polarization. Since an interest in the exotic remains a powerful motivation for Third World studies, the teacher is likely to encounter, at some point, an expressed distaste for the processes of change and the suggestion that areas should be 'left as they are'. It is critically important that this linked group of sentiments – the happy poor, survival in isolation, cultural autonomy – is squarely considered. This might most effect-ively be done by studying the two main types of demographic link-age between rich and poor countries.

It is vital that pupils grasp the nature and extent of the mortality revolution which has reduced infant, maternal and endemic disease death rates throughout the world, and still has much more to accomplish. If this fundamental change is not fully appreciated, a host of misconceptions follow – that the 'population explosion' is the result of soaring birth rates, a feckless preference for enormous families, rather than the result of improved survival rates. In particular, however, it is the mortality revolution which has destroyed the autonomy of cultures, since the alteration of vital

111

rates rapidly affects the existing ecological balance of human groups, higher densities impelling them to re-establish a new balance involving changed ways of life.[9] It is the mortality revolution, above all, which eliminates the pseudo-option that areas might choose to 'stay as they are'. The phrase, 'population explosion' is learned early, and middle school pupils will offer confident diagnoses that the poor countries are poor because they have too many people – a diagnosis with inevitable racial undertones. In view of this, the demographic component must be very carefully designed in any course of Third World studies. Some consideration of Britain's own population history is vital, to show how declining mortality rates generated our nineteenth-century population explosion. Such a study would be no dusty historical digression, but a powerful reminder that birth rates of over thirty per thousand, large families, and a wildly-unbalanced and youthful age-structure are in no sense the peculiar attributes of today's Third World societies. Some examination of the context in which our birth rate began its decline in the late nineteenth century would be equally relevant. Without in any way implying that developing countries will recapitulate the social and economic history of the West, such an examination might at least suggest that changing attitudes to family size are more related to social and economic trends than to the crusading dissemination on contraceptive advice. These two demographic linkages between rich and poor environments are central to Third World studies.

Links with the Third World are not limited to flows of commodities, profits, medical techniques and aid. The movements of people are equally significant. In terms of course-design, five broad categories of movement seem to require consideration; each of these would be most effectively presented via selected regional case studies. First, the work of the slave trade in distorting the indigenous economies of West Africa and constructing new colonial populations in the New World. No topic should be included in any Third World course that cannot be shown to extend the range of 'diagnoses' of poverty available to the student. A study of the slave trade contributes an insight into the familiar argument that 'these countries should raise themselves by their own bootstraps, like we did'. Recognition of the close connections between our own agrarian and industrial revolutions and the mercantile capital accumulated by the slave traders of Bristol and Liverpool helps to dispel this prevalent notion of wealth generated without 'help' from the outside world.[10]

Secondly, the movement of Europeans overseas represents a

response to 'population pressure' not available to most Third World countries today. Case studies of Afrikaner trekkers and Zulus, of Dakota miners and the Sioux, would effectively illustrate earlier approaches to 'Third World problems' and generate a certain healthy scepticism about the practicability of cultural co-existence.[11] Thirdly, formal or economic colonization stimulated those wide-ranging movements which have endowed Trinidad, Natal and Fiji with Indian communities, distributed Chinese settlement throughout South East Asia, and which necessarily involve most Third World states in a precarious quest for 'national identity'. Without some appreciation of their essentially plural societies, any understanding of political news from Third World states would remain imperfect. A fourth significant movement is the reverse flow from the 'poor South' to the rich industrial North; one need look no further than our own National Health Service to illustrate our dependence, not only on manual workers from overseas, but on the increasing drain, from the poorer countries, of their most able and expensively-trained personnel.[12]

The fifth and final type of movement which links the rich and poor worlds is the movement from countryside to city. This accelerating concentration, the mirror-image of the process of outward dispersal characteristic of Western urban areas, is focused on those points – Lagos, Saigon, Lima – where the rich and poor worlds meet. In such cities, 'our' environment, with its cars, refrigerators, supermarkets, air-conditioned apartments and regular wage-employment, is permanently on display to the unemployed and underfed rural migrant. A study which enlisted the talents of Third World novelists[13] to demonstrate the pressures which lead an individual to move to the town could encompass most of the vital aspects of Third World environments – the 'pull' of the 'modern' enclave with its possibilities of profit, the 'push' of a stagnant and despised rural hinterland. The teenager in Dakar, in Kingston, learns incessantly about *our* environment, from films, newspapers, the ubiquitous transistor. A grotesquely flamboyant version of Western affluence is present in all Third World cities, in the residential areas inhabited by successful businessmen and bureaucrats. The rich world is undoubtedly part of his environment; the Third World has become part of ours, and we should do what we can to try to make it intelligible to young people.[14]

References
1. Examination of the scope of a journal such as the *Bulletin of Environmental Education* would confirm this view.

2. Critical assessments of some of the values claimed for local studies are contained in: STORM, M. J., 1973, 'Schools and the Community: an Issue Based Approach', in BALE, J., GRAVES, N. & WALFORD, R. (eds.), *Perspectives in Geographical Education*, Oliver and Boyd, Edinburgh; STORM, M. J., 1973, 'The Community and the Curriculum' in *Bulletin of the General Studies Association*, 20, Spring, Longman, Harlow.

3. See, for example, MIDWINTER, E., 1972, *Social Environment and the Urban School*, Ward Lock Educational, London.

4. A useful introduction to research findings in this area is CARNIE, J., 1972, 'Children's Attitudes to other Nationalities' in GRAVES, N. (ed.), *New Movements in the Study and Teaching of Geography*, Temple Smith, London.

5. This discussion is more fully developed in STORM, M. J., 1972, 'Studies of Distant Environments in the Primary School: some Problems', in FYSON, N. L. (ed.), *The Development Puzzle, a sourcebook for teaching*, Voluntary Committee on Overseas Aid and Development, London.

6. HORE, P., in *Teaching About the Third World*, report of a discussion meeting at the Geographical Association Conference, January 1974. The report, edited by Professor R. W. Steel, will appear in a forthcoming issue of the association's journal, *Geography*.

7. STORM, M. J., 'Images', in FYSON, N. L. (ed.), *The Development Puzzle* (see above).

8. See, for example, RIVERS, P., 1974, 'Misguided Tours', in *New Internationalist*, 12 (February), Third World Publications, London.

9. Particularly interesting discussions of this topic are contained in BOSERUP, E., 1965, *The Conditions of Agricultural Growth*, Allen and Unwin, London; WILKINSON, R., 1973, *Poverty and Progress*, Methuen, London.

10. See, for example, WILLIAMS, E., 1964, *Capitalism and Slavery*, Deutsch, London.

11. Particularly stimulating sources for the teacher here are KIERNAN, V. G., 1969, *The Lords of Human Kind: European attitudes towards the outside world in the imperial age*, Weidenfeld and Nicolson, London; MASON, P., 1970, *Patterns of Dominance*, Oxford University Press, London.

12. See, for example, GISH, O. & GUEST, I., 1974, 'The Immigrant Doctor', in *New Internationalist*, 13 (March), Third World Publications, London.

13. Effective material will be found in ACHEBE, C., 1960, *No Longer at Ease*, Heinemann, London; PATTERSON, H. O., 1964, *The Children of Sisyphus*, New Authors, London; NAIPAUL, S., 1973, *The Chip Chip Gatherers*, Deutsch, London.

14. Current information is available from Development Forum, Centre for Economic and Social Information, United Nations.

11 Planning studies

John Holliday

Historically planning has come to be associated with the environment through the law and practice of town planning. Law and practice are still mainly concerned with the environment but the field is in a stage of transition in which planning as a discipline is beginning to operate in the wider social context of the community and is not necessarily restricted to the physical environment. Much work in the physical environment is and will be undertaken by scientists and the title 'planning studies' refers to the discipline of planning in education which, although to a large extent concerned with physical environment, operates in the wider social context.

Planning is that process undertaken by an individual, group, institution or other body to achieve some desired objective. As the scale of activity increases the process tends to become more complex, for the components of the system being planned are more numerous and their interactions less understood. In looking at cities, for example, studies of planning must include political, legal, economic, commercial, managerial and other fields including those traditionally associated with city planning: surveying, engineering and architecture. In this situation the recently developed work on cybernetics and systems theory is important.[1] Planning is essentially looking forward to an improved society and environment, and as such does not rely wholly on traditional academic disciplines, for it has a strong normative and practical content, and is concerned with the process of achieving objectives within a policy framework. In this chapter the concern is with public policy although private sector planning has similar generic characteristics. A recent publication *Education for Planning*,[2] gives some useful definitions as well as an analysis and recommendations relevant for anyone concerned with planning education.

Planning and environment

The most generally observed records of man's history are his works

115

in the environment, whether ancient or modern irrigation schemes, cities, roads or other features. The association of these physical features with human activity inevitably raises questions not only about the people who built them but about their organization and their planning. Clearly many developments were carefully planned and to the contemporary observer in the nineteenth-century unplanned industrial city these offered examples to be followed. Two streams of planning thought emerged from this situation. One was concerned with social reform, which in the mid-nineteenth century included improvements in environmental health through the introduction of water supply, sewerage systems, better housing and open space. The other was concerned with the actual design and construction of these physical requirements. These two streams of activity combined with public health, housing and eventually in 1909 with planning law to give a strictly physical and legal basis for planning exercised by local government. A full account of the movement can be found in Ashworth.[3]

The Town Planning Institute was founded in 1914, primarily on the initiative of surveyors, architects and engineers, but including a strong legal element and recognition of government public health and housing needs. It was not until 1947 that economics, geography and other disciplines began to inform planning education in different ways, but it was only in the 1960s that really significant changes began to emerge in planning and education. Public and sociological criticism of physical planning activity, new thinking about the planning process in society (particularly from the USA) and new disciplines such as cybernetics and management, and the use of computors, all combined to start a radical shift in the basis for planning education which is still in progress. No longer is the physical environment the sole object of study. The social, political, economic and other processes and disciplines which determine the workings of society are now fundamental to planning studies.

In addition, planning activity has widened into other fields. The relatively new local government departments of social services and the new regional health authorities are required to prepare plans. Corporate management in local government is resulting in another stream of planning activity, some of it with particular emphasis on financial planning. Many of these planning activities are not directed towards the environment. Although it is important to distinguish between planning in a generic sense and environmental planning, it must also be recognized that the latter can only be successful if it is undertaken in the full knowledge of its interaction with community objectives in wider terms.

Education

'If town planning is to meet the needs of the city's life, to aid its growth, and advance its progress, it must surely know and understand its city. To mitigate its ends, it needs diagnosis before treatment. To express its highest ambitions, it must appreciate and share them. Hence town planning and civics must be advanced together.' Writing thus in 1915, Patrick Geddes[4] distinguished technical town planning from civics or the public understanding of the city, and in talking of the city he was fully aware of its interdependence with the country. Fifty-four years later the Skeffington report[5] on public participation returned to the theme, without the depth of insight which Geddes had brought to the problem, but clearly with a view that town planning and public understanding must advance together. The Town and Country Planning Act of 1971 makes public participation a statutory requirement for planning authorities.

Only recently have environmental studies as Geddes perceived them been introduced into the school curriculum. The general public has a growing awareness of the importance of environment and planners are becoming more fully involved with the community for which they plan. A full sequence of planning education from school onwards is developing a growing civic consciousness which is replacing the dulled senses of populations reared in grinding industrial towns. But an enormous amount of education remains to be done.

Educationists as a whole, from school to higher education, must take much of the initiative, but the problem is formidable. The system of examining boards, and entry to higher education, is strongly determined by the past, and in particular by academic disciplines irrelevant to an understanding of environment. Post-war developments in early school education, freed from traditional disciplines, have shown the way, but only recently have 'O' and 'A' level syllabuses been prepared for a study of the environment.

The nature and process of educational development is often inimical to a study of contemporary problems. A fundamental problem is the reconciliation of expertise in a particular discipline with relevance of the application of the discipline to social needs.

117

Expertise tends to be conveyed in ways which have developed to meet particular problems over time. The consolidation of knowledge in text books and curricula often relates to past social contexts rather than present. The consequent apparent lack of relevance makes their study at best tedious and at worst harmful in the sense that pupils and students are not educated to understand contemporary problems. On the other hand, it is difficult to devise studies of relevance, as methods may not be adequately tested; there will be no text books, and teachers will reply in part on their own traditional knowledge.

An historical view of education suggests that there are stages when entirely new studies must invade the traditional fields and that these studies emerge as a result of new problems or developments in society. Science was a case in point in the nineteenth century. Environment is one today. At these stages some traditional disciplines may be used together with new studies to produce a new discipline. The philosophy of the Open University is both to mix disciplines within a single course, and to allow students to mix courses. Both teachers and students thus begin to fuse approaches from different traditions and in time new disciplines will emerge eventually perhaps to become traditional themselves.

Planning and environment are at such a stage today and their study will be looked at from the viewpoints of, first, professional planning and, second, general education. In doing this it is important to remember that planning exists to solve problems, and thus has an educational dimension in common with science and engineering which is not shared by many of the arts and humanities. The existence of this extra dimension makes the study different in kind, requiring different behaviours from teachers and student, and sometimes a longer period of study.

The development of professional education shows three characteristics which have existed from its inception in 1920. First, the practical problem-solving emphasis; second, the width of study and, third, the adaptation of studies to meet the new demands which continuously arise in our society. The problem-solving element was initially concerned mainly with design studies with an architectural or engineering base. These extended to the scale of the city. The development of town and regional planning has led to greater attention being given to other practical problems, such as those relating to the distribution of population and employment. In addition to the early studies of surveying, architecture, engineering and landscape architecture, studies in law, government and housing have always been of central importance to planning. The range of study was increased after the war with the fuller introduction of geographical, economic, statistical and social studies with a consequential shift to practical work which related to social processes in general. Design product gave way to planning process, often, unfortunately, forgetting what sort of environmental product the process was supposed to achieve.

Until the late sixties planning education was the prerogative of the Town Planning Institute, but increasing public criticism of planning and the academic recognition of some of its shortfalls led to the emergence of a number of new university courses concerned with planning, transport and environment. For example, higher degrees were instituted in Regional and Urban Planning Studies at the Universities of Reading and Birmingham, in Regional Studies at Sussex, Urban Studies at Salford and Transport at Imperial College. A full account of all courses in included in *Education for Planning*.[2] The emergence of management has also related to planning education and many planners see their job as the management of the city or countryside. The ramifications of education for planning are wide. The publication just referred to is subtitled *The development of knowledge and capability for urban governance*. Knowledge might be taken to cover general education (and research), whilst capability requires professional expertise of various kinds and not only that of the professional planner. The Royal Town Planning Instititute is itself moving towards a much wider view of planning education, although its emphasis remains on the environment.

However, it has already been pointed out that planning is an activity taking place in more and more areas. There are mathematical, statistical and other techniques which can fall under the heading of planning studies and which have nothing to do with the environment. Management, economics, engineering and other subjects all include planning techniques. But while it is important to recognize the generic nature of planning, there is no room in this essay to pursue planning into areas outside the study of environment.

Planning education in the UK is in many ways more developed than in other countries. Since 1946 it has been possible to take a first degree in planning and this is now the commonest way of entering the profession. But until the sixties postgraduate courses were more usual and this is still the mode in Europe and the USA. The relative merits of both forms are arguable. The fact of the first degree indicates an educational movement which has now also begun to appear in a few other countries. It may well be that Britain's advanced planning legislation and government activity in planning are the reasons for the development. But the bringing forward of planning in the chronological sequence of education will probably affect school education in the UK before it does so in other countries.

To what extent is school and teacher training education fitted to develop planning studies? There is a good deal of capital in the traditional disciplines if taught with imagination and a requirement to think rather than simply remember (unfortunately, often not the case). Mathematics is valuable, as are some aspects of geography, economics, sociology and other subjects. But the tendency to specialize in school creates problems, particularly when combinations of arts and science subjects are required. The division is inappropriate for studying the art, science and politics of planning the environment. The development of 'O' and 'A' level curricula is promising in several respects. The AEB environmental studies 'O' level syllabus spans science, social science and technology and also requires a report on change and development. The University of London Hertfordshire Mode Two syllabus in environmental studies at 'A' level actually includes a field study on 'Environmental Conflicts and Planning', but the basis for study is in some ways less adequate than the AEB 'O' level course. The three sections of the syllabus other than the field study are on energy and resources, the ecosystem and man as an organism within the environment. The emphasis is scientific and geographic, and there is insufficient study of social and organizational factors to enable students to evaluate the field problem in terms of some resolution of the conflict.

Another 'A' level syllabus, the Oxford Local Examination paper on design is a novel and very interesting attempt to study design in a wide social context. Its section on 'Man in Society' provides a strong social context for the designer's problems whether of furniture or environment. While professional criticism can be made of some of the approaches, all these courses are an excellent introduction to the kind of problems which planners have to face.

In addition to formal curricula there is a growth of local and environmental studies, including those designed to educate the child into community politics, such as the *Shelter Housing and Redevelopment Kit* (SHARK) developed at the Hillfields Community Education Centre in Coventry for local schools. SHARK has two basic aims which are : first, to enable children to reach a greater understanding of their social environment and to participate more actively in it; and second, to give pupils experiences which enable them to make their own decisions, leading to an understanding of the concept of housing and redevelopment. Communication and awareness were seen as essential developments for the child, and teachers found that such traditional disciplines as mathematics, geography and history could be brought easily into the learning process, and given more relevance (discussion on SHARK and related developments can be found in an unpublished thesis by D. Lathbury[6]). This development contains some of the elements traditionally included in planning education, in particular, practical problem-solving and breadth of subjects studied. In this there are relationships with many other contemporary approaches. The Open University's multi-disciplinary team work has been mentioned. In local government, corporate planning has been allied to programme or area teams focussing on specific issues or problems. In discussing problem solving in broad terms for society at large, Schon advocates 'pools of competence' and 'task groups' to handle policy and its implementation.[7] The behaviours required for all these activities from school to government have elements in common, in particular the ability to work in teams towards the solution of problems and an awareness of the interconnectivity of values and activity systems which allows for a more sensitive response to social needs.

The community

The increasing complexity of society means that not only is differentiation of function necessary to support it, but that overall policies must be developed, which meet many needs arising from the urban system, in ways which allow for sensible evaluation of problems. To survive, society must learn, adapt and control its activities in order to achieve general goals.

The goal of a better environment is non-controversial in certain terms. Clean air and water are essential to life. But in other terms the goal and the means for achieving it are much less clear. Why is there a movement towards the conservation of historic buildings and towns? Is the cost justified when so many are homeless and without adequate food? Whose values determine what the planner shall do? His own, his employees' or others'?

How does one deal with pluralities? The planner at all levels is faced with scores of problems relating to the investment of resources and the improvement of environment. He must be on his guard against too simple an interpretation of a good environment. The attractive façades of Venice and Paris hide a host of community problems.

The development of community politics in planning has been a strong force in the Western World over the past fifteen years. In planning, criticisms have been levelled at the clearance of slums and the break-up of communities, at high rise flats and at the destruction of city centres for road building. The public is more articulate and advocates for the deprived have emerged from many professional fields.

Progress must come on three fronts: education, research and government. By its nature research must concentrate on limited fields in order to lay bare certain truths. Research in the social sciences has barely begun compared with the traditions of science. Its growth will hopefully lead to a better understanding of society. From broad experience, understanding of central and local government policy must be improved. Effective planning will be part of and contribute to this improvement. The strands of its activity will be very varied but the community has called for laws which have put responsibilities on planning authorities and their planners and which are ubiquitous in their exercise; relatively little change in the environment is exempt from the control of planning law. But although law gives powers of control over environment, social and economic forces may be more powerful. Decisions about the development of roads and mining in national parks are not simply aesthetic, and, as in the case of north sea oil, national economic arguments will override the landscape conservation lobby. The same kinds of problems occur every day on a local scale, and planners cannot easily determine the right answer, for much of the law is open to interpretation. Policy may dictate that green belts should not be built on but the law does not, and many of the judgments to be made are interpretative of values in general.

At this stage only education of the community at large can help resolve conflict and bring understanding.[8] Education about environment without education about the organization of society and methods of government and decision-making is limited in value. Although our West European tradition in modern times has pursued objectivity in science and knowledge, it is becoming recognized, even in science, that all objectivity relates to human values and in the field of planning the achievement of objective solutions is impossible. Ethics and political philosophy are as much a part of the problem as empirical study and measurement. Nevertheless, decisions must be taken, technologies are developed, population growth demands accommodation. It is characteristic of much planning that decisions must be taken quickly and on inadequate information. A major aim in education must be to achieve a recognition about the hard realities of the processes of environmental change and development, and a willingness to accept decisions made on the basis of inadequate information. In return the planner and the politician must make plain the reasons for decisions and be open to criticism if the reasons are inadequate. Hence the planner must be educated to understand that the recognition of his solution may be withheld if he has not adequately consulted the public, either directly or by virtue of a study of social attitudes and responses to change.

References
1. McLoughlin, J. B., 1969, *Urban and Regional Planning: a systems approach*, Faber, London.
2. Diamond, D. & McLoughlin, J. B. (eds.), 1973, *Education for Planning: the development of knowledge and capability for urban governance*, Pergamon Press, Oxford.
3. Ashworth, W., 1954, *The Genesis of Modern British Town Planning*, Routledge & Kegan Paul, London.
4. Geddes, P., 1968, *Cities in Evolution* (new edition), Ernest Benn, London.
5. Skeffington Report, 1969, *People and Planning*, Report of the Committee on Public Participation in Planning, HMSO, London.
6. Lathbury, D., 1974, *Local Authority Policy-Making: the potential contribution of environmental education*, unpublished thesis, Lanchester Polytechnic.
7. Schon, D. A., 1973, *Beyond the Stable State: public and private learning in a changing society*, Pelican, Harmondsworth.
8. Forbes, J., 1974, 'Towards a Co-ordinating Framework for Environmental Education—a Planner's View', *Bulletin of Environmental Education*, March.

Bibliography
Broady, M., 1968, *Planning for People: essays on the social context of planning*, Bedford Square Press, London.
Martin, C. & Turner, E. (eds.), 1972, 'The Planned Environment' (Chapter 6), *Environmental Studies* (Blond's Teachers' Handbooks), Blond Educational, London.
Stewart, N. (ed.), 1972, *The City: problems of planning*, Penguin (for Open University), Harmondsworth.

12 Environmental sciences

Malcolm Elliott

The development of environmental science courses in the United Kingdom has given weight to Professor Keith Clayton's observation that 'the range of environmental sciences can hardly be less than that of the sciences themselves'. Widely differing courses involving 'environmental sciences' are available or in preparation for students at all levels from primary school to postgraduate. Clearly, limitations of space make a discussion of the nuances of all of these courses impossible within the present chapter, accordingly the author has chosen to consider some of the ways in which the originators of environmental science courses have varied the balance between the contributions from the separate science disciplines and the ways in which the various elements have been fused into coherent educational programmes. In the course of this survey it has been possible to recognize three main types of approach to production of environmental science courses.

(a) The development of new multidisciplinary courses.
(b) The origin of courses by broadening formerly specialized degree programmes by the incorporation of studies in other disciplines.
(c) The addition of broadly-based courses as supplements to specialized programmes of study in disciplines which have not been traditionally regarded as 'environmental'.

M.Sc. courses

At present there are few taught MSc courses in the UK which have environmental science contributions. The one year MSc course in 'Environmental Resources' at the University of Salford takes as its central theme the unstable biological conditions brought about by man-made modifications to the natural environment. Although the 'core' of the course is biological, the broad base of studies is emphasized by the fact that heavy reliance in the lecture programme is placed on experts from outside the biology department and, in fact, from outside the university. In the early part of the course, formal teaching is concentrated on a study of water resources, and other resource problems discussed later draw heavily on the lessons learned from the discussion of water resources. The first two terms are occupied with formal tuition and the remainder of the year is taken up by dissertation work. The University of Manchester offers an MSc course in 'Pollution and Environmental Control'; this topic clearly requires that students be exposed to expertise from a number of areas which were formerly taught separately. Accordingly the university has produced a multidisciplinary degree in which ecological, economic, engineering, legal and planning aspects of the subject are covered. The MSc in 'Conservation' taught at University College London is discussed in detail elsewhere, but it is noteworthy that in this course discussions of the theory and practice of conservation and of land utilization have been carefully integrated with material which, in earlier times, would have been found in the 'physical geography' part of a geography degree and in the 'ecology' part of a biology degree. This provision of subject areas in new combinations either with or without major attempts at integration is, of course, the unifying feature of first degree courses in environmental science.

First degree courses at universities and polytechnics

In the universities two approaches to production of environmental science degree courses have been evident. Some of the 'new' universities (for example, Bradford, East Anglia, Lancaster and Ulster) have set up schools or departments of environmental sciences which have produced environmental science degree programmes *de novo*. The alternative approach adopted by some of the 'older' universities has been to produce programmes in environmental sciences which are based principally on the courses offered by their separate science departments. Clearly the former approach has advantages in that all elements of the course have allegiance to one administrative group so that the balance between, and integration of, the components may be readily controlled. A problem of interdisciplinary courses arises from the fact that most of the teachers at present involved were themselves trained by means of traditional single subject honours degrees. This means that communication between teachers is difficult because of differences in training and hence of language.

Clearly such teachers, when housed together and involved in a single administrative structure, have more opportunity and need to achieve an understanding of each other's problems. Despite these points, it seems that the boards of studies of the interdepartmental degree courses in environmental sciences are successfully resolving the communications and integration problems.

The polytechnics have, at present, only one degree programme originating in a department of environmental studies (Plymouth's BSc Environmental Sciences), the remainder have been produced on an interdepartmental basis and in all cases the rigours of the Council for National Academic Awards' approval scheme will ensure that cohesion and integration will be achieved.

Some universities and polytechnics have modular degree programmes in which the student may select, from the large number of options available, modules which provide a course of study equivalent to an environmental science degree. The author has grave reservations about the extent to which the modules in this type of course may be integrated into a coherent whole but, of course, this view is hotly contested by the proponents of the broad modular degree schemes.

In the following discussion of university degree courses, the first group offers various interpretations of 'environmental sciences' in which the elements of each course have been drawn largely from traditionally separate 'pure science' courses and integrated into a coherent whole. The second group contains courses originating in engineering departments and having strongly environmental themes integrated with 'applied science' material, while the third group includes courses where an environmental science theme can be achieved as part of a broader based degree programme.

The University of Bradford admitted the first students to its BSc (Honours) degree in environmental science in 1973. The course aims to give students an understanding of the physical nature and biological aspects of the environment and the processes which operate within it. In particular, the course sets out to provide its students with an appreciation of human interaction with the environment with reference to resource utilisation and management. The course occupies four years with a year of vocational training between the second and fourth years. In the curriculum for this course emphasis is placed on the applied aspects and methodology of life sciences, economics and geography and on planning and managerial techniques. The first year of the course is designed to establish a sound scientific basis for the more applied studies of later years, it consists of an introductory study of the physical and biotic environment and the processes which take place within it and is divided up into units of:

(a) Basic science – an integrated course on physical and chemical processes in the living and non-living environment;
(b) Environmental science – an integrated course of physical geography and ecology;
(c) Environmental economics and management;
(d) Environmental statistics and experimental design.

In the second year the attention of the student is focused on the human interactions within the environment. The units in this year are:

(a) Environmental science 2 – Man and the environment; covers aspects of man's relationship to his environment from the physiological basis of life up to problems man has created by polluting the environment;
(b) Environmental economics and management 2;
(c) Environmental statistics and experimental design 2 – basic computing and systems modelling;
(d) Social philosophy.

The third year is used for vocational training and the fourth for studies of environmental management with attention being given to resource utilization and development, environmental planning and management and a special topic selected from applied ecology, land use planning or management of the industrial environment. Thus it can be seen that the emphasis in this course is at first concentrated on material from the physical and biological sciences and is gradually switched to management studies as the course progresses.

The BSc Honours degree programme in environmental sciences at the University of East Anglia had its first students in 1968. The degree programme, like all the others for which no specific alternative is stated, occupies three years of full time study and is largely concerned with the physical environment. The aim of the course is to draw together the relevant parts of the disciplines of geography and geology, together with geophysics, oceanography, meteorology, hydrology, soil science, ecology and planning, in the study of the environment.

In the first year, the student is exposed to a broad survey course which has as one of its aims his introduction to the range of topics which are included in the university's version of environmental sciences. Secondly, the student is taught the importance of experimental design and the role of intellect in tackling an experimental or observational problem. The final element of the first year course is numerical, a course in statistics, mechanical and calculus. Thus prepared the student takes three options in each of the second and third years from a range of sixteen options which are regularly offered. They include ecology, hydrology, oceanography, soil science, tropical resources and development, urban and regional planning, rock chemistry, quaternary studies and computing science.

The Department of Environmental Sciences at the University of Lancaster provides a BA degree in environmental sciences and also makes contributions to the university's joint honours programmes in ecology and in 'Physics of the Environment'. In the BA Environmental Sciences attention is concentrated on the physical and chemical structure and behaviour of the earth, oceans and atmosphere and also of the moon and nearby planets. The course integrates information from the formerly separate sciences of geochemistry, geology, geomorphology, geophysics, hydrology, meteorology, oceanography and lunar and planetry science. Basically this degree programme, like several of the others described in this section, has brought about the re-association of disciplines which has become increasingly separated since the nineteenth century. The first year course in environmental sciences provides an introduction to the study of the nature and origin of the solar system, the form and composition of the solid earth, atmospheric processes and the hydrologic cycle. This course represents one third of the first year work, the choice of subjects for the remainder of the first year work depends on the student's academic background. In the second and third years a 'core' course provides a deeper treatment of the material introduced in the first year and, in addition, the student selects an option from a range covering aspects of the solid earth, hydrology, the atmosphere and lunar and planetary studies. Students on the BA joint degree programme in 'Physics of the Environment' have their first and second years divided into studies of environmental science, physics and mathematics and in their third year they concentrate on the first two topics. The BA joint degree programme in ecology provides a fully integrated treatment of the relationships between living organisms and their physical and chemical environment.

Westfield College, University of London, will offer a new BSc (Honours) degree in environmental science in October 1974. This is a science-based course which aims to consider the natural aspects of the environment such as ecology (including conservation and pollution), the earth, its atmosphere and its natural resources. The ecology content of the 'core' will be high and the selection of option courses include 'Environmental Organic Chemistry', 'Resources and Pollution' and 'Computer Science'.

The departments of botany, geography and geology of the University of Sheffield have co-operated in the production of a BSc (Honours) degree course in 'Natural Environmental Science'. This course is designed to provide for the training of scientists concerned broadly with the natural environment and, in particular, to cross the traditional boundaries of the various disciplines involved. The curriculum includes the study of natural ecosystems and primary productivity on both land and sea, climatology, geomorphology and geochemistry, natural resources, hydrology and economic geology. In the third year half of the teaching time will be spent on options chosen by students from a wide range of topics. The general aim of the course will be to foster the management approach to natural resources.

At the University of Southampton the programme for the BSc (Honours) in environmental science has been produced by the departments of biology, geography, geology and oceanography. The course aims at a scientific study of the nature and interactions of the biological and physical components of man's natural environment. The degree is based on a system of aggregated unit and half-unit courses selected from a wide range. The combinations of unit courses available to environmental sciences students cover relevant topics from biology, geography, geology and oceanography, together with supporting work from other courses. Much of the first and part of the second year work is common to all students taking the course but later a wide range of choices are possible. Compulsory topics in the first two years include plant and animal diversity, introduction to ecology, geomorphology, climatology, earth history, earth materials and applied aspects of environmental sciences. Third year options include genetics, plant and animal ecology, geophysics, economic geology and resource management and conservation.

The BSc (Honours) Technological Economics degree of the University of Stirling has been designed to bridge the gap between technology and economics. The main contributing subjects are biology, industrial science and economics. The biological material covers the range from cell biology to human ecology, it is integrated with material on industrial science and economics (which includes industrial science and experimentation) operational research and systems analysis and management economics and economic analysis.

The University of Sussex offers a BSc (Honours) degree in environmental science which is taught primarily in the School of Molecular Sciences. The course is based on the molecular sciences, but draws upon biology and physical geography in order to describe and discuss many facets of the interaction between technical developments and the environment. The preliminary courses in structure and properties of matter, chemistry and mathematics provide a basis for a more advanced treatment of pure and applied chemistry which is accompanied by courses in physics, biochemistry, physical geography, ecology, climatology, soil science, operational methods and industrial economics.

An interdisciplinary approach to environmental science is provided by the BSc (Honours) Environmental Science of the New University of Ulster. The programme is designed as a broadly-based undergraduate introduction to the advanced study of special aspects and problems of the physical environment. The major contributions to the 'core' would formerly have been recognized as aspects of biology and of physical geography. A wide range of optional courses are available which permit the student to orientate his studies towards the study of the physical environment, environmental planning and management or ecological aspects of the environment.

Finally in this group, the University of Warwick plans a series of new joint degree courses in environmental sciences to start in 1974. Units in environmental science will make up part of the second year studies and three quarters of the final year material. The environmental science units offered will be: 'Environmental Physics', 'Quantitative evaluation of pollutants and their effects', 'The generation of pollutants and their biological consequences', 'The biosphere' and 'Law and management of the environment'.

The first of the engineering-based courses is the new interdisciplinary degree course in 'Environmental Chemical Engineering' which was first offered at the University of Exeter in 1973. The subject material embraces, on the one hand, pollution and its control and the underlying biological, hydrological and meteorological science involved in understanding its effects; and on the other hand, the management of natural resources, conservation and the recovery and re-use of materials, particularly those which are at present wastefully and damagingly discarded by civilization. The course aims to produce engineers who will be acceptable as full corporate members of the Institute of Chemical Engineers and whose training will help them to apply the basic concepts and intellectual skills of chemical engineering to the solution of problems which affect the environment. In order to achieve this aim the course will involve an integration of basic chemical engineering with aspects of biology, geography, geology and meteorology.

The University of Salford's BSc (Honours) in environmental sciences is offered by the departments of civil engineering and of Sociology, Government and Administration. The aim of the course is to carry out a study of those aspects of the environment, especially the urban environment, in which there lie hazards to the health, safety and welfare of society and of the legal and administrative means by which the hazards may be controlled. Aspects of biology and geography have been integrated into the course in order that this aim may be best fulfilled.

The BSc (Honours) in environmental engineering of the University of Strathclyde attempts to study the application of engineering and biological science to the control of people's physical surroundings. The first year of the four year programme provides the basic studies of the traditional engineering course, but in the second and third years the traditional studies are accompanied by material on environmental engineering and biology. In the final year the student may study either biological science with emphasis on environmental hygiene or engineering and physical aspects of environmental control.

At the University College of Swansea a BSc degree in civil engineering and environmental studies is offered. It includes courses in environmental analysis, environmental contamination, social and economic geography and sociology.

A broad modular degree scheme which permits students to 'pick out' an education in environmental science has been offered at Queen Mary College, University of London since 1966. In addition the degree schemes at Birmingham and Cardiff make efforts to provide opportunities in environmental sciences and are described below.

The BSc Honours programme in biological sciences and geography of the University of Birmingham aims to give a broad training in ecology and environmental science. The course offers a very wide range of options and gives particular attention to problems of conservation and to the economical, social and cultural aspects of human geography.

At the University College, Cardiff an interdepartment course in environmental studies is offered as a new development in the General Degree Scheme in the Faculty of Science. The course involves teachers from the departments of botany, zoology, geology, microbiology, biochemistry, chemistry, archeology and mineral exploitation. In order to facilitate integration of material extensive use is made of interdepartmental seminars. The environmental studies course is taught, along with one other science subject, during the second year of the course and is intended to give an integrated view of the relevance of a number of science disciplines to the human environment.

Polytechnic degree programmes in environmental science are available at Leicester, Plymouth and Sunderland.

The BSc (Honours) Science and the Environment at the City of Leicester Polytechnic had its origin in the recognition of educational and social needs. It has become clear that the traditional honours degree with its concentration on in-depth studies of a single subject has grave limitations as a preparation for careers in the fast changing employment situations of the present and future; general science degrees, however, (which may be regarded as educationally appropriate) have a limited attraction for students because of the lack of cohesion between the elements of the degree programme. In the face of great demand for courses having relevance to environmental problems the Leicester degree was designed to provide a broad science education having coherence within the framework of a study of the environment. Thus the degree has followed three main principles.

1. To base the course on a sound foundation of biology, chemistry, physics, mathematics and economics, upon which is built a study of the environment, and a consideration of the way in which man may control his environmental impact.
2. To demonstrate the interrelationship of physical, chemical and biological factors that make up the environment, with an emphasis on a quantitative approach.
3. To study the economic and social aspects of man's effect upon the environment.

In the third year of the course the 'threads' of the compulsory core are drawn together in the environmental studies module where the students will work with a team of five teachers (each from a different discipline) to produce a fully documented systems case study. Optional modules in the third year make possible specialization in ecology, toxicology or environmental economics. The possibility of in-depth study of toxicology is one of several unique features of this course, and arises from a recognition of the need for students to understand the problems which pollutants create in man and of the way in which their damaging effects occur. The course organizers feel that its graduates will, by virtue of their broad-based training, be best equipped to find scientifically and economically viable solutions to environmental problems, but also that their broad scientific background will make them better equipped to handle many non-environmental problems than are graduates of the traditional single-subject honours degree.

Plymouth Polytechnic admitted the first students to its BSc (Honours) degree in environmental sciences in 1973. At Plymouth, lecturers in biology, geography, geology and planning have combined to form the department of environmental studies, which coordinates the course, and economists, mathematicians and sociologists from other departments are co-opted as necessary. The course sets out to train environmental scientists who can state environmental problems clearly and scientifically, who can understand the interdisciplinary nature of many environmental problems and who can integrate information coming from different disciplines. In the first year attention is concentrated on bringing all students up to an appropriate level in biology, geography, geology and quantitative techniques, then in the second year students take resource studies along with either human ecology or environmental geology. In the final year there is a choice of specialization from options including ecological resource management, pollution studies, population studies and food or water resources.

The BSc (Honours) degree in environmental science at Sunderland Polytechnic aims to produce an education in the understanding and management of the environment and to provide graduates aware of the problems, scientific and social, in control and improvement of the environment. In the first year the student will have introductory courses in the earth sciences, ecology, mathematics and statistics, population studies, social sciences and the fundamentals of science. This year will prepare the student for a second year which will include consideration of 'Environmental Resources and Degradation', 'The Social Environment and Computer Studies' and quantitative techniques. In the final year students may opt for an in-depth study of either 'Environmental Control and Conservation' or 'Planning the Human Environment'.

Broad modular degree programmes allowing the student to choose a programme in environmental sciences are available at the City of London Polytechnic and at Oxford Polytechnic.

Diploma in higher education

A Dip HE course in environmental science is in an advanced stage of development at Farnborough College of Technology. The course starts with a discussion of scientific methodology with reference to biology, physical sciences, earth sciences and mathematics, then proceeds to carry out a socio-technical analysis and to make an in-depth study of the physical environment. At the beginning of the second year of the course resources are considered in more detail and the course concludes with a consideration of environmental pollution, applied systems analysis and government and conservation.

Environmental science in colleges of education

As Dr Cyril Bibby pointed out at the National Conference on Environmental Education in 1973, the Colleges of Education have included environmental studies and environmental sciences in their teaching programmes for many years and so these cannot be regarded as new curriculum developments. However, some colleges have developed special courses or special emphases in this area and these will be considered.

Alsager College of Education provides a one-term course in environmental studies for serving teachers which lays emphasis on methods appropriate for children in the eight to thirteen age range. The aim of the course is to equip teachers with skills and theoretical knowledge which will enable them to use a practical approach to studies of the environment and to impart an informed concern for the environment. Topics covered include: recent curriculum developments in environmental studies, aims and objectives of environmental education, the interdependence of soil, atmosphere, plants, animals and man, man's use of natural resources and his impact on the environment and study techniques (including soil studies, weather studies and plant and animal husbandry).

The supplementary course in environmental studies provided by Bordesley College of Education for lecturers who have specialized in history or geography includes a series of field exercises which emphasize the need for observation, recording and interpretation. Also included are a series of seminars for discussion of elementary geology, climatology, ecological techniques, analysis and presentation of data and models, role-playing and simulation exercises.

De La Salle College of Education provides the opportunity to study environmental science as one of the optional subjects in the teacher's certificate course. This course provides a quantitative and objective approach to the environment, an appreciation of man's place within it and his responsibility in the management of it. It includes discussion of the natural environment (the treatment includes earth science, geology, meteorology and pedology) and of ecology, and concludes with an examination of production in the natural environment, agricultural science and the effects of pollution on the environment. Students are required to present a report on their individual studies of some aspect of society or economics of the environment.

The environmental studies course at St Paul's College, Cheltenham can be taken at Principal Subject level but not at BEd level. This is a very broad-based course which has a significant science content in the second year when the course concentrates on natural environments (the interrelationship of plant and animal life, rocks, soils and microclimates), and environmental problems of modern society (pollution, redevelopment and conservation).

Main subject studies in environmental education at Teeside College of Education commence with a common unit designed to give an analytical appraisal of the total environment in preparation for more specialized study of subjects chosen from a wide range of unit courses which include earth science, ecology, race and population, meteorology and climate, earth resources, pollution and conservation and environmental planning.

Totley-Thornbridge College of Education offers environmental science as a component of environmental studies courses which are available at Main, Advanced Main, BEd and one year Diploma levels. In each case the environmental science components are chiefly geological and ecological and vary in depth of study according to the course which is involved.

Environmental science at school

A consideration of this topic is outside the scope of this chapter but the interested reader is recommended to The Association for Science Education Study Series pamphlet on 'The Place of Science in Environmental Education' (1974).

Bibliography

OECD, 1973, *Environmental Education at University level: Trends and Data*, HMSO, London.

ROSE, J. (ed.), 1973, *Synopses of Papers Delivered at the National Conference on Environmental Education*, Institution of Environmental Sciences, London.

WEST, R. W. (ed.), 1974, *The Place of Science in Environmental Education*, Study Series, Association of Science Education, Hatfield.

Acknowledgements

Grateful acknowledgement is made to Dr J. M. Thompson and to Dr D. R. Scott for providing access to unpublished information.

13 Human ecology

Paul Rogers

In the past fifty years the term 'human ecology' has been applied to a variety of studies involving particular disciplines and combinations of disciplines. Its use has ranged from medical epidemiology to urban sociology and from human geography to nutritional ecology. It has also been used to signify attempts to achieve a broadly based study of the human environment at individual, communal and eco-system levels of organization. Such an approach is multidisciplinary in that it involves contributions from a number of recognized disciplines. It is also interdisciplinary in that it entails a conscious effort to integrate the differing approaches of the contributing disciplines.

This meaning of the term has become more widespread in the United Kingdom over the past five years, as is exemplified by a number of university and polytechnic degree courses, by the newly established Centre for Human Ecology at the University of Edinburgh and by the work of the Commonwealth Human Ecology Council.

The aim of the present chapter is to review briefly the development of human ecology and to describe some of the recent developments in human ecology within the field of higher education in the United Kingdom.

The development of human ecology

The term 'ecology' was first used by Haeckel to denote the study of relationships existing between organisms and the living and non-living components of their environment. At the human level this necessarily involves a wide range of disciplines, yet human ecology has tended to acquire other meanings than that of a multidisciplin-ary study of the total ecology of man.

Thus in one connotation it has been considered as a branch of sociology centred on the study of human interrelationships. This human autecology probably found its most concrete expression in the human ecology school at the University of Chicago in the 1920s and 1930s, especially in the work of Robert E. Park and his students (Park *et al.*, 1925). Certainly the work of this group demonstrated the use of strictly ecological concepts, as developed at that time, applied to human urban systems and this use of the term 'human ecology' persists to the present, especially in the United States (see Quinn, 1961).

A rather differing view of human ecology sees it as synonymous with human geography, an approach probably initiated by Barrows in his presidential address to the Association of American Geographers in 1922 (Barrows, 1923), but developed also by other writers (for example, White and Renner, 1936; Theodorson, 1961).

In introducing a collection of papers on man/evironment relationships, Eyre and Jones (1966) argued that the approach of Barrows had been too anthropocentric and lacked awareness of the natural environment. Even so, they saw that geography as human ecology represented an approach which the increased sophistication of techniques of geographical study enhanced. They considered that much of the challenge of geographical studies was epitomized in the collection of papers which they had edited by the regard which those papers had for the interaction between human activity and natural circumstances. This study of interactions was the real core of human ecology.

In many ways this echoed the opinions of Quinn as expressed in an early review by that author (1940). Rather than seeing human ecology as encompassing many different disciplines, he saw its real value as picking out only those aspects of various disciplines which were relevant to the study of relationships between man and environment. On this basis it would not include meterology or anatomy *per se*, but only those aspects of such subjects thought to impinge directly on man/environment relationships.

This was at variance with the work of Bews which constitutes one of the earliest attempts to envisage human ecology as being both multi- and inter-disciplinary. J. W. Bews was a botanist by training but his main work on human ecology (Bews, 1935) was written in later life when he was Principal of Natal University College.

In introducing his book he summarized his views on human ecology thus:

The value of human ecology, as in the case of ecology generally, lies in its synthesizing effect. It not only provides a pattern into which may be fitted all the separate human sciences, but it affords a means of testing the relative value of each method of approach to the all-important, all-embracing question of how and why man is as he is, and behaves as he does. It unifies all the human sciences and enables each one to find its proper place in a generalized study of man.

Thus, for Bews, human ecology was a holistic study including a wide range of traditional disciplines such as ecology, economics, sociology and human biology. It was thus a study of formidable breadth, demanding a detailed knowledge of many conventional disciplines.

These ideas of Bews would hardly be accepted at the present time, if for no other reason than that they expect too much of any one student. But this is not to say that the idea of a multidisciplinary approach to the study of the human environment is meaningless. Rather than expect any one person to achieve the synthesis embodied in the approach of Bews, it is only reasonable to expect human ecology to encompass the *approaches* of the various constituent disciplines, coupled with a knowledge of those aspects of individual disciplines impinging most clearly on the study of man-environment interrelationships.

This kind of attitude is apparent in a number of case-studies undertaken in the past couple of decades, studies which were conscious attempts to interrelate the approaches of different disciplines in the study of man-environment interrelationships in discrete geographical areas. Perhaps most worthy of note in this regard is the work of Fraser Darling which was concerned with the West Highlands of Scotland (Fraser Darling, 1955). This work, undertaken between 1944 and 1950, is rightly considered as a pioneering study in human ecology. The survey was envisaged by Dr Fraser Darling in 1943 as a social and biological investigation into the problems of the West Highlands, and, according to the preface to the published account 'was established by the Development Commission in June 1944 in order to examine the Highland problem in the spirit of scientific enquiry, to gather a solid body of facts for analysis and synthesis, which would serve as a fountain for a future policy for the region.' Fraser Darling saw, as an essential aspect of such a policy, the establishment of an agricultural advisory and demonstration centre in the crofting areas. Sheddick (1973) described the breadth of the work in the following way:

An initial account of the non-human aspect of the problem is followed immediately by a comprehensive, ecologically orientated demographic survey and analysis. The treatment of the socio-cultural situation gives an indication of the range of factors involved and shown to be relevant. In addition to such obvious topics as land use and tenure, agricultural practice and subsistence economy, the survey looks at the social organization of settlement, the range and nature of voluntary groups and the extent of co-operative activities. Governmental and religious institutions are considered in their relation to other pertinent factors.

In many ways, Fraser Darling's work has served as a prelude for a recent expansion in interest in multidisciplinary case-studies as a means of planning the long-term management of the human environment.

The Commonwealth Human Ecology Council

In this context, the work of the Commonwealth Human Ecology Council (CHEC) is relevant. The Council, established in 1969, is a non-governmental organization formally recognized by the Economic and Social Council of the United Nations and supported by the Commonwealth Foundation. It evolved from an earlier Committee on Nutrition in the Commonwealth which recognized the need for integrative action in the effective management of the human environment based on a combined approach towards agriculture, nutrition, medicine, education, land use and human settlement.

The Council sees human ecology as the study of the interaction of human society with the environment and recognizes that such a study must be multidisciplinary. It attempts to foster human ecology approaches to development by means of an information service, establishing case studies, organizing seminars and symposia, publishing books in the human ecology field (Bowen-Jones, 1972; Rogers, 1973; Van and Rogers, 1974) and encouraging co-ordinated action and study between Commonwealth countries and in professional, academic, industrial and government institutions.

In the information field, recent developments have included an *Index of Human Ecology* (Jones and Jones, 1974) and a survey of degree-level courses in the field of human ecology throughout the Commonwealth, a survey that includes over 100 courses from 92 institutions in 16 countries (CHEC, 1974).

Recent developments in higher education in the United Kingdom

The CHEC survey lists a large number of recently developed degree courses in the United Kingdom which fall within the orbit of human ecology. Of the older courses, the Honour School of Human Sciences at Oxford and the environmental science course at the University of East Anglia are perhaps the best known. The aim of the East Anglia course is to 'draw together the relevant parts of the disciplines of geography and geology together with the related subjects of geophysics, oceanography, meteorology, hydrology, soil science, ecology and planning, in the study of the environment' (quotation from the prospectus). Although largely concerned with the physical environment the three-year degree programme includes introductory lectures on such subjects as the location of economic activity and ecology. At a later stage in the programme, options are available in subjects including ecology, hydrology, tropical resource development and urban and regional planning.

The Oxford Honour School of Human Sciences was instituted in 1970 to provide an integrated pattern of education in the biological and social aspects of the study of man. It is intended to bridge the gap between traditional courses in biology and the social sciences and to encourage the study of such important aspects of human affairs as world population growth, comparative social institutions, race relations and the concept of race.

Among a number of more recent developments are two courses at colleges in London, the degree programme in human sciences at University College and the programme in human environmental studies at King's College, while at the University of Edinburgh, a Centre for Human Ecology has been established recently. One of the courses with which this Centre is concerned is a planned diploma in human ecology. This would be available to postgraduate students of any faculty who wished to enlarge and deepen their knowledge of human ecology by studying in other faculties. It would be a one-year course involving participation in selected undergraduate courses in various faculties together with a project or dissertation. The curriculum would be specified for each individual student to suit his interests and otherwise enable him to achieve a balanced study. A graduate in a biological science might, for example, pursue a programme of study in politics, economics and sociology, whereas a sociologist might study ecology, international law and urban and regional planning. The merit of this kind of course is that it utilizes the already considerable resources of the university, tailored to meet the needs of the individual student.

One of the most recent developments in the human ecology field is the BSc Human Ecology degree at Huddersfield Polytechnic starting in 1975. This four year CNAA sandwich degree reflects the interdisciplinary approach of human ecology by including studies in human biology, ecology, geography, the behavioural sciences and economics with considerable emphasis placed on integration.

In the first six months all students take an introductory course in human ecology along with four foundation courses taken from economics, geography, quantitative analysis, physical science or biological science, this arrangement allowing an intake of students with widely differing educational backgrounds. For the rest of the year, all students then pursue courses in ecology, human biology and further elements of quantitative analysis.

The second-year course is common to all students and is in three parts. 'Geography for Planning Studies' is mainly concerned with resources and resource economics, settlement studies and physical environment processes affecting human activity. A human biology course covers applied human physiology, demography and environmental health and a behavioural studies course includes elements of psychology, social anthropology and sociology.

The third year is the 'External Experience Year' when students work for twelve months in any of a diverse range of occupations varying from a fisheries laboratory to the personnel department of an industrial complex and from a field centre to a housing association. The aim will be to give first hand experience of human environment problems and solutions.

Then in the final year all students will participate in an interdisciplinary course in 'Human Environment Management' concerned with the economic, physical and ecological approaches to the planning and management of the human environment. There will be a project, possibly related to the 'External Experience Year', and each student will also be able to select two from the following list of optional courses:

Human Reproduction Studies
Social Organization
International Development and Environmental Studies
The Built Environment.

Three aspects of this course are worth emphasizing. First is the integration of the component disciplines. This is perhaps what human ecology is all about – the recognition that it is rarely possible to overcome problems concerning the human environment from the confines of a single discipline. Effective integration is therefore a key aspect of the course. Some parts of the course are themselves consciously interdisciplinary, for example the 'Human Environment Management' final year course; but integration will also be furthered by a series of inter-disciplinary seminars in the second and final years, a residential field course involving ecological and geographical studies in the second year, and the project, which will be a practical example of the integration of the various components of human ecology. Extra-mural participation will involve the participation of experts from industry, local and regional government organizations and institutes and organizations concerned with environmental management and human relations in seminars, special lectures and 'on site' study. The location of the Polytechnic in an area of diverse industrial and rural activity lends itself to this aspect of the programme.

Another aspect of the course is the 'External Experience Year'. Of the many new human environment degree courses now operating in Britain, only those at Bradford University (B.Tech in environmental science) and Huddersfield have a sandwich element. This, we feel, is an essential component of the course and one which will make the whole course more realistic in its approach to the study of the human environment.

Finally, an international outlook permeates much of the course. This is not just reflected in the final year development studies option, but is to be found in many of the components in all years of the course. This is felt to be an absolutely essential aspect of the course, especially at a time when there is a rapidly growing realization of the importance of the changing relationships between the developed and less developed countries of the world.

The Huddersfield course is only one of many degree courses on the general theme of the study of the human environment, and there is no doubt that an interest in this subject area is found in all sectors of the educational system. The three aspects of the course just mentioned can be applied to any study of the human environment at any level. Just as in further and higher education, the study should be interdisciplinary, realistic and aware of the international context, so also should it be in schools. The methods may vary but the aims should be the same. Unless this is appreciated, it is only too easy for human ecology to become an 'ivory tower' study, unconnected with the pressing problems of the human environment which face us now and in the future.

Bibliography

BARROWS, H. H., 1923, 'Geography as Human Ecology', *Ann. Assn Amer. Geog.*, **13**, 1–14.

BEWS, J. W., 1935, *Human Ecology*, Oxford University Press, London.

BOWEN-JONES, H., 1972, *Human Ecology in the Commonwealth*. Charles Knight, London.

CHEC, 1974, *Survey of Human Ecology Degrees in the Commonwealth*, Commonwealth Human Ecology Council, London.

EYRE, S. J. & JONES, G., 1966, *Geography as Human Ecology*, Edward Arnold, London.

FRASER DARLING, F., 1955, *The West Highland Survey*, Oxford University Press, London.

JONES, J. O. & JONES, E., 1974, *Index of Human Ecology*, Europa Publications, London.

PARK, R. E., BURGESS, E. W. & MCKENZIE, R. D., 1925, *The City*, University of Chicago Press, Chicago.

QUINN, J. A., 1940, 'Human Ecology and Interactional Ecology', *Am. Sociological Rev.*, **5**, 713–722.

QUINN, J. A., 1961, 'The Nature of Human Ecology: Re-examination and Re-definition', in THEODORSON, G. A. (ed.), *Studies in Human Ecology*, Harper and Row, New York.

ROGERS, P., 1973, *The Education of Human Ecologists*, Charles Knight, London.

SHEDDICK, V. G., 1973, 'The Contribution of Anthropology to the Study of Human Ecology', in ROGERS, P. (ed.), *The Education of Human Ecologists*, Charles Knight, London.

THEODORSON, G. A., 1961, *Studies in Human Ecology*, Harper and Row, New York.

VANN, A. & ROGERS, P., 1974, *Human Ecology and World Development*, Plenum Publishing Company, London.

WHITE, C. L. & RENNER, G. T., 1936, *Geography: an Introduction to Human Ecology*, Appleton-Century, New York.

Section 3

Environmental education as an international movement

This section describes the work being done to implement environmental education objectives not only in Britain, but also in Australia and the United States. The following chapters therefore demonstrate the international nature of environmental education, and provide a review of developments in those countries which could catalyse similar action in education here. The section is concluded with an account of the work of the IUCN, the most important of the international organizations working towards environmental education throughout the world.

14 Environmental education in Britain

Carol Johnson

Activities in Britain relating to the broad field of environmental education are extremely diverse, and a brief summary can focus on only a sample of these activities. It is certainly true that interest in environmental education has grown rapidly over the past few years, and the situation in Britain is now reaching the stage where increased co-ordination between interested parties is vital to avoid duplication of effort.

An encouraging number of organizations, educational institutions, commercial concerns, government departments and individuals are now expressing an interest in environmental education. For some, the change in attitude has occurred fairly recently, while others have maintained and developed a long-standing interest in the investigation of ways in which man can acquire a greater understanding of himself, his society and his surroundings. The motives and methods of these groups often differ greatly and the broad term 'environmental education' is consequently given a great many interpretations. To some the term is synonymous with conservation education, countryside interpretation or even a modern form of 'nature study', while others see it as an approach to education which helps to develop individual potential and promotes a sense of responsibility for the consequences of personal and social actions.

The use of the blanket term 'environmental education' to describe all the many activities involving the use of the environment for educational purposes has inevitably created many uneasy bedfellows, and any discussions on the subject can provoke conflicts between groups with similar basic aims but differing emphases. Much of this conflict is unnecessary, for in a country which prides itself on allowing individual freedom of choice, it is often preferable to offer several interpretations and allow the individual to choose the one with which he has the most sympathy. This lack of uniformity and central dictation is perhaps most evident in the British education system. British schools and colleges are allowed a fair measure of autonomy and, within the broadly unifying limits of resource availability, community expectations and regional examination systems, are allowed to function independently. For this reason it is appropriate that a wide range of methods and interpretations are made available to the teacher.

Although unnecessary conflict between the various interest groups can result in a great deal of frustration, and wasted effort, valuable debates are often initiated in this way, thus ensuring that ideas and developments are never allowed to stagnate but are maintained in a healthy state of flux, open to critical reassessment and modification.

Environmental education within the formal education system

The ideas and methods of environmental education are now gaining a foothold in the schools and colleges throughout the country. Again, because of the inherent diversity within the British education system, there is great variation in the degree of commitment, the methods employed and even the titles used to describe relevant courses and activities. In some schools a well-equipped and staffed environmental studies department will exist, and a considerable proportion of the timetable will be devoted to work with a broadly environmental theme. In other schools the pioneering efforts of teachers concerned with traditional environmental subjects, such as geography and the natural sciences, are creating new interdisciplinary courses based on the study of an environmental situation from several related angles. Increasingly, it is the humanities or liberal studies teachers who are beginning to see local environmental studies as a useful means whereby students can be encouraged to take an interest in the affairs of the community. It is unfortunate that in some schools the existence of a full and rigid timetable means that environmental education is relegated to discussions within VI form general studies periods, to religious education lessons or even to after-school activities initiated by an enthusiastic teacher. Even in this situation, however, the individual teacher can still contribute a great deal by broadening his own outlook and that of his students beyond the rigid boundaries of his subject. Examination syllabuses in environmental studies/science now exist at all levels,[1] although some are as yet only at the trial stage. Although the development of examination syllabuses is often deplored by those who view environmental education as an approach to education rather than a subject with a defined syllabus, the existence of examination syllabuses does at least allow those schools which emphasize the importance of examinations to attempt some form of environmental education.

Several curriculum development projects have been initiated recently which have a bearing on developments in environmental education. Many of the Schools Council sponsored projects in the geography/social science/humanities/science areas have generated ideas and materials appropriate to environmental education while, conversely, the very real interest in environmental education has no doubt flavoured the proposals and methods developed by the project teams. Two of the Schools Council projects have been specially concerned with environmental education. 'Environmental Studies 5–13' looked at the contribution which the ideas and methods used in local studies could make towards the educational development of young children, while 'Project Environment', which was primarily concerned with the upper-age levels, reassessed the whole of traditional rural studies in the light of newly developing attitudes towards environmental awareness.[2] A third major research project, funded by the Leverhulme Trust, has been set up to carry out an evaluation of current developments in environmental education at all levels, identifying areas of uncertainty and conflict and attempting to resolve them with the aid of working groups of teachers throughout the country.[3] The project is based at the University of Sussex and commenced in October 1974.

Resources for environmental education

In his search for information on environmental education, the enquiring teacher could find himself faced with a bewildering array of handbooks, conference papers, policy documents and other publications produced by a surprising variety of agencies who have declared an interest in the subject. Again, the contradictions and differing emphases expressed in these publications is inevitable, and can be confusing to newcomers to the field.

The teacher whose enthusiasm for environmental education has been fired by one means or another can find a great deal of practical support for his course in the form of teaching materials. Several teachers' centres, libraries and museums have now developed resource packs of maps, documents, photographs and background information on features in the locality, which provide invaluable material for enquiry work. A number of organizations and industries with a vested interest in some aspect of the environment have developed teaching aids on topics within their sphere of interest, while commercial publishing companies have added a vast array of teaching aids on broadly environmental themes. Again, the problem here is not so much a lack of teaching material, but more the headache of selecting the most appropriate, most effective and most economical materials from such a wide choice. It is perhaps worth while to stress here the importance of each teacher deciding upon the fundamental aims which he hopes his course will achieve. Without a clear idea of the true purpose of a course, even the most expensive and elaborate teaching aids can be ineffective, while a good teacher with clear objectives in mind can achieve excellent results using nothing more elaborate than the local newspaper to spark off enquiry work.

The most important resource for environmental education is, of course, the environment itself, and teachers and their students are leaving the classrooms for the wide-open spaces in ever increasing numbers. In fact, so great has the pressure on popular study sites become in recent years that there is a danger that the environment which we seek to preserve will disappear through being trampled underfoot by enthusiastic students. Nor is it only the precious flora and fauna which can suffer – in popular villages, shopping centres and local communities, it is the residents and shopkeepers who can find themselves inconvenienced, and even intimidated, by students engaged in survey work involving the use of questionnaires and interview techniques. As with any activity, the inconsiderate behaviour of a minority of field parties is beginning to try the patience of all those affected by outdoor study work in all its forms. Codes of conduct for those involved in practically any outdoor activity from mountaineering to wildlife photography have been produced and widely advertised, but it is becoming increasingly apparent that exhortation to better behaviour is not enough. Consequently, there is now a proposal for the initiation of a Certificate of Leadership in Field Studies[4] to ensure that leaders of parties are fully aware of correct fieldwork techniques, safety precautions and the necessity for considerate behaviour.

Changing attitudes to environmental study work, coupled with inevitable restrictions on travel as transport costs increase, have brought about an increase in the use of the local environment for a range of activities. For over 80% of the population in Britain today, the local environment is a town or a city, and the urban situation provides a host of starting points for valid inter-disciplinary studies. In most towns, new buildings rub shoulders with those of previous centuries, providing a visible reminder of the changes in lifestyle and attitudes which shape the environment. Often studies of the locality can incorporate the investigation of complex issues of current interest which will affect the life of the community – for example, redevelopment proposals, the provision or removal of amenities, or plans to regulate traffic flow. Through studies such as these, students can not only learn to understand and interpret their surroundings, but also have the chance of forming their own opinions and exploring the avenues by which these opinions can be conveyed to planners and decision-makers. The Town and Country Planning Association's Education Unit, through its monthly publication *BEE* (*Bulletin of Environmental Education*)[5] has been largely instrumental in promoting ideas such as these, and one of its particular successes has been the development of 'Town Trails' – selected routes through urban areas along which items of historical, architectural, social or visual interest are pinpointed. Trails such as these, particularly when devised by the students themselves, can provide students with new insight into the interesting features of their surroundings which they may previously have overlooked.

The potential of the school site itself for basic enquiry work has not been overlooked, and a considerable amount of research has been devoted to the development of the school site to provide more varied study areas.[6] Nevertheless, large numbers of school and college parties still make use of the many field centres which now exist throughout the country, often situated in rural areas or mountainous regions which provide a contrast to the student's home environment.[7] The Field Studies Council,[8] who were pioneers in this sphere, now manage one day centre and nine residential centres in England and Wales. Each centre is fully provided with laboratories, equipment, reference books and local resources, as well as being staffed by a qualified teacher/warden and several assistants who are able to provide tuition and specialist courses for visitors to their centre.

The majority of field centres in this country are now owned and managed by local education authorities, often for the exclusive use of schools within the managing authority. Equipment and facilities vary – some centres are purpose-built and well-equipped, while others have been developed in existing buildings and suffer from the inevitable restrictions of conversion. Some centres are purposely primitive, and are used as combined field study and 'adventure' centres, where the emphasis is more on the development of self-reliance and the broadening of personal experience than on academic field work. For many children a visit to a residential centre can be their first experience of community life in a strange situation, and the educational value of this aspect should not be overlooked. Nowadays, the term 'field centre' does not necessarily have a rural connotation, for several centres are situated in sub-urban, industrial and semi-urban areas. Nor are the activities carried out at field centres exclusively concerned with the 'natural' environment. Courses and resource materials on topics such as industrial archaeology, local history and the built environment are available at many centres. The development of true 'urban studies centres' is being actively encouraged by the Council for Urban Studies Centres.[9] Already negotiations are under way in several major towns and cities which may result in the provision of suitably equipped buildings for urban centres. In addition to their value as bases for school and college groups engaged in 'street-work (urban fieldwork), urban studies centres are envisaged as being community centres which local residents can visit on a casual basis to learn more about their town through lectures and displays, and where planning proposals can be advertised and explained in detail with the aid of maps and models. The centre would also have a valuable function as a central meeting place for residents' associations and other local interest groups. Staffed by a knowledgeable warden and containing a central store of resources of local interest, the centre would also provide an invaluable starting point for visitors from other areas engaged in comparative studies.

The large and small landowners in Britain, both private and statutory, have co-operated in providing field parties with access to their lands. Statutory bodies, such as the Forestry Commission, the Nature Conservancy Council and the Countryside Commission, continue to develop special education areas within forests, nature-reserves and country parks, often linked to information and interpretation centres which cater both for school parties and members of the public. The information provided at such centres has undergone a change in emphasis in recent years – visitors to forests, for example, are provided with information on the woodland ecosystem as a whole in addition to details on the commercial production of timber, while information provided at nature reserves has developed beyond the traditional confines of natural history to encompass problems of land management and habitat maintenance.

Organizations with an interest in environmental education

A great number of organizations concerned with environmental matters now exist in this country, some long established like the Botanical Society of the British Isles, and the Society for the Promotion of Nature Reserves, and some newer and more concerned with today's pressing environmental problems, such as Friends of the Earth and the Conservation Society. Many of these organizations have begun to realize the important role of education in promoting environmental awareness and have appointed education officers or committees. The Nature Conservancy, for example, has had an education advisory section for several years, while the Town and Country Planning Association and the Royal Society for the Protection of Birds both have full time education officers. A wide range of environmental organizations such as the Conservation Society and National Farmers' Union have set up committees and working groups to consider educational policies. Conversely, many educational bodies such as the Association for Science Education and the Geographical Association have organized workshops, conferences and study groups to discuss environmental problems and to consider new ideas on environmental education. There are obvious mutual benefits in bringing together environmentalists concerned with education and educationists concerned with the environment, and in 1968 the Council for Environmental Education (CEE) was formed for this purpose. Its membership embraces educational and environmental organizations, as well as the two teacher organizations specifically concerned with environmental education – the National Association for Environmental Education (NAEE) and the Society for Environmental Education (SEE).

NAEE,[10] which grew out of the long established National Rural Studies Association but which now attracts members from a variety of disciplines, still maintains its network of affiliated local associations which are able to give help and support to teachers in their immediate area. SEE,[11] which was founded in 1968, brings educationists together at nationally organized conferences where techniques, objectives and the basic philosophy of environmental education are fully discussed. Both organizations publish journals and papers which give wider circulation to the ideas under discussion.

CEE, in addition to its function as a co-ordinating body for organizations interested in environmental education, also acts as a central agency for enquiries relating to environmental education. Its publications include a monthly teachers' news-sheet and a loose-leaf guide to teaching aids.[12] The council is a registered charity, and the primary source of its funds is now the grant-aid which it receives from a number of local authorities, some of whom have expressed enthusiastic support for the council's aims. The majority of the local education authorities which support the council are co-operating in the distribution of the monthly news-sheet to every school, college and teachers' centre within the authority.

Informal environmental education

Public awareness of environmental issues has increased in recent years, and is reflected in the number of television and radio broadcasts, books and magazine articles which now deal with environmental topics. There is also evidence of an increasing demand for more detailed information, and evening classes and leisure courses on aspects of the environment are developing in response to this demand. Most are well attended. The marked growth in the number of voluntary groups and societies which are dedicated to environmental improvement is also firm evidence of a desire for practical action. Informal film shows and specialist lectures on environmental issues now feature on the programme of meetings for groups such as Women's Institutes, Scout and Guide troops, church organizations and youth clubs, while several nationally organized competitions with an environmental theme which have been directed at out-of-school groups, have met with a good response. Certainly much public interest has been stimulated by government-backed events such as European Conservation Year (1970), Tree Planting Year (1973) and World Population Year (1974).

This year, 1975, has been designated European Architectural Heritage Year by the Council of Europe, and it is hoped that this event will arouse public interest in the preservation of fine historic buildings and may even encourage a general reassessment of the attitudes shown towards our crowded towns and cities. The co-operation and communication with other European countries which is stimulated by activities like this is extremely valuable, for it aids the growing realization that problems relating to the environment and to environmental education are not peculiar to Britain, and that there is much to be gained on both sides by pooling information and suggestions with other countries. Certainly, the co-ordination of ideas and activities at national, European and world level is essential if the full aims of environmental education are ever to be achieved.

References

1. Examination syllabuses in environmental studies/science are offered by the following boards: *CSE:* Associated Lancashire Schools Examining Board; East Midland Regional Examination Board; North Regional Examinations Board; Southern Regional Examinations Board; West Yorkshire and Lindsey Regional Examining Board. *GCE:* Associated Examining Board ('O' and trial 'A' level); Cambridge University Local Examinations Syndicate ('O' level); University of London ('O' level rural environmental studies and trial 'A' level); Oxford Delegacy of Local Examinations ('O' level).

2. For further information on all Schools Council curriculum development projects, contact Information Section, Schools Council (for address see list at the back of this book). Material from 'Environmental Studies 5–13' has been published by Rupert Hart-Davis (1972), 'Project Environment' material by Longmans during 1974/75.

3. For further information contact the Project Director, Education Development Building, University of Sussex, Falmer, Brighton, Sussex.

4. This proposal is currently under discussion, but preliminary information is available from the Secretary of the Council for Environmental Education (for address see list at the back of this book).

5. *BEE* is available on subscription from The Education Unit of the Town and Country Planning Association (for address see list at the back of this book).

6. For example, the 'Planning the School Site' project (Institute of Advanced Studies, Manchester Polytechnic, Hilton House, Hilton Street, Manchester, M1 2FE) and the work of the 'Project Environment' team (published by Longmans in 1974/75 as *The Outdoor Resource Area in Schools*). Leaflets on the subject include *Planning an Outdoor Study area* (free from Council for Environmental Education) and *School Grounds: A Resource for Teaching Environmental Studies* by E. A. J. Buckhurst (Town and Country Planning Association).

7. Details of over 300 field centres in England and Wales are contained in the Council for Environmental Education's publication *Directory of Centres for Outdoor Studies* (1973).

8. Information Centre, Field Studies Council (address is given in the list at the back of this book).

9. For further details contact The Secretary, Council for Urban Studies Centre, Town and Country Planning Association.

10. See list at the back of this book for address of National Association for Environmental Education.

11. See list at the back of this book for address of Society for Environmental Education.

12. For full details of the Council's membership and publications, contact The Secretary, Council for Environmental Education (for address see list at the back of this book).

15   Environmental education in Australia

David L. Smith

It is impossible to outline adequately the wide diversity of activity that is occurring in Australia within the scope of environmental education. At present, an extensive research report that analyses the development and present state of environmental education is being compiled.[1] Because of such wide diversity this chapter will attempt to identify some of the general trends and then to illustrate them using a number of selected case studies in environmental education.

General trends

The move towards environmental education probably began owing to influences outside Australia during the 1960s, although certain aspects of its content have been a feature of curricula taught in Australian schools for a number of years. The growing concern that man's actions upon the earth were contributing to grave unbalances in his relationships with the environment were heralded by Carlson,[2] Ehrlich,[3] Commoner et al.[4] With increasing problems occurring, especially in Sydney and Melbourne, due to the concentration of population through intensifying urbanization, the events in other countries became more real to the Australian experience.

In 1970[5] there came a plea for a comprehensively organized programme of environmental education. However, Boyden and O'Neill,[6] in 1971, concluded that there had been no real coordination, and there was little evidence of Australia taking the lead in environmental education. This was again reinforced by Reid[7] in 1973 who observed that the practical responses had been somewhat confused with a wide range of isolated and unco-ordinated activities occurring in schools, colleges and universities. Much of this confusion and lack of organization may be inherent in the nature and scope of environmental studies, as they are difficult to define, and for this reason widely diverse activities, organizations and experiences have been interpreted as being part of environmental education – such as programmes of study about 'plants and animals' and 'getting along with others'.[8] However, no matter if the experience is diverse, the challenge of environmental education has certainly raised issues in curriculum development, especially concerning the place of the traditional subject disciplines and their relationship to inter-disciplinary programmes of study.[9]

Linke (1974)[10] using a review of Australian literature in environmental education, and questionnaire research, has attempted to define this form of education in terms of four distinguishable characteristics. The first of these is an awareness of the complex and detailed inter-relationships of man with his environment, especially the awareness that man's actions are repercussive. Secondly, this awareness promotes a concern for the quality of life at a scale determined by the referent. The concern instils a feeling of responsibility for conservation of the environment which, finally, leads to a decision to take some action in line with that awareness and concern. It is these four characteristics that, for Linke, define the nature and the objectives of environmental education in Australia. Using this schema, it could be argued that the traditional disciplines, both scientific and social, have been involved in certain aspects of environmental education. It may also be argued that these disciplines are capable only of examining some aspects, and to achieve the broader aims requires a more inclusive framework than those the traditional disciplines can provide.[11] Johnson,[12] in fact, has suggested that one of the major factors inhibiting the growth of environmental education in Australia has been the rather rigid disciplinary structure of the school organization. Some progress in reducing this rigidity has been made, especially at the primary school level, with the introduction of 'open plan' classrooms, more flexible timetabling, greater independence of teachers and the possibility of introducing integrative programmes.[13] A further reason for slow development in the field has been the lack of suitably trained teachers, and the absence of suitable resource material. This has been partly remedied, in the last two years especially, by the development of a number of programmes in environmental education at both college and university levels, and by the appearance of materials suggesting strategies that might be adopted to achieve the objectives of environmental education in the classroom.[14]

It may be that in reviewing the development of environmental education in Australia one should only be concerned with that which occurs in formal educational institutions. However, there is

no doubt that for many Australians the objectives outlined previously have been achieved through experiences outside these formal
institutions, especially by involvement in community-type action.
There have been numerous instances where citizens, confronted with
planning decisions that implied a reduction in their quality of life,
have formed groups to translate awareness into action.[15] As well,
there have been numerous issues concerning the use of resources that
have led to the formation of pressure groups in an attempt to effect
a change in government policies.[16] Trade unions have been at the
forefront of this movement and an environmental consciousness by
their leaders, if not by all their members, has resulted in a number of
'green bans' being imposed in various Australian urban areas, thus
preventing any destruction or modification of selected environmental locations. In most instances this has involved a confrontation
with land developers and with large industrialists. These movements
have existed alongside the more traditional organizations such as the
Australian Conservation Foundation, the National Trust, the 'Keep
Australia Beautiful' Committee, National Parks and Wild Life and
the Departments of the Environment. In all of these experiences
many Australians are confronted by problems resulting from man's
use of the environment and are thus becoming involved in the
process of environmental education.

One final, general trend is the 'band waggon' effect that has been
produced by a non-rational and often 'emotive' approach to man
and his environment, caused to some extent by the media. In some
ways this has produced negative attitudes associated with the idea
that the problems mankind now faces are a 'passing fad'. However,
this effect has been offset by a rapidly expanding group of
Australians who have become genuinely concerned about the
environment and their quality of life and have been willing to act to
preserve them.

General trends in primary education

Linke's review at the primary level showed there was great confusion about the nature of environmental education and little study
that was undertaken was explicitly concerned with the environment.[17] Most of the work at this level is incidental, concerns a
'nature study' type of approach, that introduces basic concepts, but
tends to remain at the awareness level. There are numerous

instances of primary school students being involved in 'Litter Campaigns', 'Clean-ups', collections of bottles and cans for re-cycling, and the development of nature areas or school gardens, involving the clearing of the site, planning of the environment and the planting of trees, shrubs and plants, and setting of stones, bark areas and leaf litter. These types of activities are supported by the observance of occasions such as Arbor Day and Wattle Day which in themselves include some concepts of conservation, as well as visits by some students to environmental field study centres. Other long established organizations such as the Gould League of Bird Lovers have also contributed in certain ways to achieving the objectives of environmental education. However, there has been no move towards an integrated approach to environmental education.

General trends in secondary education

At this level, there are certain 'spin offs' that occur from teaching syllabuses in the traditional disciplines, but courses in environmental education are rare, and limited to schools that possess a much greater flexibility in organization of curricula and greater freedom for teachers to develop their own programmes.

One of the most important developments associated with students in secondary schools has been the formation of INSPECT.[18]

INSPECT was the idea of Dr Peter Ellyard of the Society for Social Responsibility in Science (Australian Capital Territory, Australia) who also sponsored the programme. INSPECT was held first in Canberra in 1970, a relatively clean and well planned city with embryonic environmental problems. INSPECT is an acronym for *IN*quiry into the *S*tate of *P*ollution and *E*nvironmental *C*onservation by *T*houghtful people. It is a programme in which a public symposium or 'teach-in' is held as a culmination of many weeks research work by high school students. INSPECT's aim is edu-cational, designed to stimulate awareness of environmental prob-lems, encourage thoughtful inquiry into the problems and explore courses of action. The idea involves students because it was felt that this group is concerned, has time to carry out research and is an effective medium for the spreading of ideas about the environment. INSPECT programmes have been based in a number of schools, colleges and universities and a suggested method for organizing a programme is outlined in the annual reports[19] as well as the

INSPECT handbook. A programme begins with a lecture/discussion series with visiting speakers for teachers and students, from which students select problems and commence research. Guidance in this is available from experts in various fields and may involve questionnaire or experimental work. The programme concludes after a number of weeks or months with a symposium where the 'non-experts' enter into dialogue and discussion with experts and other members of the community. Through this type of programme 'non-experts' may realize that they can make a significant contribution to the understanding of man's relationship with the environment and may be important forces in bringing about change of policy. Some of the projects completed include a conservation attitude survey, waste disposal attitude survey, air pollution over Canberra, survey of relative levels of noise in Canberra, pesticide-use behaviour survey, water pollution attitude survey and research into foaming and phosphate concentrations of washing powders, traffic, transport and planning in the ACT. These activities all occurred in Canberra in 1970. From there INSPECT grew to commence programmes in Adelaide, Albury, Brisbane and Sydney during 1971 and in 1972 Hobart, Melbourne, Armidale and Newcastle joined in the 'idea' which expanded and diversified in 1973 and 1974. In 1972 a rock musical, *Earth and Sun*, depicting man and his balance in the environment was originated, produced and performed in the ACT.[20] In 1971 studies from a number of broad areas were completed; four major themes were resource recycling, land and water conservation – use, transportation, and pollution. Under the auspices of INSPECT, high school students are fully involved in a rational, thorough and mission-oriented way which involves them not only in the collection of data and the analysis of problems, but also in the suggestion of policy decisions for action programmes.

Apart from INSPECT students have also taken part in a number of aspects of planning and evaluating their own environment via their participation in Junior Council.[21] 'Project Environment', a competition organized annually by the New South Wales Geography Teachers' Association, involves students in investigating aspects of their environment and their quality of life.[22] Similar projects occur in other competitions and organizations. Involvement at this level of education tends to be more rigorous and more concerned with an objective analysis that results in a deeper understanding of the complex interrelationships and a more planned strategy for environmental action.

General trends in tertiary education

In a number of ways it is in the colleges and universities where the strongest move towards environmental education has occurred. This is partly because of greater autonomy and also the greater influence of students in helping to create courses that are relevant to them and to their perception of the present society. Thus a number of specialized courses and seminars in environmental education have developed, aimed at a higher level of understanding and analysis and based upon a much more rigorous and scientific approach, but still vitally concerned with the associated problems of values and attitudes concerning man's transformation and use of the environment. There is still an absence of programmes devoted to designing curricula in environmental education, concerned with educating teachers for this interdisciplinary approach.

Traditional faculties and departments have widened their scope to include courses in environmental law, environmental architecture, environmental geology, air pollution and meteorology, and environmental musicology. In addition, new departments have been established with their emphases upon environmental studies.[23]

Case studies in Australian environmental education

Case study 1: The social sciences programme – Education Department of Tasmania

The aim of this programme,[24] set for grades 1–6 in Tasmanian primary schools, is stated as being to develop in children attitudes, skills and knowledge that will create satisfaction and understanding of the society and environment in which they live. There are four stages in the programme. Grades 1 and 2 make up stage 1, grades 3 and 4 stage 2 and grades 5 and 6 form stage 3. Stage 4 continues some of the themes in the first year or two of high school. The social sciences programme is integrated into the rest of the primary programme, with the child as the centre to achieve certain knowledge, skills and attitudes/values.

In stage 1 the main themes are Families, The School, and Communities. In this stage there is only passing reference to what might be called environmental education. Students study how native animals reflect the environment in which they live and also how physical factors affect communities and environments. In addition, some of the relationships between soil, climate and rural production are considered. Finally, students are concerned with recognizing how the characteristics of clothing, food and shelter reflect the environment. Thus in stage 1 a major objective is awareness that the physical environment affects any type of community.

In stage 2, students begin to understand that any region on the earth's surface is a composite of a number of physical and human elements, and the working activities of the inhabitants of the region reflect the natural resources and the regional environment. Since man lives in many different regions working patterns and activities are extremely varied. Once again, the main emphasis is a basic awareness with the emphasis upon man as an adaptor rather than a transformer of the environment. However, toward the end of this stage students examine the impact of mineral discoveries upon the Australian colonies and the resultant transformation.

Stage 3 is concerned with facilitating the development of advanced inquiry skills and value judgements. Students are confronted with the task of evaluating the suitability of man's settlement areas, especially the quality of life in large urban environments, examining issues such as congestion, pollution, waste disposal and recycling and crime. These studies are concerned also with the way man perceives his environment, explores it and, on the basis of increasing feedback, makes decisions about establishing some settlement pattern.

By the end of the primary school in Tasmania, students have studied a number of man/environment relationships, even if at a fairly basic level. This foundation is built on in the secondary school as a continuation of the spiral approach to curriculum development. Later studies are concerned with man's place in determining the significance of the environment, and the value problems concerned with the growth economy and capitalist society.

From this case study it may be seen how, even at very junior levels, students are grappling with basic concepts and questions associated with the environment.

Case study 2: Secondary education

All the science and social science curricula in some way reflect some of the relationships that exist between man and his environment.

Two new courses approved under the more open approach to curriculum in Queensland are very much concerned with man and his environment. These two courses, called 'The Living Environment' and 'Man and the Environment', are outlined for grades eleven and twelve and are part of the senior school geography programme.[25]

The first course seeks to help students to understand the distinctive aspects of the geography of vegetation and animal life, and develop attitudes relating to the maintenance, restoration and improvement of environmental quality. Unit 1 introduces the interdependence of vegetation and animal life, while units 2, 3 and 4 deal with particular spatial environments at both the local and world levels. The course concludes with a series of regional studies introducing value questions of man's environmental impact, his resource usage and his quality of life.

'Man and the Environment' is designed to help students understand that man is an inseparable part of the system consisting of himself, culture and the biophysical environment. Man has the ability to modify and alter the relationships within this system but in so doing often confronts environmental problems of impact, pollution, resource depletion and resource competition. The activities of the course also attempt to engender concern for environmental quality and skills in commitment and action. Section A involves a historical survey of man's impact on the biophysical environment. Section B studies areas demonstrating different degrees of environmental impact, beginning with minimal impact upon an area and gradually increasing the emphasis upon alteration and deliberate transformation. Section C examines conflicts of environmental usage, while Section D concludes by examining current problems of demography, the third world, world income, resource consumption and global patterns of waste disposal, as well as considering the future prospects.

Victoria has just introduced a course in environmental science[26] at the senior level which has as one of its main aims 'to contribute to environmental education by providing a course concerned with scientific attitudes applied to environmental management and planning'. More general aims are an understanding of man's social and biophysical environments, concern for environmental consequences of science and technology, and an increased awareness of the issues and values involved in natural resource usage. The course uses a systems viewpoint and consists of three sections:

(a) Introductory Service Units – these are compulsory and deal with the biophysical environment, the socio-economic environment and ecosystem management.

(b) Alternative Study Units – three out of fourteen units are chosen. Some of the units are heavily agricultural in emphasis and some are very physics-oriented.

(c) Case histories based on others' or students' own research.

With this sort of framework students grapple with various aspects of man's occupation and the decisions that are involved. In this programme there is a conscious attempt to facilitate experiences in which a number of the objectives of environmental education may be realized, although a criticism may be made that it does not concern itself enough with the value problems of environmental decisions.

Case study 3: Tertiary case study

At Macquarie University there are three levels of environmental studies. Undergraduate students are encouraged to take courses in one of the disciplines plus supporting courses related to basic environmental issues. As well, there is the possibility of pursuing Master's or PhD study in matters relating to the environment. In March 1973, Macquarie University began a Diploma in Environmental Studies,[27] which is a part-time two-year programme taught by permanent academic staff and non-university based professionals. The programme is described as interdisciplinary and is administered by a team drawn from a number of academic schools; it is hoped to appoint a full time director in 1975. The diploma was born from the belief that the university could play an important role in developing expertise directed towards the solution of environmental problems. There is close co-operation with the Natural Parks and Wildlife Service and the New South Wales Department of the Environment. Students have already undertaken studies for the department and have given it access to their work, while a number of members of staff have been appointed to various committees concerned with environmental problems.

The aim of the Diploma in Environmental Studies is to give candidates of widely differing backgrounds the opportunity of widening their knowledge of environmental issues and, by the interchange of ideas and studying particular systems, of arriving at more effective ways of solving current problems. A particular feature of the course is the opportunity to participate in, and develop approaches to, the assessment of proposed actions on the environment.

The diploma consists of the following courses: General Principles of Environments, Environmental Impact Assessment, Management of Natural Ecosystems, Chemicals in the Environment, Urban Ecology. The intake is limited to thirty, which allows case study approaches such as the environmental impact assessment of an inner city peninsula area of Sydney. There are also three nine-day field trips to study ecosystems of the Rangelands-Desert, Sclerophyll heath and Rainforest, and Forest and Alpine areas.

As already stated, this field of interest is beginning to become an important research area and the university's role as consultant is also increasing. Also, in November 1973, a small workshop was planned to consider the indices of quality of life in urban environments. The university has encouraged professionals to go in for recurrent education and has also attempted to play some role in educating the public about their relationships with their environments.

In this way Macquarie University has made an important contribution to environmental education at the tertiary level. Similar courses or programmes take place at Monash University, Griffith University, Melbourne University, the State College of Victoria and the University of Western Australia.

Conclusion

In conclusion it may be said that:

(a) there has been a slow movement towards the establishment of separate programmes in environmental education, although a general environmental consciousness has influenced the development of a number of curricula;

(b) although there is a wide diversity of environmental experience, the plea for a comprehensively organized programme of environmental education has not been realized, and perhaps may never be necessary;[28]

(c) the approach has often been piecemeal, lacking rigorous analysis and characterized by confusion due to a failure properly to identify the implications for the curriculum.[29]

Australia in the past has been a lucky country. However, environmental problems are increasing and with them is a growing concern for man's use and modification of his environment.

References

1. (a) LINKE, R. D., *Environmental Education in Australia*—An Outline of the Final Report on a National Survey of Environmental Education in Australia 1973–1974, Faculty of Education, Monash University, Victoria, Australia. (b) LINKE, R. D., *Environmental Education in Australia*—Final Report on a National Survey of Environmental Education in Australia 1973–1974, Chapter 1, Faculty of Education, Monash University, Victoria, Australia.
2. CARSON. R., 1962, *Silent Spring*, Penguin Books, Harmondsworth.
3. EHRLICH, P., 1971, *The Population Bomb*, Ballantyne Books, New York.
4. COMMONER, B., 1971, *Science and Survival*, Ballantyne Books, New York.
5. EVANS, J. & BOYDEN, S. (eds), 1970, *Education and the Environmental Crisis*, Australian Academy of Science, Canberra, Australian Capital Territory.
6. BOYDEN, S. & O'NEILL, J., 1971, 'The Role of Environmental Education', *Educational News*, Number 13, pp. 15–17.
7. REID, A. J., 1973, *Problems of the Development of Environmental Education*, a paper presented to the Australian and New Zealand Association for the Advancement of Science, 45th Congress, Perth, Western Australia.
8. LINKE, R. D., *op. cit.* (1a), p. 8.
9. See, for example, SHORTLE, D., 1971, 'Environmental Ethics and Geographical Education', *Geography Teacher*, **2**, 2, 79–101; SHORTLE, D., 'Whither Geography? Curriculum Development in the 1970s', *Geography Bulletin of the Geography Teachers' Association of New South Wales, Australia*, **4**, No. 3, September, pp. 62–82; EMERY, J., DAVEY, C. & MILNE, A. K., 1973, *Environmental Education: the Geographer's Contribution*, paper presented at IGU/UNESCO Regional Workshop on the Teaching of Geography in South East Asia and the South West Pacific, Sydney, September (to be published in *Journal of Geography* (USA), May 1974); SMITH, D. L., 1974, 'Education for Pollution', Parts 1 and 2, *Bulletin of the NSWGTA*, **4** and **5**; SMITH, D. L., 1974, 'Social Relevance in Geographic Education: For Whom? For When?' *Geographical Education* (Australian Geography Teachers' Association).
10. LINKE, R. D., *op. cit.* (1b), p.l.
11. SMITH, D. L., *op. cit.*, *Geographical Education*.
12. JOHNSON, T., 1972, 'Education and the Environment', in RAPOPORT, A. (ed.), *Australia as a Human Setting*, Angus and Robertson, Sydney, Australia.
13. See various issues of *The Primary Journal*, Department of Education, New South Wales, 1972–74.
14. See, for example: ROMBERG, F. & SMITH, D. L., 1973, *The Decline of the Environment*, Cassell, Australia; SHORTLE, D., 1972, 'Environmental Quality and Environmental Education', *Bulletin of NSWGTA*; NOAD, B., 1973, 'Environmental Education: A Review of Current Literature', *Geography Bulletin of the NSWGTA*, March, **5**, No. 1, pp. 7–16; SMITH, D. L., *op. cit.*, 1972; SPICER, B., 1974, *Planning for Westernport*—A Role-Play Game, Cassell, Australia; *Environmental Studies*—The Pollution Problem, Resource Kit, Practical Aids for Classroom Teachers, Pymble, NSW.
15. For example: (a) Action by community citizens prevented Sydney's second airport being sited at Galston, an area of rural/urban fringe to the north-west of Sydney. (b) Protest by community groups has delayed the building of a large coal loader near Wollongong on the New South Wales coast about sixty miles south of Sydney.
6. (a) A most lively campaign was organized to attempt to save Lake Pedder in Tasmania from electricity development. It would seem that the Tasmanian

government will continue its original plan, in defiance of the Australian government's support for saving the lake. (b) Similar campaigns have been fought to save Bungenia Gorge in southern New South Wales from coal mining leases and Myall Lakes on the New South Wales central coast from sandmining for rutile.

17. LINKE, *op. cit.* (1a), pp. 6–7.
18. For further information see: GIFFORD, R. M. & ELLYARD, P. (eds), 1971, *Bad Luck, Dead Duck* (the Report of INSPECT 1970), Dalton Publishing Company, Canberra, ACT; GIFFORD, R. M., 1972, *What a Mess Let's Confess* (the Report of INSPECT 1971), Dalton Publishing Company, Canberra, ACT.
19. *Ibid.*
20. *Ibid*, p. 1, 1972.
21. For further details see: DEER, C. E. & SMITH, D. L., 1975, 'Student Participation in Planning', in WHEELER, K. & WAITES, B. (eds), *Environmental Geography*, Rupert Hart Davis, London.
22. See various editions of the *Sydney Morning Herald* from March to May, 1972–74.
23. For example, the new Department of Australian Environmental Studies, created at Griffith University, Queensland. This is an interdisciplinary department gathering scholars from traditional earth science and social science disciplines.
24. Curriculum Branch, Education Department of Tasmania, 'Social Sciences Programme', Stages 1–3, Grades 1–6, 1970–73; Curriculum Branch, Education Department of Tasmania, 'Secondary Social Sciences Programme', Junior, Units 1–7 (Trial Version), September 1972–73.
25. Queensland Curriculum Branch, 'Man and the Environment', Approved Geography Semester Course, Grades 11–12; Queensland Curriculum Branch, 'The Living Environment', Approved Geography Semester Course, Grades 11–12.
26. Victorian Curriculum Branch, 'Higher School Certificate, Environmental Science', 1973.
27. Centre for Educational Research—'Innovation, Project on Environmental Education at University Level', May 1974 Case Study Evaluation Conference (Case Study of the Macquarie University Programme in Environmental Education).
28. TERRY, M., 1971, *Teaching for Survival*, Ballantyne Books, New York.
29. For further discussion see: LUCAS, A. M., 1972, *Environment and Environmental Education: Conceptual Issues and Curriculum Implications*, unpublished Ph.D. thesis, Ohio State University.

16 Environmental education in the United States

James L. Aldrich & Anne M. Blackburn

In many parts of the world, environmental education concentrates on the study of natural systems. Such programs generally have two primary goals: to instill a reverence for non-human forms of life, and to develop a consciousness of human dependence upon the intricate and delicate natural support systems. In the United States, as well, educational use of Wilderness Areas, Wildlife Refuges, Environmental Study Centers and Outdoor Laboratories on school sites is becoming increasingly popular. Evaluated by this measure alone, environmental education in the US would compare favorably with efforts elsewhere.

But environmental education in the United States cannot limit itself to this pleasant, but narrow view, nor to the formal education system as its only target. The message it must convey is far too serious. The United States could be thought of as an environmental time bomb primed with three volatile elements: a political system in which public opinion chooses leaders, and shapes much governmental policy and action, an economic system concerned with growth, profits and short-term goals, and a population whose affluence, attitudes and values encourage gross over-consumption and dismaying waste. Somehow, and quickly, the message must be communicated to the American people that headlong pursuit of many of the policies and beliefs that heretofore have guided our individual and collective behavior means eventual disaster for all.

If the US is to meet its environmental responsibilities to the nation and the world, the American consciousness will literally have to be reprogrammed from competitor to co-operator, from consumer to conserver, from independent to interdependent, from planning based on small political jurisdictions to that which corresponds to boundaries of natural systems and, within the formal educational system, from 'hands-off' to 'hands-on' learning experiences and from single to multi- or trans-disciplinary approaches. We must come to understand the ramifications of limited resources, the pressures produced by exponential population growth and the effects of population concentrations on energy, air, water, waste disposal and land resources. We must learn that we have been paying falsely low costs for many products and services, costs that did not accurately reflect the use of resources in production, or the ultimate costs of disposal after use. Most important, we must come to understand that protecting our environment will require that each of us provide active support for new costs, policies and protective restrictions.

It is naive to expect that such major attitude and behavior changes will be achieved by appeals to moral responsibility or our natural altruism. The only way sufficient attitudinal and behavioral changes can be stimulated in a broad enough segment of the American population to produce a measurable effect will be to convince the people, one by one, that what will occur if we fail to act in accordance with ecological principles poses a worse danger to each of them than the threat that many of them now perceive environmental restrictions to be upon their personal freedom and freedom of choice. Environmental education in the US must provide this process, the process through which environmental concerns are made meaningful to each citizen in terms of his lifestyle, his own levels and patterns of consumption. Each must become aware and knowledgeable about his total dependence upon the natural support systems, aware of the toleration limits of segments of the support systems and of the threats we consciously and unconsciously are placing upon them, conscious of our personal impact upon natural resources and the environment and aware that we are active agents in these processes, capable of doing both great good and great harm.

The late 1960s and early 1970s saw a sharp rise in the numbers of Americans who experienced a decreasing quality in their personal lives and in their surrounding environment. Nothing really new was taking place; the problems of air and water pollution, overcrowding, inadequate public services and land surfaces scarred by spreading populations, mining and agricultural and lumbering processes had always been present to a degree. The natural systems have long had to contend with these side-effects of human activity, but the bulk of the human population could still 'escape' by moving somewhere else, traveling to the nearest shore or mountain area, or seeking out a nearby parksite as a quiet retreat. For those who were fortunate enough, their escape was a daily one. The negatives that accompanied a high-paying job in the city were eliminated by the 'five-pm-flee' to an oasis in the suburbs. Slowly, however, these escape spots themselves were becoming overcrowded, trash-strewn aesthetically displeasing, mental and physical health hazards.

The current environmental movement in the US has been

criticized as being a middle-class, elitist effort. The point that proportionately large numbers of this segment of the population are involved is a valid one. What is often incorrectly assumed, however, is that the fact lessens the value of their concern, and negates the seriousness of the problems. What actually occurred was that it was this broad group whose lives were most affected by the acceleration in the deterioration of the environment that became evident in the late 1960s. It was their commuting to work that doubled in time because of increasing numbers of people, inadequate transportation and poorly planned road systems ... it was their 'view' that was bulldozed away and replaced with more housing, shopping centers and roads ... often their lake or shore retreat that became too polluted to swim in or fish from ... their taxes that rose higher and higher ... and their patience that also became overtaxed. Finally, it was their dismayed collective cry that merged with the previously ignored voices of ecologically-sensitive scientists and conservationists, and brought responsive legislative action from Congress.

The critical clue to the seriousness of the American environmental dilemma emerges at this point: it was only after broad citizen outcry that federal environmental protection measures were enacted. The dissatisfaction of many *individual* citizens about problems they encountered in their daily lives produced enough *collective* pressure to cause remedial legislation, as these distressed citizens looked to their government to solve the problems of environmental degradation they were experiencing. But most individual citizens who had participated in that public outcry were concerned primarily about the single personally-experienced problem that had motivated their initial interest. Those individuals admittedly wanted something done about their specific concerns, but they were little prepared for the fact that in many cases the necessary solutions would have a more profound impact on their lives than the problems had.

Thus, while the philosophical goal of protection of the environment is accepted as praiseworthy by the country as a whole, the attitudinal and behavioral changes that implementation of that goal requires are regarded as threats, threats which challenge the accustomed freedom and lifestyle of the individual citizen – his right to consume, to acquire, to 'outdo' his peers, for many, the right to dream. It is the failure to confront this dichotomy that has left many environmental education efforts in the United States fragmented, and lacking in focus, substance, defined goals and identified targets – barely beginning to meet the massive responsibility they face.

G

In the passage of legislation such as the Air Quality Act, the National Environmental Protection Act, the Environmental Quality Education Act, Coastal Zone Management Act and the Water Pollution Control Act and its Amendments of 1972, Congress, in essence, has redirected the social and economic goals of this nation, placing these broad commitments to the protection and preservation of a liveable environment for all above the unlimited rights of the individual to use and abuse natural resources. These laws infer a new, radically different, social ethic and value system, as well as costs and controls that eventually will affect the life of every American.

In October 1970, the Environmental Education Act was passed by Congress, establishing an Office of Environmental Education specifically to guide the development and implementation of additional programs to educate the American citizens about environmental concerns. The Act, Public Law 91–516, was hailed as a tremendous environmental victory, for it ranked as a national education priority 'the educational process dealing with man's relationship with his natural and man-made surroundings including the relation of population, pollution, resource allocation and depletion, conservation, transportation, technology, and urban and rural planning to the total human environment.' The Act provided support for and an opportunity to expand the educational emphasis that had previously been confined to the efforts of a few conservation-oriented groups and agencies, and singularly dedicated teachers.

Despite governmental rhetoric in support of environmental education, nine months passed before a director was named for the new Office of Environmental Education. In addition, the Advisory Council for OEE, mandated by the Act, did not hold its first meeting until 14 months after the statute had become law. The Office of

	Proposals	Grants	Authorization	Appropriation	Granted
1971	1925	74	$5 000 000	$2 000 000	$1 725 000
1972	1650	162	$15 000 000	$3 514 000	$2 999 040
1973	1130	54	$25 000 000	$3 180 000	$1 143 185*
Totals	4705	290	$45 000 000	$8 694 000	$5 867 225

* Approximately $2 million was lost from OEE'S 1973 budget because of alleged illegal backdating of 19 72 grants.

Environmental Education (OEE) finally began its crucial efforts in 1971 with a minimal budget which permitted funding of only 4% of the 2000 proposals the Office had received. (See Table 1).

Through OEE and other dedicated groups, the past two years have witnessed a mad scurry on the part of conscientious educators and scientists to meet this unparalleled educational challenge. Unfortunately, the situation has also precipitated a great outpouring of largely useless materials and programs labeled 'environmental education' – as opportunists rush to take advantage of the country's growing interest and concern.

Despite the development of some excellent programs, and some available materials that are finally 'on target', the process that is environmental education in the US still resembles the Tea Party in *Alice in Wonderland;* for, the Environmental Quality Education Act not only gave education the serious responsibility of communicating to the American people the need to redirect their attitudes and behavior; the philosophy of the new laws also required tremendous changes in the educational process itself, changes as yet unrealized.

The role of our educational system has been that of 'translator': to study the past, and to pass on the accepted values and social goals of the nation. The formal education system has come to operate to a great extent through single discipline approaches, and has often restricted itself to broad interpretations of problems in which the student at best becomes 'intellectually aware' of the elements of a problem. No amount of study about environmental concerns that uses these obsolete approaches will be adequate: our past is no longer capable of teaching us how to direct our future, and the student who experiences only the single disciplinary approaches or the sweeping overview of environmental concerns will not fully understand the scope and complexity of these problems; worse yet, he will not see himself as an agent of responsibility and change within the situation.

This means that whether the target group of an environmental education effort is students, citizens of a particular community, teachers participating in training sessions, key policy and decision-makers, or an interaction of all of these, certain components should be tied into the learning experience:

REAL PROBLEM EMPHASIS

The problem under study and/or discussion should be tied into local or personal examples, so that there is a sense of reality to the considerations

171

and the participants are motivated because they can identify with the situation.

MULTIDISCIPLINARY APPROACHES AND VALUES CLARIFICATION

A wide range of possible present courses of action should be discussed, with the implications of each alternative examined – implications in the environmental, political, economic, sociologic, aesthetic and ethical spheres.

A FOCUS ON THE FUTURE

Promotion of a 'future orientation' examining the long-range considerations and options that are involved; stimulating the habit of long-range planning that allows consideration of alternatives at a time when positive choices still remain.

There is no limit to the type or number of subjects that can and should be approached within such a framework. We agree, however, with R. Thomas Tanner's point in *Ecology, Environment, and Education*. He states that 'whereas EE may range across a diversity of topics and all subject-matter areas, it must not lose its central focus, which is the maintenance, for present and future generations, of a healthy, varied, and pleasant life-support system in the good Spaceship Earth.'

For the US student of environmental education we should sharpen the focus even further, carrying each study to the examination of the role of the single individual in the 'maintenance of a healthy, varied and pleasant life-support system.' For, in this wealthy democratic system based on free enterprise it is truly the citizens and only the citizens, acting singly but producing collective results, who will ultimately determine the quality of the future environment. It is their purchasing power that will decide which products will sell, their attitudes towards consumption that will determine the allocation of resources, their vote that will decide who is elected. The future will be decided by them – whether this will be by design or default depends upon the quality of education they receive about their environmental responsibilities.

To prepare citizens to be capable, conscious participators in structuring the future, environmental education must go well beyond the traditional role of translator. It must provide an arena of awareness in which the student comes to understand himself as a responsible force in shaping the future; it must become a forum for alternatives, providing the student with opportunity to imagine, design, test and devise ways to move towards a desirable future.

172

An education for survival is an education for change and social action, directed towards a future we seek. To educate for change is to educate for instability, versatility and adaptability.

HURD

The US will not become an environmentally conscientious country by passing legislation and developing environmental protection policies based on scientific soundness and sociological platitudes. Preservation of a quality environment will only become a reality if we can develop broad citizen understanding of the short-range and long-range objectives of sound environmental management, and citizen acceptance of the financial and personal commitment necessary to achieve those objectives. The gap between goals and actuality is the one to be filled by environmental education and the following pages indicate some noteworthy attempts to do so.

While there has been a lot of activity under the environmental education label, there has been little progress toward the kind of education that is needed. There are some excellent programs available; but these represent only segments of a *continuum* – only segments, because most of the programs and materials so far produced have stemmed from some individuals' or groups' need to promote their interests. Materials coming out of these special interest focuses, however well-intended, are in essence public relations materials, not the open-ended total-systems approach needed to educate the public about their environment and its interacting and interrelated problems.

In preparing a brief overview such as this on a topic which is evolving as rapidly as environmental education, you encounter at least two constraints when you get to providing specific examples of activity. First, there is not enough space to provide a reasonable and useful description of the exemplary programs that the authors have identified. Second, we wanted to avoid the instant obsolescence that threatens recommendations that become outdated between the submission of final manuscript and publication. Many first-rate projects and programs fail to achieve the promise that seems guaranteed when they are initiated. For example, four years ago the Public Broadcasting Environment Center was on its way to contributing significantly to the 'environmental movement' in this country. It had received a substantial planning grant, it had a heavy emphasis in the maturing medium of television and it was riding on the crest of the wave of public recognition of our environmental problems. It no longer exists. And there are few people that are aware that it ever did. The list of program fatalities is far longer and for the most part less spectacular than the Center's story, but the point remains in attempting to prepare something that would be of some continuing value to you, the reader. It seems more useful, therefore, to provide some selected resources, a compendium of sources of additional information which could be used for monitoring and sampling this growing education opportunity.

The following are six selected information sources which will help in identifying a wide range of environmental education activities with experiences worth sharing:

DISINGER, JOHN F., *A Directory of Projects and Programs in Environmental Education for Elementary and Secondary Schools,* ERIC Information Analysis Center, December 1972.

Environmental Education Programs and Materials, PREP Report No. 33, U.S. Department of Health, Education, and Welfare, reprinted, Aug. 1972.

Environmental Conservation Education, compiled for The Conservation Education Association. (Order from The Interstate Printers & Publishers, Inc.) A selected, annotated bibliography. Useful in building an environmental conservation library, as well as for single references.

Programs in Environmental Education, compiled by The National Science Teachers' Association. This publication is a 1969–1970 survey of programs being offered by various states. A brief description of each program with appropriate addresses is included. Copies of the survey are available from NEA Publications Sales.

The Environment Film Review, available from the Environment Information Center, Film Reference Department. An extensive guide which reviews hundreds of films and is to be updated annually. The reviews are annotated and include rental and purchase prices and distributors' addresses. The films are organized under various categories which is helpful for users.

QUIGG, P. W., (Ed.), *World Directory of Environmental Education Programs,* R. R. Bowker (publishers). There are entries from 70 countries, including each of the 50 United States. 660 programs in 440 US post-secondary institutions are listed with a detailed profile of each program.

In addition, the publisher of Dr. Disinger's report, ERIC/SMEAC

(Educational Resources Information Center/Science, Mathematics, and Environmental Education Information Analysis Center), provides a continuing service in the form of abstracts and reports on the subject.

The Journal of Environmental Education offers continuing in-depth coverage of programs and developments in the field. It is available from Dembar Educational Research Services, Inc.

The Environmental Education Report is a 16-page monthly publication that provides up-to-the-minute coverage of news and in-depth articles about events shaping the course of environmental education both in the United States and in other parts of the world. It is published by Environmental Educators, Inc.

As a sampler of more detailed program statements the following will provide considerable useful information and guidance :

GIESE, R. L., PARKER, G. R. & BINHAMMER, B. F., *Environmental Education for the Seventies,* Natural Resources and Environmental Science Program, School of Agriculture, Purdue University, Sept. 1973. This manual outlines the philosophy, methods for lesson planning, and lists resource materials for some activities in terms of a kindergarten through secondary school program.

STAPP, W. B., *Development, Implementation and Evaluation of Environmental Education Programs* (K-12), April 1973. Available from the Office of Education, Division of Technology and Environmental Education. (A similar statement by Dr. Stapp is included in the previously noted manual.)

ALDRICH, J. L. & KORMONDY, E. J., *Environmental Education: Academia's Response,* Publication no. 34 of the Commission on Undergraduate Education in the Biological Sciences. Contains a collection of statements from several programs which suggest the range of responses occurring in higher education.

The resources cited above offer innumerable exploration points for those of you interested in knowing more about and applying environmental education. Appended at the end of this chapter is a list of other publications directly used in preparing these pages. In these 'mines' of information are the references to the various government agencies, the growing number of private organizations and the noteworthy efforts of and materials available from selected industry sources which need to be considered but could not be included here.

As we have tried to suggest throughout these pages, environmental education in the United States is a dynamic, evolving area fraught with unfulfilled promise and confronting a staggering gap between the rhetoric of the committed educators and the reality of too many classrooms. Environmental education is a significant opportunity for education renewal in this country; not the only opportunity; not the only priority on the agenda of education. But the other side of the coin of unfulfilled promise is great potential. It is not a question of should we, or shouldn't we, teach environmental education, only how should we teach it.

Bibliography

TANNER, T., 1974, *Ecology, Environment, and Education*, Professional Educators Publications, Inc., Lincoln, Neb.

Department of Health Education and Welfare, *Environmental Education Projects*, Fiscal Year 1973 (DHEW Publ. No. (OE) 74–15000), Washington, D.C.

BURDIN, J. L. & SUTMAN, F. X., 1972, *In Defense of Man: Educators and Environmental Action*, ERIC Clearinghouse, Columbus, Ohio.

The American Institute of Biological Sciences, *Environmental Education, the Adult Public* (Report of a Workshop Conference), Washington, DC.

HENDERSON, M. T., *Environmental Education*, Publication # 136 of the Social Science Education Consortium, Inc., Boulder, Colo., 80302.

'Title III in Environmental Education', *The Title III Quarterly*, Spring 1972.

Office of Education, *The Case for Environmental Awareness*, US Department of Health, Education, and Welfare, Washington, DC. 20202.

The Conservation Foundation, 1973, *Support for Environmental Education: Where Do We Go From Here?*, Washington, DC.

World environmental education:
the role of the IUCN

Tom Pritchard

Environmental education and conservation

'Environment' denotes immediate surroundings, but the term has acquired a more specialized meaning in ecological usage to describe the sum total of all the external conditions which may influence organisms, including man. In conservation circles, the word is used to describe the human environment in this wider sense but with emphasis on its natural resources. The conservationist is interested in environmental education because it is concerned with instilling an awareness of the value of such natural resources for man's overall welfare, cultural and aesthetic as well as material, and of the necessity for their proper management and conservation.

The International Union for the Conservation of Nature (IUCN) has, from its inception in 1949, devoted much attention to environmental education. In the early days it was called conservation education (the term environmental education was not used until the mid-sixties) and it focussed on the protection of fauna and flora and their habitats. The Union's Commission on Education played a prominent part in promoting such education, notably the evolution and cross-fertilization of ideas and development of new methods. Discussions were arranged, mainly at a series of seminars held over the years in several parts of the world, which provided IUCN with a firm grasp of the global position and enabled it to develop a working relationship with educators operating in widely different environmental, cultural and social situations, as demonstrated in its publications (for example, IUCN 1965, 1967, 1968, 1968, 1971, 1972, 1972). These activities encompassed problems ranging from those encountered in countries with small populations and environments little affected by man, on the one hand, to those in densely populated, industrialized states with few, if any, areas of natural landscape, on the other.

The issues examined have included the following:

(i)   the significance of the natural resources of land, water and wild-life in providing material benefits, cultural values and opportunities for leisure;

(ii)   changes that have taken place, and which are occurring at an increasing rate, affecting the supply and quality of such resources;

(iii)   the educational needs, to prepare society to regulate those changes so as to ensure more rational use of natural resources;

(iv)   the value of natural features of the environment (such as undisturbed ecosystems, physiographic and geological features) in the educational process;

(v)   measures taken in different countries to develop studies of natural environmental processes;

(vi)   promising educational developments that might be explored further or adopted more widely.

Publications and recommendations on these and other issues arising from IUCN-sponsored meetings have indicated very clearly to governments the need for action. It is now accepted in many countries of eastern and western Europe, North America and elsewhere that the environmental approach has a place in all levels of formal education and in out-of-school activities.

Considerable attention has been given to the means of preparing young people, in environmental terms, to live in tomorrow's world. The objectives are best defined by determining what is likely to be expected of today's youth when they enter adult society. There will, inevitably, be groupings of people (such as the land-linked professions) who exert a greater influence than others on environmental policies and actions. But everyone will have an impact, directly or indirectly.

The functions of environmental education should be considered in relation to such groupings; the following analysis demonstrates the point.

(i)   *Those who will obtain their livelihood directly from the land*, particularly farmers and foresters. The education and training of these people should be a priority task in countries such as India where serious agrarian problems are encountered.

(ii)   *Those who will embark on a career in professions related directly to the management of natural resources* such as earth scientists, ecologists, agricultural and forest scientists, civil engineers and landscape architects. Inadequate interest in the conservation of natural resources among these professions would have serious repercussions. Furthermore, some parts of the world face a desperate shortage of these skills in any form.

(iii) *Those destined to become scientists and technologists* whose research and development work may severely affect the environment. There is evidence to show that some of the damage caused by industry today has stemmed from decisions taken by people who were given no education about the environment at any stage in their careers.

(iv) *Those who will become the future statesmen and public servants, and leaders in industry and commerce,* who, locally, nationally and internationally, will formulate policies and authorize actions having far-reaching effects on the environment.

(v) *Those who will become teachers,* probably the most important of all the groups in the long-term.

Apart from such professional involvement, every member of society will have some influence on the environment – as a consumer and through his action (or non-action) in persuading those who formulate policies. If he is ignorant and apathetic, he will contribute towards the creation or perpetuation of a low-quality environment; if informed and alert, he will be listened to, sooner or later. European Conservation Year 1970 demonstrated how the surge of public interest in environmental affairs subsequently brought about substantial changes in the attitudes and priorities of governments, industry and other institutions.

Environmental education, therefore, functions in two ways. It is an important part of the liberal education of all people; and it is a special part of the vocational training of those who will engage in planning, use, development or management of natural resources. Thus it provides an understanding of the political, economic and technological power which can now be wielded by most nations in the process of wresting basic needs from diminishing natural resources. Such education should, however, go further than creating an understanding of man's relationship to his environment. It should show how people, as individuals or communities, can conserve natural resources, indicating that conservation involves matching the use of such resources to the changing demands of human populations. In other words, the concept of care of the environment should become an integral part of modern cultures. IUCN believes this can best be achieved by incorporating appropriate education and training within existing curricula rather than by seeking to have conservation of the environment singled out for separate treatment by educators, thus the significance of investigations of curricula, syllabuses, and educational methods, such as those referred to below.

Recent developments sponsored by IUCN

International Workshop on environmental studies in higher education and teacher training

Since the IUCN seminar on education at the university level, Lucerne 1966 (IUCN, 1967), several new courses and other developments have appeared. Another review was arranged by IUCN in September 1972 at an International Workshop at Althouse College of Education, London, Ontario. This considered three names: environmental programmes in higher education; in teacher education; and in professional fields. Resolutions of widespread interest included the following:

(i) *Data Bank* There is need for the collection and dissemination of information. IUCN has a limited capacity for this and the workshop suggested, as guidelines for expansion of the clearing house, that (a) selected discipline material from all countries should be sought, compiled and made available for distribution, and should include lists of institutes and individuals active in environmental education; (b) a programme of international visits of experts would be useful; and (c) a periodic newsletter would also be useful.

(ii) *Conference on goals and objectives* It was recommended that a working conference should be arranged to develop specific educational goals, covering at least two levels: for the education of all citizens; and for the education and training of environmental specialists.

(iii) *Teacher education* was covered comprehensively; development of methods handbooks were recommended, a subject subsequently to be dealt with at an IUCN Workshop in Wales in 1975 (see below). Emphasis was placed on several recommendations made at the Rüschlikon Conference (see p. 184); and the need for a clearing house for teacher training information was stressed.

(iv) *Environmental programmes in the professional fields* received exceptionally thorough analysis. Recommendations covered a range of important topics, including in-service training and re-shaping of existing professional courses. The formation of a National Centre was also proposed as follows:

Every nation should develop a National Environmental Centre (or Centres) within one or more Universities, with a team of specialists active in a broad range of disciplines. These centres should operate with as much independence as possible in order to encourage and actively foster teaching and research of an interdisciplinary nature. They should interact with all other units within the University, and maintain close contact with environmental affairs at all levels of the nation's activities. The breadth of disciplines that need to be involved cannot be overemphasized, and their freedom to investigate independently and advise the government, the public and industry on environmental concerns must be ensured.

The National Environmental Centres, although essentially academic, would be expected to fulfil a role within the University and in the public and private sectors. They would develop and teach courses at the post-graduate and under-graduate levels, provide public education-programmes, develop in-service courses and briefing packages on special topics, provide facilities for environmental research, and assist in solving problems in a consultative capacity. The development of courses for public education, information for the communications media, and industrial consultation must be recognized as essential activities of the Centre, and must be implemented at the outset.

Such Centres should enjoy international recognition and be given all possible support, particularly in developing countries, in order to allow for the exchange of personnel and ideas more easily.

Universities and other institutions should also be encouraged to develop in-service programmes, organize study sessions and seminars, conduct research and pursue other activities to promote better understanding and management of the environment.

An important role of the Centre would be the development of long-range forecasting techniques. This would require the compilation of existing data and acquisition of new data on the environment.

International course for teacher training in environmental conservation and education

This project covered a ten day course in August, 1972 at the Drapers' Field Centre situated in the Snowdonia National Park, Gwynedd, North Wales, under the joint sponsorship of IUCN, the British Field Studies Council and the Nature Conservancy in conjunction with the Prince of Wales' Committee.

Emphasis was placed on the development of techniques for teaching environmental studies. Much of the course consisted of fieldwork, but time was also allotted for exchange of information and discussions relating to the variety of teaching situations experienced elsewhere. The three main themes covered were:

(i) *Teaching from the environment* with emphasis on open-ended environmental work in which there is no pre-conceived syllabus, but where the main concern is investigation and enquiry and the development of the learning process. This is most commonly associated with studies by younger children.

(ii) *Teaching about the environment* covering studies based on a specific topic or a restricted area in which the main consideration is academic study to gain information and comprehension. The major part of the field studies at secondary level in Britain fall in this category.

(iii) *Teaching for the environment* where conservation, visual amenities, environmental quality and wise use of resources were the main objects.

The course was directed by the staff of the Drapers' Field Centre and the Nature Conservancy together with specialists from IUCN and invited contributors.

A second international meeting will be held at the same venue in 1975 to give more detailed attention to these issues.

International seminar on environmental education in the schools in eastern European countries

This meeting was organized to bring attention to environmental conservation education at the primary and secondary school levels in eastern European countries, and to find ways of increasing the amount of such education in school programmes. The seminar was held at Pieniny National Park (Poland) in June, 1972. It was organized by the East Europe Committee of the IUCN Commission on Education.

Filmstrips on conservation

The project covers the preparation of a series of filmstrips to be used as teaching aids. It has been felt for a long time that IUCN should prepare and produce materials of this kind.

Popular publications on conservation

The project covers the preparation, publication and distribution, in three selected countries, of small booklets for young people on environmental conservation problems and solutions. Kenya, India and Venezuela are the countries selected for the project. Free distribution of the publications is being considered.

The books will be locally written and produced, and will be designed specially for each country. Local experts are collaborating with the Secretariat to produce the booklets. UNESCO, through its Gift Coupon Programme, has included this project in its programme.

Workshop on environmental education for mountain areas, Aosta Valley, Italy, held in September, 1973 prepared a teaching manual with three major chapters on :

   (i) Which principal qualities or elements of the mountain environment should receive attention in order to maintain an overall equilibrium?
  (ii) What are the principal dangers which menace the mountain environment?
 (iii) What are the measures to be taken for maintenance and restoration of the mountain environment?

Each chapter will be divided into sub-chapters covering natural values and cultural values.

Other activities

Projects being promoted at present include a proposed world conference on environmental education (with UNESCO); a pilot seminar on education methodology to be held in East Africa; completion of the *Multilingual Dictionary of Conservation Terms*; establishment of education programmes in French-speaking countries; and, in collaboration with the United Nations Environment Programme (UNEP), a project to extend and make more effective the existing mechanisms for informing and educating citizens throughout the world about conservation.

IUCN's comparative studies in Europe

The North-West Europe Committee

In 1960, the Commission on Education established a North West Europe Committee to consider education, training and public information relevant to conservation in that region. Belgium, Denmark, Federal Republic of Germany, Finland, Great Britain, Netherlands, Norway and Sweden participated, and contributed to a comparative report of environmental education sponsored by the Council of Europe (Pritchard, 1968). That report provided a useful basis for further investigations and discussions of the position in Europe, culminating in the European Conference at Rüschlikon in December, 1971. A summary of its findings is given below.

Definition of environmental education

The exact limits of environmental education in Europe are imprecise because it covers such a broad field. It includes studies undertaken as parts of well-defined disciplines, such as geography, geology and biology, but also embraces nature study, rural studies, ecological science and conservation education. Some of these subjects, such as ecological science, are relatively new, but others, such as nature study, have been taught from the early days of organized education systems.

Environmental studies should not be regarded purely as part of school, college and university courses. There is a strong extra-curricular component, included in the activities of clubs, societies and further education groups and in popular books, magazines, films, television and radio programmes.

The major characteristics and functions of environmental education at different levels, from primary school upwards, are outlined below, together with a summary of the principal methods employed.

Young Children

Environmental studies are a characteristic feature of primary education in northern Europe. They often include studies of plants and animals, with the aim of stimulating the child's interest in living organisms and in the earth, air and water. One opinion, widespread amongst progressive teachers, is that such studies should be treated as a gateway to education. If imaginatively taught, they can embrace not only simple biology and earth science but also mathematics, chemistry, physics, history, art and literature. They have the advantage of offering children many opportunities for active participation and experiment, and can be introduced even at kindergarten. Several innovative teaching methods now being tested in different countries are providing guidelines for widespread improvements along these lines in primary schools.

Older children

The unity of approach found in primary schools is more difficult to maintain at the secondary school level. In practice, the main elements of environmental education are usually found in biology and geography (where they have to compete with a wide range of other studies). Thus, environmental education occupies a confused and unsatisfactory position; at the lower secondary levels it is part of both liberal and scientific education but, at the higher levels, it is usually only provided for those who intend to obtain professional or academic qualifications in the environmental sciences.

At primary school level interest in environmental subjects is easily maintained. However, there are serious problems in sustaining this interest at lower secondary level, where the broad, environmentally-based studies of the primary school tend to be abruptly replaced by circumscribed disciplines, some of which are arbitrarily chosen and of a narrow and specialist kind. Biology, for example, which is an important component of environmental education, may become separated into the compartments of taxonomy, morphology, anatomy, physiology and genetics. Then there are organizational difficulties in providing time and facilities for studies out-of-doors.

The average secondary school child in northern Europe is not, therefore, given much opportunity of developing an interest in the world of nature. This situation, however, is less widespread than it used to be; in some countries rapid progress has been made towards interrelating biology, geography and social studies, thus maintaining the characteristics of the best primary school approach while achieving advanced educational standards.

Reference has already been made to the social value of environmental education. If its value as a medium for creating a better society in the future is accepted, then much more attention should be given to this subject at secondary school levels. What kind of dividend could be expected? For example, can environmental studies contribute toward achieving more widespread scientific literacy, which is one of the challenges of our time? Can these studies also enable young people to obtain greater satisfaction out of their environment both now and later in life?

Young people growing up in urban surroundings, and without easy access to open air facilities for spontaneous recreation, are being faced with complicated emotional problems and some are finding great difficulty in adapting themselves to existing social patterns. Sociologists might consider whether the boredom of these young people may not be related to their inability to obtain any mental or physical satisfaction from their environment. They might also consider the potential for a joint study of the problems by sociologists, educationalists and environmentalists.

At senior secondary schools the biological sciences, taught as the basis for entering higher courses, contain varying amounts of ecology. It may be argued that there should be a much larger ecological component, but this leads to arguments on the merits or otherwise of early specialisation. The options emerging from curricular studies and other educational development work, have provided opportunities for reform in many places, leading to a more effective secondary school education in environmental subjects both as an end in itself and as a base for advanced studies and vocational training.

Higher education and professional training

Universities and other institutes of higher education in many European countries are becoming increasingly conscious of their responsibilities as centres which utlimately have a tremendous impact on the way in which the human environment is treated. They are principal centres of fundamental and applied research and they exert a dominating influence in educational circles because their entrance requirements determine the pattern of teaching in secondary schools, quite apart from the fact that they train the majority of teachers for them.

The approach to education and training is greatly affected by the location of the institute concerned, its historical background and the specialized interests of its professors and other staff. It is, therefore, exceptionally difficult to provide an overall view. Environmental education normally comprises a range of subjects which are either taught separately as distinct disciplines or as an integrated course. In first degree courses, such education usually takes the form of ecology for biologists and environmental studies for geographers. Some courses for town and country planners, landscape designers, civil engineers, foresters and farmers also incorporate ecology.

New courses in ecology, environmental studies, natural resources and related subjects have been appearing in many countries during the last few years. They are orientated towards conservation and the management of natural resources.

The growing demand for specialists with a scientific background to deal with environmental problems has undoubtedly affected the degree to which conservation philosophy is entering into current syllabuses. However, vocational considerations are unlikely to be the only reason for professors to include a larger component of environmental education in their teaching programme. Probably of greater significance has been the recognition that the management of natural resources is developing as a science in its own right. Greater emphasis on these subjects may, in some institutes, also have resulted from reassessment of the content of courses in biology and the earth sciences.

Ecology and related subjects have been drawn into a debate about the value of broader-based studies at first degree levels as opposed to early specialization. Further, it has been argued that ecology and other environmental studies are particularly important as a bridge between botany and zoology; similarly, there are geographers and geologists who wish to see closer relationships between their subjects and biology.

Clearly, there are educational problems and teaching techniques which are common to many countries. Others have hitherto been characteristic of certain places only, but the lessons learnt in these places could profitably be adopted in a modified form to meet the needs of many other institutes. There is a need for greater efforts in educational research, particularly on the relationships of higher education and training to the patterns of vocational requirements that are emerging. One proposal studied by IUCN is for the establishment of an advisory and consultative service in higher education and training in the environmental sciences. Such a service should facilitate communication between experts and gather a fund of information to be made available to those who ask for it, particularly educationalists proposing to develop new courses in their institutes.

There is clearly a need for an appraisal to be made in Europe of the following:

(i) the present position in higher education and professional training, with special emphasis on obtaining information about major types of courses and techniques of teaching which are aimed at achieving distinct educational objectives and at meeting widely varying vocational requirements;

(ii) the existing, projected and potential demand for environmental scientists and other key personnel.

This appraisal should include an investigation of the extent to which different types of training are suited to existing and anticipated vocational requirements. The need for a global appraisal, and a data bank and consultation service was also identified at the London, Ontario Workshop in September 1972 (see pp. 180–1).

Nevertheless, the land-linked professions, covering a range from the pure ecologist at the one end of the scale, to the practical planner, farmer or civil engineer at the other, still comprise only a tiny proportion of the total population. Indeed, these professions are only a relatively small part of those engaged in the overall design and management of the human environment. The statesmen and civil servants, the owners of land, industrialists, builders, sportsmen and many others all have a strong, and often overwhelming, influence on policies and practices regardless of the advice and opinions available from the land-linked professions.

Rather little has been written about the contribution environmental education makes to the training of those who enter professions which cannot be directly labelled 'environmental'. This is mainly because there has so far been little attempt to develop this aspect of environmental education. The knowledge public officials, industrialists and other leaders have of their environment has either been obtained in the form of a superficial and little-heeded part of general school education or as a result of having a hobby interest in some country pursuit, or through the public information media of radio, television, newspapers, magazines and books.

Teachers

The training of teachers can be considered in two categories – that carried out in universities and that at the teachers' training colleges. Those trained at universities have followed one of the normal academic courses and have then received some special training in educational theory and method. Methodology, however, rarely contains much specific guidance about techniques of teaching environmental education. There seems generally to be more emphasis on methodology in the training colleges, though again little attention is paid to means of undertaking environmental education and, particularly, the conducting of field studies courses. Attempts are being made to develop more in-service training for existing teachers, but many more specialist courses are still required.

In each country, limitations are imposed on the extension and improvement of environmental education by the inability of many teachers to deal with it due to inappropriate or insufficient training or because of a lack of interest. There has been a vicious circle, in that neglect of environmental studies, particularly field work, in the training of teachers means that most of the schools send on to the universities and training colleges students whose interest in such studies has not been aroused in earlier, formative years.

Extra-curricular activities

The growing interest in the out-of-doors has resulted in a much greater demand in recent years for interpretative services relating to the countryside and particularly to wildlife and its conservation. Thus, the boundaries of environmental education are continually extending beyond the formal education system. Courses for adults, including field studies, are available, some of which also contribute towards refresher training for teachers. Although many existing opportunities are taken up by those who are already interested in the environment, there are exceptions, such as television programmes and the more sophisticated interpretative services being developed in such places as national parks, which stimulate the curiosity of large sections of people who previously were little interested in environmental matters.

Young people have more opportunities than ever before, for visiting the countryside, either individually or as members of organized groups, for a wide range of outdoor pursuits, which at the same time provide them with experience of and insight into the natural environment as an integral part of these recreational activities.

The hobby interest in environmental studies is likely to become even more firmly established as a leisure element in future. In every European country, many people have in recent years turned to outdoor pursuits, including nature studies, for their main recreational outlet and have found them an important source of refreshment. Many more people might enjoy these activities if they were initiated into them at an early age.

The use of field studies

In the early development of environmental studies, the principal approach to teaching was a combination of theoretical work, observation and survey in the field, and follow-up studies of materials collected out-of-doors. This was an observational and descriptive approach, and experimental studies were undertaken only in isolated cases. Several refinements in these basic methods have been made during the last decade, and techniques developed which place field studies on a more scientific basis and enable more efficient use to be made of the time spent on outdoor work. These new methods have also brought about closer integration between field studies and indoor work.

Field studies are not only essential to the understanding of environmental problems but they are also becoming recognized as an important educational tool in their own right thus contributing fundamentally to the educational process. For example, they offer opportunities for encouraging students to widen their experience by exploring unknown material rather than being concerned merely with a factual exposition by the teacher and then obtaining the 'right answer'. Although this is a subject in which much educational research is needed, the experience of teachers in many parts of the world strengthens the view that outdoor activities offer enormous scope for the intellectual, social and physical development of young people. The following are among the arguments put forward by European educators to support this view:

(i) Field activities offer scope for exploration of highly variable situations, allowing quite simple observation to be original and thus to contribute to knowledge. This brings satisfaction to the pupil and an early interest in original study. At the same time it strengthens confidence in his ability leading to a progressive development of a spirit of enquiry.

(ii) Active pupil participation in turn leads to the need for the teacher to respond by providing the pupils with guidance for further development of their activities. This helps to break down the old fashioned concept of 'teacher' and 'taught'. In the more successful field exercise, the teacher forms part of the 'team'.

(iii) The breadth of most field study projects encourages the team approach, but it also provides opportunities for participants to initiate their own projects and to adopt some facet or other as their own specialism.

(iv) Diagnosis of problems and accurate recording of observations in the process of finding a solution or arriving at a judgment is another important aspect. Objectives are defined and methods designed to attain them. In the case of a biological study, for example, quadrat or transect analysis of vegetation, or taxonomy, need not be ends in themselves but part of the process of understanding an ecological problem.

(v) Field activities also involve approaches common in many subjects and can demonstrate in practice the relationship between the humanities, sociology, science and many other disciplines.

Conducting field studies

Most field work is undertaken during short excursions lasting from about two hours to a full day, that is during visits which do not require sleeping accommodation. These excursions are easier to arrange than those lasting for a period of days because the cost is usually limited to paying for transport and because they can more readily be fitted into the time-table.

The type of work depends partly on the characteristic of the environment near the educational institute. Those situated in urban areas are normally poorly provided with accessible natural areas and must depend on sites severely modified from their natural condition, such as municipal parks, botanical and zoological gardens and industrial wastelands. This has resulted in the development of some specialized teaching techniques. Visits to farms are, however, a well-established feature of education for both town and country schools.

Longer excursions, such as school expeditions and visits to school camps, may last several weeks though one week courses are common at residential centres set up specifically for field studies and other outdoor activities. The aim is to offer facilities for participants to obtain experience of environments rather different from those to which they are accustomed. Many of the visits are to natural and semi-natural landscapes and much of the time is devoted to exploration and survey. Individual experience is a common objective in exercises of this kind, but the emphasis on intellectual or physical attainment varies widely. Even in excursions where physical recreation is the main objective, there is an increasing tendency to encourage observation of natural phenomena. A small, but increasing amount of time is spent on experimental and analytical studies. For these purposes, there is pressure on places of natural scientific interest, including nature reserves and it is now becoming necessary to set up special reserves for educational purposes, sometimes linked with field museums and centres providing basic equipment and reference material.

Among the techniques used to obtain greater benefit from field studies, one which has grown in popularity is the nature trail. A nature trail is a route through an area of natural history interest which enables people to see its major features easily and to be guided in their interpretation. These features may be explained by signboards, by paragraphs in a pamphlet corresponding to numbers on the trail route, or personally by a guide.

Supporting methods

Much of the value of field studies will be lost unless there is preparation beforehand and follow-up afterwards. The use of illustrative and reference material is essential and may involve visits to museums and libraries. School visits to museums can be of particular importance and museums are increasingly supplying materials on loan for use in schools.

A wide range of reading material, including books, magazines and pamphlets, is available for background and follow-up, and this is being supplemented by radio and television programmes, records, tapes, films, film-strips and slides. There is, however, still a shortage of material specifically produced to guide teachers, youth leaders and others in the methodology of environmental education.

The European Working Conference on environmental conservation education

This conference was held at the Gottlieb Duttweiler Institute, Rüschlikon, Zurich in December, 1971. The objectives were to assemble, for the first time at European level, specialists working in environmental education in order to exchange information, clarify concepts and formulate specific recommendations for programmes related to primary and secondary schools, teacher training, higher education and out-of-school activities. The conference was attended by 105 specialists – teachers, scientists, administrators and other experts – from 21 European countries, 11 international organizations, Canada, Australia and the USA.

In spite of some diversity of approaches to problems, particularly towards implementation of environmental education, much cooperation and involvement developed as participants found common ground to promote their points of view and to make recommendations. These are included in full in the Proceedings of the Conference (IUCN, 1972).

Like many other IUCN working meetings, the European conference was invaluable for exchanging information on the methodology of environmental education in many countries, and practical programmes suited to education systems in a variety of situations were proposed.

Looking ahead

In those regions and countries where the concepts and methods are already understood, educators have the responsibility of extending, and improving upon, the experiences gained in the last decade, in many parts of the world, to meet their own circumstances. IUCN has already made a very substantial contribution by gathering information, making contacts, stimulating international cooperation, identifying principal issues needing investigation in depth, and providing training and other facilities, on a pilot scheme basis. It will continue this work, giving special regard to the needs of developing countries. In so doing, it will extend and strengthen its contacts with government, professional institutes, other international organizations and, above all, the individuals who participate in the challenging, and urgent, task of promoting environmental education throughout the world.

Bibliography

IUCN, 1965, 'Conservation education', *Supplementary Paper No. 7, IUCN Publications, New Series*, Morges, Switzerland, 75 pp.

IUCN, 1967, 'Conservation education at the university level', *Supplementary Paper No. 9, IUCN Publications, New Series*, Morges, Switzerland, 74 pp.

IUCN, 1968, *Proceedings of the Conference on the Conservation of Nature and Natural Resources in South-East Asia* (Bangkok, Thailand, 1965), Morges, Switzerland, 550 pp.

IUCN, 1968, *Proceedings of the Latin-American Conference on the Conservation of Renewable Natural Resources* (Bariloche, Argentina, 1968), Morges, Switzerland, 517 pp.

IUCN, 1971, Papers and Proceedings IUCN Eleventh Technical Meeting, Vol. IV, *Environmental Conservation Education among Populations of Rural and Woodland Areas* (New Delhi, India, 1969), Morges, Switzerland, 156 pp.

IUCN, 1972, Final Report—*European Working Conference on Environmental Conservation Education* (Rüschlikon, Switzerland, 1971), Morges, Switzerland, 58 pp.

IUCN, 1972, Final Report *International Course for Teacher Training in Environmental Conservation and Education* (Betws-y-Coed, Wales, 1972), Morges, Switzerland, 19 pp.

PRITCHARD, T., 1968, *Environmental Education—its social relevance in North-West Europe*, Council of Europe (unpublished report CE/Nat (68) 67), Strasbourg, 148 pp.

Discussion Questions

These discussion questions should be attempted after reading the insights provided by each of the contributors to this book, and followed up by further reading of the references or bibliography given at the end of each chapter.

1. Account for the 'dilemma of definition' inherent in the present concept of environmental education. How do you suggest this problem may be resolved?
2. Assess the contribution of 'conservationists' to the development of environmental education.
3. Suggest a syllabus for a school course in environmental education up to either (a) CSE level, or (b) 'A' Level.
4. Make a list of all the streetwork projects you can suggest for a CSE course in environmental education.
5. Compare and contrast the curriculum content of Australian environmental education with environmental education in either Britain or the USA.
6. Evaluate the contribution of IUCN to environmental education.
7. Draw up a list of all the resources you can find in your college library dealing *specifically* with environmental education. How adequately does it cover the full range of studies possible?
8. Examine the concept of 'conservation education', and outline a scheme of work for one of (a) top primary school children; (b) 4th year CSE Candidates, or (c) a Sixth Form General Studies Course.
9. Study a selection of planning documents dealing with your own locality. How far do they offer ideas for projects in environmental education?
10. John Burton, in Chapter 3, argues that the main concern of environmental education should be to establish an 'environmental ethic'. How far do you agree? How might this be done?
11. 'The environmental revolution, amid which we live, has a double face. It can be seen as a man-made change, sudden and

world wide, in our natural environment. It can equally be regarded in the light of a transformation in our attitude to that environment.' (Max Nicholson) Discuss.

12. Critically assess your own education in the light of the objectives for environmental education set out in this book.

13. Explain how you might adapt a school syllabus in history, geography or biology to contain environmental education objectives.

14. Bryan Waites explains the reasons for including education about historic conservation in the curriculum. What are these reasons? How far do you agree with them?

15. Planning education must inevitably involve political education. What do you think?

16. In what ways can community education involve young people in concern for the environment?

17. 'The environmental education movement possesses enough definition problems without adding a global dimension.' (Chapter 10.) Discuss.

18. Design a Secondary school syllabus in either (a) Human ecology or (b) Environmental science.

19. Argue the case for introducing human ecology into the school curriculum.

20. Establish a check-list for identifying criteria to be used in assessing the environmental education content of a particular syllabus. Apply it to a subject or inter-disciplinary course you have experienced in either a Polytechnic or a College of Education.

21. How far do you consider an 'international outlook' should be part of a course in environmental education?

22. Draw up a 'genealogical tree' showing the development of environmental education since 1889.

23. 'Urban Studies offers the possibility of unifying the academic and social elements in education which would motivate pupils of all ages and abilities.' How far do you agree?

24. In what ways can a course in design education provide awareness of problems of environmental planning?

25. Collect newspaper information about an 'environmental problem' currently occurring in Britain. Outline a scheme of work to teach this topic to any selected age range of pupils.

26. Assess the problems you might encounter when introducing an environmental education course into a secondary school.

27. Discuss the meaning of the word 'environment'.

28. Explain your environmental philosophy to the other members of your discussion group.
29. How far do you consider that English is a foundation subject in a secondary school curriculum for environmental education?
30. In what ways should a primary school curriculum be orientated towards environmental education objectives?

Useful Addresses

The Association for Science Education, College Lane, Hatfield, Herts.

The Civic Trust, 17 Carlton House Terrace, London, SW1Y 5AS.

Council for Urban Study Centres, 17 Carlton House Terrace, London, SW1Y 5AS.

Council for Environmental Education, 24 London Road, Reading, RG1 5AQ.

The Conservation Society, 12 London Street, Chertsey, Surrey.

Conservation Society/Conservation Trust Joint Education Working Party, 246 London Road, Earley, Reading, RG6 1AJ.

Field Studies Council (Information Centre), Preston Mountford Field Centre, Mountford Bridge, Shrewsbury, SY4 1DX.

Friends of the Earth, 9 Poland Street, London, W1V 3DG.

Geographical Association, 343 Fulwood Road, Sheffield, S10, 3BP.

Institute of Biology, 41 Queen's Gate, London, SW7 5HU.

Institution of Environmental Sciences, 14 Princes Gate, Hyde Park, London, SW7 1PU.

International Union for the Conservation of Nature, 1110 Morges, Switzerland.

National Association for Design Education (Gen. Sec. P. H. Roberts), Manor High School, Copse Close, Oadby, Leicester.

National Association for Environmental Education, Offley Place, Great Offley, Hitchin, Herts.

Nature Conservancy Council, 19–20 Belgrave Square, London, SW1X 8PY.

Schools Action Group for the Environment, Dr Challoner's Grammar School, Amersham, Bucks.

Schools Council (Information Section), 160 Great Portland Street, London W.1.

Schools Eco-Action Group, 28 Wood Lane, Highgate, London, N6 5UB.

Society for Environmental Education, City of Portsmouth College of Education, Locksway Road, Milton, Portsmouth, PO4 8JF.

Town & Country Planning Association (Education Unit), 17 Carlton House Terrace, London, SW1Y 5AS.

United Nations (Centre for Economic and Social Information), Palais des Nations, CH–1211 Geneva 10, Switzerland.
Voluntary Committee on Overseas Aid and Development, Parnell House, 25 Wilton Road, London, SW1V 1JS.
Watch, Trumpington Street, Cambridge, CB2 1QY.

US Addresses (Chapter 16)

Conservation Foundation, 1717 Massachusetts Avenue NW, Washington, DC 20036.
Dember Educational Research Services Inc, Box 1605, Madison, Wisconsin 53701.
Division of Technology and Environmental Education (Office of Education), 400 Maryland Avenue SW, Washington DC.
Environmental Educators Inc., 1621 Connecticut Avenue NW, Washington, DC 20009.
Environment Information Center, Film Reference Department, 124 East 39th Street, New York, NY, 10016.
ERIC Information Analysis Center, 1460 West Lane Avenue, Columbus, Ohio 43210.
Interstate Printers & Publishers Inc., 19 North Jackson Street, Danville, Illinois 61832.
NEA Publications Sales, 1210 16th Street NW, Washington, DC 20036.
US Government Printing Office (Superintendent of Documents), Washington, DC 20402 (for US Government Publications).